Complete

Puppy
Care

AMY SHOJAI

Copyright

ISBN-10: 1-944423-28-1
ISBN-13: 978-1-944423-28-5

Second Print Edition, March 2017
Furry Muse Publishing

IMAGES & GRAPHICS from DepositPhotos.com (in order of appearance)
Cover image © khunaspix, @Laures (dedication silhouette), @scropp, @eriklam, @martyhaas, @phase4studios, @willeecole, @lifeonwhite, @lunamarina, @nanka-photo, @mdorottya, @cynoclub, @ alvenmod, @lifeonwhite, @oksun70, @lifeonwhite, @FotoJagodka, @sommaill, @FotoJagodka, @FotoJagodka, @Sheikoevgeniya, @willeecole, @ gurinaleksandr, @willeecole, @classpics, @alexeys, @ feedough, @ eriklam, @lifeonwhite, @willeecole, @lufimorgan, @Klanneke, @hurricanehank, @firstbite, @phase4studios, @Laures; PART 1-4 Graphics: @yupiramos & PART 5 Graphic: @fizgig; Dog-Heart Chapter Heading: @deskcube; Dog Face Icons: @funwayillustration

IMAGES & GRAPHICS from © Amy Shojai (in order of appearance)
Puppy chewing, Magic GSD, woman with Chihuahua, woman with mixed pup, Aussie pup in outdoor crate, blond woman cradling pup, GSD with litter, blond girl with pup, puppy nose, GSD pup in leaves, 2 pups sleeping, GSD in car, GSD sniffing cat, Golden tugging torn ball, GSD rolling in leaves, boy with several puppies, woman training GSD to sit, white pup chewing bracelet, pup chewing stuffed toy, GSD in flower field, guilty black pup; Illustrations: parasites, ear cleaning, tapeworm life cycle, puppy body language

First Published by Cool Gus Publishing
First Printing, August 2014
COPYRIGHT © Amy Shojai, 2014

FURRY MUSE
PUBLISHING
P.O. Box 1904
Sherman TX 75091
(903)814-4319
amy@shojai.com

AUTHOR NOTE

Dedication

For the people who make a difference—

Dedicated shelter staffs,
Caring veterinarians and volunteers,
Loving fanciers, responsible breeders,
Devoted dog-parents everywhere.

And for the puppies who share our lives—

Those from planned births and "accidents,"
Throw aways and foundling strays,
Chosen fur-kids and rescued waifs,
All those serendipity sends our way.

But most especially,
For the puppies that never find a home.

In loving memory.

Contents

PART TWO: BRINGING HOME BABY

PART THREE: PUPPY CARE 101

9: Preventing Puppy Health Problems

PART FIVE: CANINE FASCINATIONS

APPENDIX A: Favorite Puppy Websites

APPENDIX B: Resources

INTRODUCTION

Welcome to *Complete Puppy Care*, the most easy-to-use, up-to-date reference available on one of the most endearing and extraordinary pets you could choose.

First and foremost, this book celebrates puppies. And a celebration of all things fuzzy goes beyond cute stories, and cuter pictures—although you'll find lots of that here as well. Most importantly, this book's solid information arms you with the tools you'll need to build a lasting, loving relationship with the special dog babies in your life.

Puppyhood is a unique period that demands special attention. Puppies are works-in-progress that must receive proper care if they are to achieve their full potential. The physical and emotional needs of puppies are very specific and not only impact the present, but also the future. What happens to your baby dog today—for good or ill—defines everything she can expect to be as an adult.

And so, cherish these days, weeks, and months, for puppyhood is a fleeting treasure. It comes only once in each dog's life, and is even more precious because of its transient nature.

Puppyhood is the foundation upon which affection takes root. With the proper care, affection blooms into a lifetime of shared love.

Nothing Beats Puppy Love

I have known this forever, and have testified to puppy love in countless articles and quite a few books over my twenty-plus years as a pet writer. Puppies are different than their adult counterparts. Not better—just different.

Obviously, puppy looks and behaviors set her apart from her parents. But more than that, adult dogs have already developed many habits, whether good or bad, and their personality traits become more fixed as they mature. Puppy personality and habits, on the other paw, remain malleable and can be shaped by the world around them. The most important difference between dogs and puppies, though, is that the tiny puppy brain is a sponge with an insatiable thirst for knowledge. As responsible caretakers, we must make the most of this wonderful opportunity.

Puppies aren't born knowing how the world works or what's expected of them. A puppy is dependent upon the humans in her life to offer guidance and structure as she matures, and help her develop positive personality traits and habits. It's up to you to mold that non-stop dynamo into a respectable and affectionate member of your family.

You will be repaid a hundred-fold in loving wags, furry snuggles and slurpy-kisses, and unquestioned trust and respect. Puppy compliments don't come any higher than that!

Love 'Em and DON'T Leave 'Em!

Loving puppies is easy—especially when they cry for attention, they chase the ball with full-tilt energy, or curl into a sleepy ball of fluff on your lap. You don't need a book to tell your heart how to feel.

But puppies have no off-switch. Their high jinx can turn tolerant human smiles into nervous tics, especially when they want to play bite-your-nose at three a.m., their teeth target your furniture, or they leave bathroom "deposits" under the potted palm.

Puppies can't explain why they do the things they do. And humans don't automatically know how to teach puppies acceptable behavior. We don't speak the same language, and our cultures are foreign to each other. That's why thousands upon thousands of puppies lose their homes—and their lives—every year. People love 'em and then leave 'em because of unrealistic expectations, misunderstandings, and miscommunications.

That's where this book comes in. Consider *Complete Puppy Care* as the Miss Manners for teaching proper canine etiquette to your puppy, and a handy guide for you to understand what makes Puppy tick. Believe me, the more you know about the extraordinary creature you've chosen to love, the stronger becomes the attachment, and the greater your commitment to fix any transient "problems." That's the best way to ensure your relationship endures.

The Cute Factor and Disposable Pets

"The Cute Factor" protects even the most mischievous canine prankster from a scolding. Human scowls and anger dissolve into helpless amusement with one look from an innocent, big-eyed puppy face. She didn't *mean* to gnaw your TV remote—or ruin your pantyhose—or drink from the toilet. It doesn't take these babies long to learn to clown for our enjoyment, or just how far to push the limits of human patience.

But as puppies mature their "cute quotient" changes. While allowances may be made for the fuzzy eight-week-old baby who grabs your pant leg or swipes your house slippers, the nine-month-old adolescent puppy receives less tolerance when she knocks down Grandma or gnaws the baseboards. People may even characterize normal puppy antics at this age as "vindictive" behavior.

Once this desirable "cute factor" fades away, the puppy finds that everything that worked before to gain loving attention from her special human now lands her in the doghouse. And there's nothing worse for a dog, especially when the baby hasn't a clue what she did wrong. A large majority of the young dogs relinquished to shelters are these in-between "juvenile delinquent" puppies—not yet adults, but disposable because their cute factor has betrayed them.

When I still worked as a vet tech, it wasn't unusual for us to see new puppies (at that "cute-icity" age) appear time and again with some families. When asked what happened to the previous pet, sometimes evasive excuses or matter of fact explanations revealed the adolescent destroyed too much property, or required too much time, and so was "given away." Now they had a do-over pup, sure that this time things would work out better. This attitude promotes disposable pets, and the idea that puppies are replaceable, and sadly this attitude has become all too common. I know readers will be horrified, as am I, by those who routinely "trade in" these wonderful creatures to shelters and then seek out another baby that better fits their notion of the perfect puppy.

Puppyhood lasts about a year—and up to 18 months or so for some breeds. But all dogs retain that puppy-on-the-inside attitude even when they are mature on the outside, especially when the furry baby receives the proper attitude-shaping attention at the right time.

Puppy attitude—outrageous curiosity, boundless energy, unlimited affection, and unending trust—is so fragile, often fleeting, and so easily destroyed. That makes understanding and providing for the physical and emotional needs of your puppy even more important. It's up to us to preserve the best parts of puppyhood for all of a pet's life.

Puppy Preparedness: Why You Need This Book

Loving puppies seems simple, but it gets complicated if you want to do things right. A whole lot more goes into puppy preparedness than plopping food in the bowl or setting up a crate.

There are some terrific guides out there for dog care—but as we know, puppies are different than adults, and have quite specific requirements. Care information constantly evolves and improves, and expert recommendations of the past often give way to more current knowledge, as it becomes available. And quite frankly, there's no one right way of doing things, no matter what some books may tell you, because every puppy and every owner and every home situation is unique.

Complete Puppy Care has been written with such flexibility in mind. The book also incorporates the expertise and latest recommendations from over 300 veterinary experts in behavior, conventional care, holistic treatments, and emergency protocols I've been fortunate to interview over the past twenty-five years. It's important to offer a consensus of opinion and the available options to consider, rather than forcing a one-size-fits-all-puppies philosophy.

Of course, puppies can't read—and even if they could, they would probably prefer to chew up this book than learn from it. You, on the other hand, are able to educate yourself to learn about and choose the best options available to care for your puppy.

The purpose of this book is to help you arm yourself with knowledge. Take the time to evaluate your own expectations and abilities, and what you can and cannot offer to a puppy in the way of commitment. That, more than anything else, will help you choose the "perfect match" for the life time of that pet. That's the smart way to choose, and then raise your puppy.

Education isn't dry, paint-by-numbers facts you must commit to memory, either. Lots of fascinating tidbits of information about dogs and puppies season our knowledge, the same way salt enhances the flavor of meat and potatoes. It's fun to know how to describe your puppy's unique coloring, or figure out what that tail-talk means. That's right—wags communicate a variety of messages.

Of course, those meat and potato facts are vital, and can be a matter of life and death when choosing proper toys or healthy food. And knowing why dogs chew, turn into sniff-aholics and bark like crazy provides the basis for preventing some of the biggest dog behavior problems before they ever develop.

I want you to not only understand your puppy, but also appreciate her unique and odd and mysterious puppy-ness. In my experience, it is this understanding that prompts us to do the right thing, more than anything else.

Puppies don't stay puppies forever, though. They grow up and develop into beautiful, amusing, affectionate adult dogs with their own individual foibles and special needs. Even as a puppy's cute-factor gives way to maturity, her love for you also matures and grows stronger. *Adoption is for the lifetime of the dog*—that can be 8 to 18 years or more when proper care is taken. And just as the puppy changes during these years, our own lifestyles and home situations may also change over time.

I hope you'll keep *Complete Puppy Care* handy as your furry baby matures, because lots of the information applies to adults, too. And of course, puppies can be addictive and likely you'll want another one before too long. First-hand experience offers a great background for the proper way to bring up dog babies. You'll know better what to expect and how to react with subsequent puppies.

Organization of the Book

The book is divided into five parts. Begin with the chapters on making informed puppy choices, the best places to look, and how to prepare for Puppy's homecoming. Already have your perfect match? Check out the chapters on preventative care and training basics.

Complete Puppy Care contains all the must-knows of puppy care and behavior to ensure your relationship remains a positive, rewarding one. You'll notice throughout the book that puppies are referred to as "he" or "she" (usually in alternating chapters, just to be fair). Each chapter also includes fascinating lore, fun facts, and insiders' training tricks. I expect you'll keep the book handy to find out why your puppy's favorite games include your underwear, the importance of timing, and how you can imitate Mom-Dog to teach Puppy some manners—and more!

Part 1: Why a Puppy?
Puppies have traveled a long road reach the level of popularity and place they hold today in our hearts. In the past, puppies and dogs have been not only celebrated as gods, as in ancient Egypt, but also reviled and persecuted as demons during the Middle Ages (that's right, cats weren't the only ones!)—and some myths about them persist even today. You will appreciate and understand your puppy even more when you learn how and why she evolved the way she did and the way this helps her interact with you and the world today.

Although every puppy is deserving of your love, some may be more suited to your particular personality, lifestyle or household situation than others. Are you a single apartment-dwelling professional, or do you live with a spouse and children? Perhaps you are retired, have a large house, and will be home all day. Or maybe you need to integrate the puppy with other pets, and won't have the time to provide daily grooming. I want you to know what to expect from the various puppy options available so you can make choices that best suit your needs.

There's a rainbow of colors and patterns, in smooth coats, fluffy coats, curly coats—even bald! Choosing the perfect puppy goes beyond the outside package. But if you're drawn to a particular look, there are many purebreds that can offer a bit more predictability in terms of appearance and attitude. For instance, you need to understand that the Border Collie probably will prefer herding your kids, cats, and even you rather than sitting in your lap.

After you know what you want, you need to know all the best places to look for the puppy-of-your dreams—from breeders to rescues, or even the waif on your doorstep—to choose a puppy that has the best chance of being physically and emotionally healthy. I've also included some checklists for evaluating puppy potential to help you narrow your choices. And—because I know the heart doesn't always listen to the logic of the brain—you'll also find helpful guidelines and suggestions to consider when dealing with the at-risk or less-than-perfect baby you're determined to rescue.

Part 2: Bringing Home Baby

After you've chosen your new family member, you'll need to figure out how to prepare for the little one. In this part there's a fun section on choosing a name for the little one (hint: puppies often seem to name themselves!). And you'll also find information about protecting the puppy from unexpected household dangers by puppy-proofing your home.

You also need a list of all the "must-haves" for puppies to make him feel at home—everything from food and bowls to toys and grooming supplies. Today there are so many choices available that choosing the "right" product for the puppy can be tough. I provide a discussion of the pros and cons of some of the most popular canine accoutrements so you can choose the one best suited to your puppy needs.

This part also explains all about the canine social structure. Understanding how and why puppies act and react to other dogs, as well as strange animals, people, and places lets you smooth relationships and speeds up the training process. That gives you the tools you'll need to introduce your puppy to all the important things in your life like other adults, children or pets.

Part 3: Puppy Care 101

In this part, health issues are addressed, starting with proper nutrition. After all, puppies must eat to live--and establishing proper eating habits early can keep them from developing finicky or gluttonous habits that damage their health. What food should you feed? How much and how often should your puppy eat? Are treats okay? You'll find the answers to these and other tasty questions in this section.

Puppy grooming concerns are also addressed. You'll learn how to keep your puppy looking spiffy and feeling her best, what grooming supplies you need, from flea combs and shampoos to tooth brushes and nail trimmers—and most important of all, *how* to groom the baby so she enjoys the process.

Veterinarians agree that preventing health problems is much easier than treating illness once it develops. This part tells you how to choose a veterinarian, the signs of good puppy health, and key prevention care like vaccinations, parasite control, and elective surgeries like spay, neuter and ear cropping or tail docking procedures—and the truth about what's involved. I'll also give you a list of the top puppy health concerns, and how to recognize possible health problems. Puppies often do need medicine, just like human babies, so you'll find step-by-step instructions on home-medicating your puppy when needed. And because puppies do grow into adults, there's also information on what to expect as your baby grows up, from physical signs of maturity and the behavior changes you'll see, to recommended prevention care as well as some of the most common health concerns.

Chapter 11 covers the most common puppy emergencies and what to do. If the worst should happen—your puppy runs in front of a car, eats the wrong medicine, or is bitten by a stray dog—you are the first line of defense. This chapter explains how to prevent danger, and how to save your puppy's life. I pray you'll never need to do so.

Of course, no book can replace the expertise of a veterinarian. Never hesitate to call on the experts, don't leave it to chance. Better a false alarm than the puppy becoming sick (or worse).

Part 4: Puppy Sociability and Training

One of my favorite topics is canine behavior, and in this section you'll learn all about how your puppy sees, hears, smells the world, tastes her food and feels when you pet her. That's important, because senses rule the why, when, and how of puppy behavior, from growls and barks, to wags and body wiggles.

This section also celebrates and explains the purpose behind puppy play. You'll learn how you can make play-sessions work for you as training tools and bonding therapy to bring out the best personality in your pet.

Puppies especially are eminently trainable and I want you to know all the key elements for teaching your new baby the rules of the house, from crate training to leash walking. What kinds of rewards work? How do I stop "bad" behavior? You'll find step-by-step instruction on these issues as well as humane and effective cures for problem behaviors like biting, chewing, digging, and hit-or-miss potty problems. So many people routinely travel these days that puppies often need to learn some rules of the road. You'll find information on keeping your puppy safe and comfortable during travel whether she goes with you, or stays at home.

Part 5: Canine Fascinations

Dogs have partnered with humans for centuries, and I've had a great time compiling some of the most entertaining information I could find in this section. Fanciful legends offer explanations for everything from distinctive looks to how dogs even had a paw in creation of the world.

You can discover even more fun legends, canine facts, puppy care products and dog chat communities by surfing the Internet. I've included a chapter listing some of my favorite puppy web destinations.

We love dogs because of their unique abilities and foibles. This part also celebrates and explains many of these fun facts. Why do dogs drink from toilets, and roll in stinky stuff? Find out in Chapter 17.

PART ONE

WHY A PUPPY?

1: Considering Your Options

Rainbow Coalition

If you've purchased this book, you already *know* why you want a puppy. There is nothing quite as endearing as that furry imp, or as heart-warming as the trust embodied by this loving creature dependent upon you to shape his life. Puppies complete the empty places inside we didn't know were missing. They make us laugh, they offer us companionship, they listen to our complaints, and wag us out of bad moods, celebrate our successes and are with us through setbacks. Puppies love us bad-breath and all, and they never, ever lie.

There is a puppy to suit every taste and circumstance. Puppies come in a kaleidoscope of coat colors, patterns, and fur length. Each is a unique work of art formed by nature, and like snowflakes, there are no two exactly alike.

Boy Versus Girl—Does It Matter?

There are exceptions to every rule, but generally speaking, boy dogs tend to be bigger at maturity than girl dogs. And as they reach sexual maturity, they can develop belligerent attitudes toward other males when they test their status. They can also wreak havoc when they leg-lift to deposit urine to mark their territory. Intact females develop a messy bloody discharge when they go into heat—that period when they can get pregnant. Practically speaking, it usually costs a bit less to have a boy dog neutered than it does to have a girl dog spayed. You can read more detailed information about the canine facts of life in Chapter 9.

During puppyhood, though, both boys and girls act very similarly. They eat the same, play the same, sleep the same, get into the same mischief, and generate the same amount of love.

Gender does matter when introducing your new puppy into a household that already has an adult dog. Unless the dogs have grown up together, it's almost always better to introduce a puppy of the opposite sex to an adult resident dog, because the older dog tends not to feel quite so threatened with this arrangement.

Everything else being equal, gender does matter in some specific circumstances, but should not be the defining issue for choosing the baby. Rather, the puppy's personality—that spark of recognition that says you were meant for each other—is much more important than gender.

Pedigreed Pooch or the Dog-Next-Door?

I confess I am an equal-opportunity pet lover. I fall in love with each puppy I meet, be it a random-bred beauty or pedigreed show puppy. We were on a waiting list for nearly three years before we got our Magical-Dawg (a German Shepherd). But my first doggy love was a random bred pooch who still fills my heart.

There really is no right or wrong choice between these two groups. It comes down to a matter of taste. However, there are advantages and disadvantages to both options that you should consider before you make your choice.

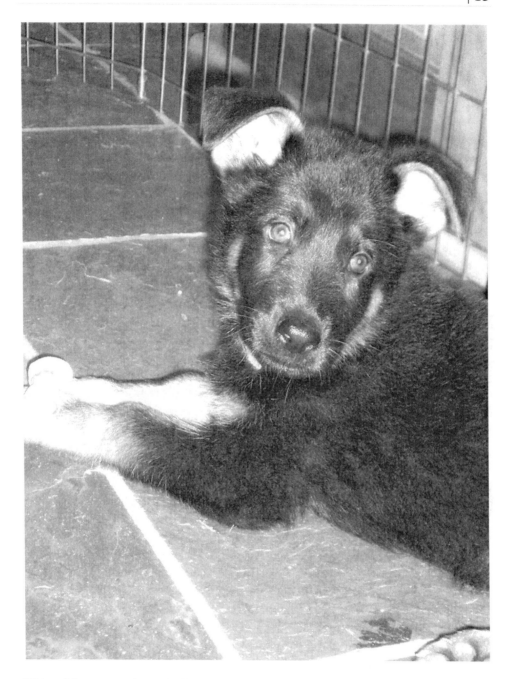

This is Magic, an eight-week-old German Shepherd puppy, on the second day he came to live with the author.

Canine Breeds

Dogs come in all shapes and sizes, and specific types are called "breeds." Very generally, a dog is considered a particular breed when a mating between two dogs of the same type produces puppies of identical type. In other words, mating two Pekingese dogs produces Peke puppies that will have the same long fur and large round eyes as their parents. And breeding two Vizsla dogs produces shorthaired red coated puppies similar in type to their parents.

Dogs have been associated with humans for at least 15,000 years, with recent genetic research pointing to as early as 100,000 years ago. Dog "types" like the Alaskan Malamute and Saluki appeared in nature, and changed very little over the centuries. Many of the breeds we know today have been around for 3000 years or longer and selective breeding by dog fanciers refined these breeds.

Dog looks and behavior evolved when people selectively bred dogs to suit their needs—to improve herding or scenting ability, for example. Breeders still experiment by creating hybrids and designer dogs. In the past when a new "type" appeared through an accidental breeding or mutation, early people promoted it.

"Spontaneous mutations" are accidents of nature that change the look or other aspects of the dog. Happy accidents include body shape and size, ear placement and tail carriage, scenting and sighting ability, or even hair coat and color. Despite the great variety in size and shape, all dogs are easily recognizable as canines. Dog breeds range in size from teacup sizes, to pony-size 200 pound plus canines.

Giantism (acromegaly) mutation created breeds like the Great Dane and Saint Bernard. These mastiff-type breeds not only are larger, they tend to be more heavily muscled and cobby—have a compact, short-bodied structure. By comparison, sighthound breeds like Greyhounds are no less muscled but appear more lithe—and there are a wide range between the two extremes.

Small breeds developed when a normal-sized dog simply miniaturized. The Whippet, for example, looks like a scaled down Greyhound, while the Poodle comes in three sizes including the tiny Toy Poodle. It may be hard to believe, but the Pug is a mastiff-type and so is the Chihuahua, often with a similar attitude as their larger counterparts.

The other "little" dogs aren't always so small—but instead, simply short. Dwarfism (achondroplasia) results in shortened, somewhat curved leg bones but leaves the body proportional. Examples include breeds like Dachshunds, Basset Hounds and Corgies.

Some dog breeds arose naturally in certain parts of the world, while others were developed by the careful selection of dedicated dog fanciers. Meticulous records of these canine family trees, called pedigrees, are kept. Educated breeders use pedigrees to help predict what kind of offspring a particular mating may produce. They strive to preserve and improve the integrity of a given breed through careful matchmaking of prospective dog parents. Today there are more than 400 different dog breeds recognized throughout the world.

Adopting a pedigree puppy from a reputable breeder offers the advantage of a known ancestry. You'll likely be able to meet at least one of the parents, which can help you predict future personality of your little one. Specific dog breeds are also known for certain personality traits, so you may be better able to choose a puppy that matches your own high-energy or laid-back demeanor. Purebred puppies also tend to have an above-average health care history because good breeders are sticklers for preventative care, such as good nutrition, vaccinations and worm medicine for the parents and the babies.

Finally, purebred puppies raised "underfoot"—that is, as members of the breeder's pet family—have the huge advantage of being properly socialized. Socialization refers to the period of time during early puppy-life when the baby learns to accept people (and other animals) as safe, happy, and normal parts of his life.

This Chihuahua puppy is the perfect choice for many pet lovers. Purebred puppies may be found from rescues as well as breeders.

There are some drawbacks to pedigree puppies. The most obvious is the cost—you can expect to spend much more on a purebred baby, in the hundreds or sometimes thousands of dollars. That's because some breeds are quite rare, and may not be available for "pet homes" because they are expected to compete in shows and contribute to their breed as future moms and dads. The cost also often includes some sort of limited guarantee, though, because of the investment the breeder has made in the health of the puppies.

After investing their time, money, and love producing high-quality puppies, breeders can be quite selective about who gets their babies. They also may limit your ability to breed the puppies, especially if they consider the puppy "pet quality" and not a show or breeding contender. After all, their reputation is at stake and they only want folks breeding their puppies who know what they're doing.

Another potential downside of adopting purebred puppies is certain health problems that may be present in a given breed. Overall, dog breeds have many more potentially inherited problems than do cats, and reputable dog breeders are honest about these concerns.

The greatest drawback to adopting purebred puppies is when the breeder is not reputable. In these instances, not only the puppy, but you suffer the consequences. Paying lots of money does not guarantee a healthy, well-bred and happy puppy. For more details about how to find and identify good breeders and quality purebred puppies, see Chapter 2.

A Look at Dog Shows

The earliest record of a dog show dates to June 1859 in England, with only 60 hunting dogs (Pointers and Setters) shown. These exhibitions evaluated dogs based on looks and ability to function.

Today the sport of dogs has grown to include more than 400 separate breeds (depending on the registering body), and expanded beyond pedigree-only dogs to embrace mutts in a variety of shaggy competitions. But a conformation dog show is exclusive to purebred dogs.

Show judges are experts in the breeds they judge. They may be qualified to judge only specific breeds, specific types, or be qualified as an "all breed judge." The judge must know what constitutes the breed "ideal." That includes the coat type and color, size, way the dog moves, temperament, and other specifics designated by the breed standard. Dogs destined for the dog show ring should be trained and properly socialized to accept handling by strangers in strange environments.

Dogs are judged against the standard. The dog that comes closest to the judge's mind's eye vision of perfection is awarded the win. Besides looks, the dog's health, ability to move, and even personality must be up to snuff. Many judges say that winning dogs have an attitude that "asks" for the ribbon.

Not every breed will be entered in all shows. Different types of shows offer entry to different selections of breeds. A "specialty show" features only those dogs of a designated breed or breeds. The room may contain a hundred Pugs, for example. A group match features all the breeds that belong to a general "type" of dog. For instance, a group match might specify the Toy group or the Terrier group. The American Kennel Club (AKC) divides the groups by function and purpose for which the dogs were bred, or by size.

- Sporting Group consists of Labs, Setters, Spaniels, pointers, retrievers.
- Hounds includes sighthounds like Greyhounds, Beagles, Foxhounds—any breeds with "hound" in the name (plus a few surprises).
- Working group includes the sled dogs, draft dogs, and dogs such as Akita and Doberman.
- Terrier group consists of nearly any breed with 'terrier' in the name plus the Miniature Schnauzer.
- Toys are by size—the little guys—from Chihuahuas to Maltese.
- Non-sporting examples include Chow Chow, Dalmatian, Bichon, Lhasa Apso, and Boston Terrier
- Herding are all the shepherds, sheepdogs, and cattle dogs.
- Miscellaneous Class is sort of a stepping-stone category for dogs that have not yet been accepted into one of the other groups, but which may in the future.

The United Kennel Club (UKC) is another very large registry of purebred dogs. The UKC recognizes many of the same breeds plus additional ones, or calls them by different names. For instance, the UKC recognizes the American Pit Bull Terrier—while the AKC calls the same breed the American Staffordshire Terrier. The UKC groups breeds slightly differently with eight groups based on purpose: Gun Dogs, Scenthounds, Herding Group, Guarding Dogs, Sighthounds, Terriers, Companion Dogs and Northern Breeds.

"Mutt" Dogs

They are called mutt dogs, random-bred puppies, or mixed-breed canines. Unlike their purebred brethren, non-pedigree dogs do not produce predictable puppies from any given mating. But whatever they're called, our dog-next-door canines are without a doubt the most popular "type" of pet dog in the world.

The biggest advantage to "everyday" puppies is that they are always available, and for a reasonable cost. Be advised that no dog is free! Even the puppies that appear on your back porch require preventative and routine maintenance health care. The cost for wellness care for your new puppy is the same whether he's a purebred or shelter rescue.

These popular puppies can be every bit as beautiful, healthy, and well socialized as their purebred counterparts. But they are at higher risk for health and behavior problems, because they may not have the advantages of being born to a healthy and pampered Mom-dog, or handled by loving dog advocates.

Random bred or "mutt" puppies come in as many varieties as their pedigree cousins, and are just as lovable. Siblings can look very different. Because these puppies are so available, there are far too many of them. That means, when you adopt a random-bred puppy it is often an act that saves the baby's life. That's the biggest advantage of all.

What's A Designer Dog?

The term "designer dog" refers to a hybrid. Hybrids are created by combining existing breeds to form new ones. Most existing dog breeds were created in this way and likely are hybrids. Many are so ancient, though, their origin is obscure.

A recent example of a designer dog is the Labradoodle, purposely bred to create a low-shedding dog (Poodle) with the temperament for a guide dog (Labrador). Because Poodles come in three sizes, Labradoodle pups also vary in size and may be more like the Poodle or Labrador side of the family. Breeders dedicated to establishing the variety as a true breed work to establish a predictable type, working with generations of dogs.

The designer dog label today is used to market hybrid dogs, which may (or may not) be more healthy, cute, trainable or other fill-in-the-blank claim. Shelters sometimes label mixed breeds as a designer breed to promote adoptions. Puppy mills jumped on the designer dog bandwagon to create boatloads of interesting mixes they sell for high prices.

The health and temperament of a puppy trumps cute factor and marketing ploys every day. Don't let a designer label or popular puppy fads get in the way of choosing a healthy companion—whether pedigree, mutt or designer breed, listen to your head as well as your heart.

Puppy Care

Considerations

Other options to consider with choosing your puppy include personality, activity level, and care requirements. All puppies play and are active, and certainly every puppy needs grooming attention. But some puppies have no off-switch while others like to lap-snuggle after a romp, and a number of puppies—especially purebred dogs—have very specific hygiene needs.

Although there are exceptions, terrier-type breeds developed to go after "critters" may not be able to control their instinct to chase and kill. Sighthounds such as Afghans or Greyhounds may also feel the urge to chase scurrying creatures.

Other dog breeds have been developed to take advantage of predatory behavior, but stop short of killing. Herding dogs chase joggers, bicyclist, sheep, and cats, for instance—it's a natural instinct, so be prepared for careful training if you share your life with one of these go-getters.

There are always exceptions, but Kerry Blue Terriers, American Pit Bull Terriers and other dog aggressive breeds may not get along with another canine. Most dogs follow the lead of the human family member they respect, though, and if YOU say the new guy is okay, King often accepts and endorses your decision.

Even friendly dogs could prove dangerous if there's a great size disparity between the pets. An 80-pound pooch could accidentally sit on your Chihuahua puppy or hurt the smaller pet if play gets too rough.

On the other paw, a jumbo-size Great Pyrenees baby might injure your old-lady Lhasa Apso when he puppy-pounces on her arthritic frame. Study the breeds and talk with professionals to help you make informed choices. It can work, but requires more supervision and care on your part.

2: Looking for Your Dream Puppy

Give Me Shelter

One of the best places to look for your dream puppy is the local animal shelter. These organizations often have puppies available by the armload, especially during the spring "puppy season."

Puppies from the best shelters have the advantage of being cared for by a knowledgeable staff and an army of caring volunteers. Animal welfare services often take great pains to handle and properly socialize these babies to ensure they will fit into your family and become the best pet possible.

Veterinary exams also screen shelter puppies for health problems, offer preventative care, and sometimes a discounted cost for future treatment. Many times, a history of the dog's life is available, and may include any medical treatments, personality traits (likes other dogs or cats) and behavior foibles (loves to dig). Shelters want these adoptions to be permanent ones, and so may also offer counseling and support services to guide you through correcting or preventing any behavioral difficulties that might arise.

There is a wide range of shelter options from which to choose. Nearly every part of the country has access to some type of facility that handles unwanted excess dogs and cats. They go by many names, from Rescue Leagues, Animal Control or City Pound, to Humane Society and SPCA (Society for the Prevention of Cruelty to Animals).

Some shelters are very large and have paid staff and a variety of services. Many are private facilities, others are city-run operations, and some are quite small. There are even shelters for dogs only.

They may be further divided into those that euthanize animals not adopted within a set time limit, or that are deemed unadoptable due to illness, injury, or temperament; and those that are no-kill facilities that rehabilitate and house the pet indefinitely, until an adoptive home is found. Euthanasia of unwanted pets is a sad fact of life for the majority of shelters, but saving all adoptable dogs and cats is an admirable goal. Until pet owners take responsibility and prevent the births of these unwanted animals, it will remain so. And unfortunately, all shelters (especially no-kill facilities) have limited space and aren't able to accept as many as they'd like.

I've traveled a great deal and visited shelter facilities all across the country. Most are run by dedicated pet lovers who want to help the animals and the people they serve. Visit your local shelters to see how the puppies are housed, handled, and treated. The best situations will have clean, sanitary-appearing facilities with staff eager and willing to answer your questions.

Clean kennels and cages are necessary to help keep puppies healthy and happy.

Some cage puppies individually to help prevent illness, often in a room segregated from other animals. Others house pairs or litters of puppies together. Still more provide play areas that allow them to interact with each other. This more natural setting can be healthier for the emotional life of the dogs, but does risk exposure to communicable illnesses if they don't receive proper health screenings.

Visit with the staff and find out their adoption policies. Although most shelters are not for profit, they must charge adoption fees to offset the cost of vetting the animals and running the facility. Often, the adoption fee includes to-date vaccinations, veterinary health exams and worm treatments, and spay/neuter surgeries. Some also microchip the adopted pet for identification purposes.

Depending on the facility, puppies may be spayed or neutered prior to you taking them home, or you may be required to schedule an appointment at a later date. Often they will either have a veterinarian on staff, or a group of dedicated local veterinarians who offer lower cost spay/neuter services.

Shelter staff often require that you complete a questionnaire, or be interviewed about your pet history to determine what you want in a pet. That helps them match you to the perfect puppy. In some instances, a shelter may refuse to allow a person to adopt a pet if they don't feel the home environment is appropriate, or if the applicant's pet history is less than ideal.

For instance, some shelters won't adopt out puppies unless they are assured the pet will only have access to a fenced yard. They may also deny an application if the person plans to give the pet as a gift to a third party—usually shelters require the prospective owner be the one to choose their perfect puppy. An exception may be made for parents adopting for children—but even then, some shelters may not be comfortable adopting very young puppies into homes with youngsters who may not know how to properly and safely handle a pet. Finally, some shelters may actually require a home visit to be sure you have an adequate place for the puppy. In the case of apartment dwellers, often shelters require a letter from the landlord that grants permission to keep a pet.

Breeder Sources

Maybe you've got your heart set on a regal Great Dane like Uncle George's, or fell in love with the Japanese Chin at a dog show. Shelters may have purebred dogs or puppies available, although they typically won't have registration papers. There may also be puppies that look similar to some of the purebred puppies, of course.

The best place to find a purebred puppy is from a reputable breeder in your area. Many of the specialty dog magazines list dog breeders and kennels in the back of their publications. Not every breed will have a kennel near you, and not all kennels will be listed in these breeder directories, but this is a good place to start.

Looks can be deceiving. Be sure that your prospective puppy also enjoys interaction with people, and isn't just a pretty face.

Another resource is websites that feature various breeds. Many of the dog registry association homepages offer a list of breeders and kennels that are available in different parts of the country.

Breed rescue organizations are another place to find purebred dogs. Individuals dedicated to taking care of a particular breed may pull dogs from shelters. They may also accept pooches that didn't work out in their first home, and attempt to find better second homes. Breed rescues more typically handle adult dogs, though.

Purebred puppies are not cheap. You can expect to pay in the hundreds of dollars for one of these selectively-bred babies. But unless you plan to compete in dog shows, a "pet quality" puppy can be the perfect and more economical choice for you. These are babies that for one reason or another—perhaps the puppy has the wrong color or less-than-perfect markings—are not judged by the breeder to be good show or breeding prospects. Often the breeder reduces the price on these pet quality puppies.

Once you have narrowed your search to nearby breeders and kennels, call and talk with the owner/breeder and arrange for a visit. Puppies won't be available all the time, and you may need to place your name on a waiting list. More important than cost or getting on a waiting list, you want to evaluate the kennel facilities where your potential new puppy family member is born and raised. It should be clean, the dogs should look healthy and happy, and the breeder should be interested in you and willing to answer any questions you have.

In fact, you should expect to be interviewed thoroughly by the breeder. These folks invest a great deal of time, money, and emotion into their puppies and won't sell to just anybody. Just like you, they want puppies to go to a forever-home, one that will love and take care of the puppy in a responsible way. A good relationship with your puppy's breeder not only offers a good resource for answering any puppy questions that may arise down the road, they can turn into lasting friendships. And if you are at all interested in showing your puppy, you can't do better than the friendship and mentoring relationship with an experienced responsible breeder.

At least some of the dogs should have run of the household—*raised underfoot* in other words, which means they are treated and handled like pets and family members. The male dogs may not be onsite, and very young puppies may also be segregated for their protection.

But if the facilities aren't clean; the dogs are all caged; the puppies and adults appear ill, unkempt, very shy or frightened; and the breeder seems more interested in getting your money than the well-being of the puppy—*RUN, DO NOT WALK, AWAY FROM THIS FACILITY!*

Sadly, there are bad apples in most any barrel, including dog breeders. Often, these establishments are referred to as "back-yard breeders" and the folks involved typically care more about making money on their furry livestock than furthering the welfare of the puppies.

It can be hard to tell the good from the bad or ugly simply from browsing an Internet or magazine listing. That's why it's so important to actually visit the site and personally choose your puppy and visit with the breeder. References from those you know and trust also can be very helpful.

Breeders do, upon occasion, ship puppies across the country. That's not something I'd recommend, even from a reputable kennel. Puppies are easily stressed and traveling as cargo on a plane puts them at risk. If your perfect breed isn't available locally, and you'd like to pursue this option, be sure to receive strong personal recommendations from people you trust about the breeder in question.

Pet Stores—Be Informed!

Many years ago when I still worked as a veterinary technician, a new client arrived, proud-as-punch over her brand-new $400 puppy purchased from a local pet store. As I filled out the history card, she corrected me from calling her puppy a mixed breed. "My puppy," she told me, "is a registered Teacup Malti-Poo. I have the registration papers right here."

I didn't argue with her—the $400 piece of paper made her happy. But there is no such breed as a "teacup" anything (that's a marketing term). This was in the days before "designer dog" combos became so popular so the Maltese-Poodle cross could not be registered with the AKC or UKC and the paperwork saying so was worth less than the ink it was printed with. She was fortunate in that her baby was healthy, and her little random-bred puppy was lucky to have found a loving home. The take-away message here is, *buyer beware!*

Reputable breeders of purebred puppies—and of pedigreed kittens, for that matter—recognize the importance of screening the new owners. Reputable breeders do not sell through pet stores. Period.

Yes, some pet stores do offer purebred puppies for sale, and it can be hard to resist that big-eyed fuzzy face in the window. The store may

WARNING!

If reputable breeders won't supply them, where do pet store purebred puppies come from? To be blunt, some come from the back-yard breeders mentioned above. They also come from establishments loosely described as *puppy mills*. The tragedy of the puppy-mill industry has been extensively covered by both print and television journalist. It is shameful that such facilities exist to serve as little more than factories for producing fuzzy cute babies for impulse-buy markets. By its very nature, puppy mills have little regard for the animal's health, comfort, safety, or wellbeing.

even have legitimate registration papers available. A few offer some type of health guarantee that could help defray veterinary costs in case the purchased puppy gets sick or dies shortly after you bring her home. Be aware that puppies generated by this industry have a much higher chance of developing health problems due to less-than-ideal breeding and hygiene practices. And as the puppy matures, behavior problems are also likely because they have not been socialized. Buying a puppy mill puppy, no matter how altruistic, supports the industry.

There is good news about pet stores, however. A number of the most progressive establishments like the superstores PetCo and PetsMart have taken steps to set a new standard for their industry. Instead of selling puppies and dogs (or kittens and cats), they have formed partnerships with local shelters and animal rescue organizations to showcase adoptable animals in their facilities. This puppy (below) won his forever-home at such an adoption event.

These liaisons offer a great opportunity for shelters, pet stores, and prospective owners to make educated choices, and have pet product resources available. Of course, the puppy benefits the most.

Friends and Neighbors

There are always neighbors, friends of friends, and family members who have rescued a pregnant dog or abandoned puppies—or have accidentally delayed spaying the family dog until she's in the family way. During the spring and fall puppy season, your local newspaper will be filled with advertisements for puppies "free to good home."

When the puppy comes from someone you know, you have the advantage of finding out more about the baby and even making several visits to be sure which one strikes the chord in your heart. You also will know your family and friends' background and how well they've cared for your prospective pet. The history of the people raising the puppies—they've loved and successfully kept dogs for the past 30 years—offers a great endorsement of how your new puppy will fit into your family.

Advertisements in newspapers may also offer good options—but here, you'll want to evaluate the environment just like you would a shelter or breeder. Are the animals clean? Well fed? Loved? Have the puppies been "raised underfoot?" Or do they live in the back yard with their mother, with no people contact?

Some people will want to ask you questions and interview your potential as a prospective pet parent—that's a very positive sign. More often, though, people are simply anxious to unburden themselves and you will have free choice of the babies, no questions asked.

Remember, too, that such situations have hidden costs involved. That "free puppy" probably has had no veterinary health care. That may mean extra expense down the road, in addition to routine vaccinations and other preventative attention. You'll find tips and information on how to evaluate puppy personality and health status in Chapter 3.

The Waif on the Doorstep

Sometimes the puppy finds you rather than the other way around, particular when someone with no heart dumps a litter and they wander up to your back patio. Adopting a stray puppy offers the most potential for problems for several reasons.

These puppies often have been on their own for some time, without any type of preventative health care. They therefore often are stressed, or already sick, when you find them. Stray puppies likely have not had the benefit of handling by humans. That can make it difficult for the baby to bond closely with you. Behavior problems could develop down the road as a result of missing this important socialization. Also, when you go in search of a puppy, you can be prepared in advance before bringing home your furry wonder—not so with an unexpected bundle of joy.

Adopting an ill, needy puppy will require a much greater investment of your time, money, and emotions. You must be prepared for those sad instances where the best of intentions and veterinary care will not save the puppy's fragile life.

But when it works, it's magic. Rescuing a lost puppy, and watching her thrive, is incredibly rewarding. The found puppy can be a viable place to meet your perfect puppy.

This Australian Shepherd puppy and her littermates was offered for sale in the parking lot of a local Wal-Mart. It's hard to resist these offerings, but be cautions before you adopt.

Know the Score—Puppy Source Check List

There are many places to find your dream puppy, and some are clearly better options than others. Of course, your heart can overrule logic if you are smitten by a needy baby. Take a moment to ask the shelter staff, breeder, or other source these questions. That will give you an idea of potential risk involved in adopting or buying from that establishment. For each question below, a yes answer receives one point, and a no response gets zero points. Tally the score when you finish to see how the puppy source rates—the higher the score the better.

10 Questions to Ask Puppy Sellers

1. Can you tell me about the temperament of at least one parent (the mother)?
2. Can you tell me about the temperament of my puppy?
3. Has the puppy been handled, so she's socialized to people?
4. May I visit the facilities to see where my puppy has been raised? Are facilities clean?
5. If she's a purebred, were health screens done on parent dogs? Is registration and pedigree information available?
6. Will you provide a medical history of to-date vaccinations or other care given?
7. Does the purchase price/adoption fee include health guarantees?
8. Do you provide a list of references/testimonials from satisfied adopters/purchasers?
9. Have you ever turn down a potential purchase/adopter?
10. Will you be available to offer help and advice as my puppy grows?

SCORES of 8 to 10 = **IDEAL**
SCORES of 5 to 7 = **FAIR to GOOD**
SCORES of 4 or less = **PROCEED WITH CAUTION**

3: Pick Of The Litter

No matter where you find your puppy, you can use the same criteria to evaluate his health and emotional status. Not every furry baby will have stellar health or start out with the best socialization. You may choose him anyway, and that's fine—these babies often are the most needy and deserving of a loving home. But it's important that you recognize problems so you know what to expect, and can take steps to make up for any false starts and give the puppy every opportunity to thrive.

The Head-to-Toe Physical

The puppy's skin is the largest physical structure of his body, and along with fur, is a barometer of puppy health. Pet the puppy all over. Short fur should be shiny and clean, long fur fluffy and without tangles, and there should be no bald spots or sores anywhere on his body. Skin sores or lost fur can be a sign of parasites like fleas, fungus infections like ringworm, or poor nutrition. All are treatable with prompt veterinary help.

The skin of the ears should be pink, clear, and clean. Any sort of discharge could indicate either an ear infection, or more commonly, parasites like ear mites. Ear mites are very contagious between pets, but are highly treatable.

Puppy eyes should be clear, have no squint, and show no discharge or crust. His nose also should be clean, with only a small amount of clear discharge, if any. Discharge from the eyes and/or nose could be a sign of serious illness like distemper, a highly contagious dog disease that can be devastating to young puppies. Veterinary attention and home nursing care is often necessary to help the baby recover.

Look inside the puppy's mouth. The gums above the teeth should be pink—if they're very pale, the baby may be anemic or dehydrated from hookworms or fleas. If you suspect dehydration, check by grasping the loose skin at the baby's neck (scruff) and lifting, then release. The skin will "tent" and stay elevated when the baby is dehydrated, rather than springing back immediately when he's normal.

Check the area beneath the puppy's tail, to be sure it's clean and has no signs of diarrhea. Diarrhea can result from a wide range of health problems, from viruses to intestinal parasites. It can also cause dehydration very quickly in a tiny puppy.

A healthy puppy has only one speed when not sleeping—ZOOM! Any time the youngster acts depressed or weak is cause for concern. Anemia, dehydration, fever, and a wide range of illnesses put a damper on puppy energy.

WARNING!

Many puppy conditions are quite contagious. Even if the one you choose appears healthy, if any of his siblings (or his mom) have signs of illness, your puppy may be incubating the disease and could become sick after you take him home.

Emotional Evaluation

Puppies in a litter not only can look very different, they can have a wide range of personalities. It's a good idea to first evaluate all the babies together—with the Mom present, when possible. There's security in numbers and the puppies often will show their true colors when they have other dogs nearby.

To get a good read on personality, sit on the floor and let the puppies come to you. You're a huge giant-creature compared to the baby and you'll be more approachable once on his own level.

The ideal puppy meets the world with curious eyes wide-open, ready to explore, and with a courageous, take-no-prisoners curiosity. They seem to thrive on new experiences. Look for a baby who, after perhaps a brief hesitation, comes forward to meet you with his tail wagging and ears pricked. He recognizes people as safe, but all-powerful beings and defers to you.

A certain amount of caution is healthy, of course. But the shy or scared puppy that hides under the bed or cowers and shivers at your touch will need lots of help to become better adjusted. Others may actually be so terrified they whine, shiver or even snarl and try to attack and can require more attention than you have to give. For shy babies, try enticing from a distance by rolling a ball to them or dragging a sock along the floor to see if they'll forget their reticence.

Interact with your prospective puppy with these tests, to help predict personality.

Puppy Temperament Tests

Think of puppy temperament testing as a canine crystal ball used to identify your puppy's personality to predict—and so manage—potential future problems. Temperament tests measure a puppy's stability, shyness, aggressiveness, and friendliness.

There's no one-size-fits-all test. Some are used by breeders to assess Schutzhund performance or tracking ability, for example. Shelters use temperament tests to measure general temperament and suitability for adoption. Still others test dogs for their therapy or assistance dog potential. Most also test for aggression.

Ask your breeder or shelter what temperament tests, if any, have been performed and the result. They may use these to choose your puppy for you, based on what you're looking for or your experience level/home environment you're able to provide. For instance, an experienced owner would do better handling a pushy puppy, and a fenced yard might be required for a "nosy" breed obsessed with running off after scents.

Personality and temperament aren't cast in stone at birth. Early experience, socialization, development and the consequences of learning all impact your puppy's future behavior. Resistance to handling, possessive aggression, territorial vocalization, excessive reactivity and many forms of fear might not emerge until the dog is older. Testing puppies as late as possible—at three to four months—may be more accurate. If you can recognize the potential for negative behaviors, you can diminish the impact.

Shelter pups (especially older ones) may test with fearfulness or aggression in the shelter, and behave very differently once out of the stress of an overwhelming environment. Socialization and training can overcome many potential problems so what's predicted doesn't always HAVE to happen.

You can also perform modified tests yourself. Use the following basics to see how your puppy performs. Tests for puppies between seven and ten weeks of age often include these basics:

- Cradle pup on his back like a baby, place a hand gently on his chest and look directly in his eyes. Pups that accept this handling are considered biddable, while those that resist are more likely to be independent-minded.
- Hold pup suspended under her armpits with hind legs dangling, while looking directly in eyes. Again, those pups that submit are said to have a low score for willfulness, while those that struggle may want to do things their own way.
- Drop keys or tin pan to test him for noise sensitivity.
- See how pup reacts to a stranger entering the room—or to being left alone in the room. Does he run to greet, or cower and cry?

Here's one more test helpful especially for older puppies. Place the individual puppy with his breeder (or shelter worker) in a room with new toys, and see how the pup reacts when the person leaves. Pups usually fall into three broad categories:

- **Couldn't care less** when owners left or came back perhaps indicating a tendency toward more independent, willful behavior or improper bonding
- **Super needy** who whined and ignored toys when owners left and clung to owners when present, suggesting over-attachment predictive of future separation anxiety
- **Middle of the road** paid attention to owners' coming and goings, but not traumatized and enjoyed toys, suggesting a healthy attachment and easygoing personality without need of either firmness or coddling.

Is He Old Enough?

What age is best to adopt your new puppy? The majority of professional dog breeders and many well-respected dog behaviorists say that dog babies should stay with siblings and Mom-dog for *at least 8 to 12 weeks*. Of course, that's not always possible.

Maturity has as much to do with emotional development as it does with physical growth. Physically, puppies are able to eat and thrive on commercial food as early as three weeks of age and most are weaned by six to eight weeks of age. That's the most common time puppies leave and go to new homes, primarily I believe for convenience's sake. Places that have puppies available, like shelters, often have limited space. So as soon as puppies reach that six to eight week mark, are able to eat, and have a set of preventative vaccines, they're out the door.

But by that age, puppies are just beginning to learn to be proper dogs. And no matter how well intentioned, human caretakers aren't able to do as good a job as furry siblings and dog-parents.

Puppies learn from other dogs how to play nicely and inhibit bites; use and understand body language and verbal cues; and to defer to older canines. They also take their cues from other dogs about what's safe—like people and other dogs or cats—and what's scary and to be avoided. That means if Mom-dog shows puppies a positive reaction to a friendly dog, they'll be more likely to get along in a multi-pet home.

Puppies adopted too early often bite more than those who have been corrected by Mom and siblings. They also may be fearful or less tolerant of other dogs, because they don't understand all the proper canine etiquette of the social structure. And because dogs tend to consider their human to be part of their family, it's important for the puppy to respect you and defer to your rules of the house, just as he would a dog-in-command.

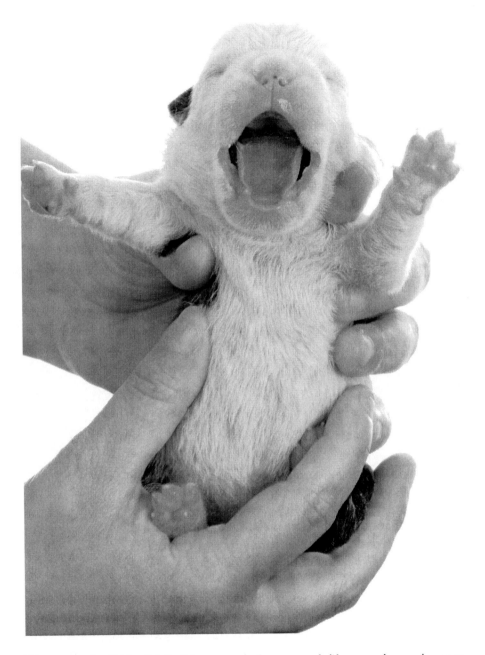

This one-week-old English Bulldog puppy looks very much like any other newborn pup. With eyes and ears still sealed, she relies on her mother for everything.

A 2012 British veterinarian study looked at the behavior problems in dogs based on the age they'd left their litters. They concluded that the chance of destructiveness, excessive barking, fearfulness on walks, noise reactivity (thunder/fireworks), food or toy possessiveness, and attention-seeking behaviors increased significantly when pups had been separated from the litter *earlier than eight weeks of age.* That argues for leaving puppies with their mother and littermates for at least this extended period to potentially reduce the chance of behavior problems as adults.

Proper socialization not only includes interaction with other dogs, but positive handling by people during this critical period. That ensures the baby is well adjusted, confident, and emotionally healthy.

Many times we do not have the luxury of adopting our puppy at the "ideal" age. That means that you, the human parent, will need to do your best to do Mom-dog's job and teach Junior how to be a proper dog. Each age has particular challenges, too. After all, a puppy is a puppy from birth until he reaches his first birthday—that's a lot of physical and emotional growth and development!

This German Shepherd mother takes care of her many babies. The author's dog Magic is one of the puppies in this litter.

Puppy Growth Progression—What to Expect
Neonatal Period = Birth through week two
Transitional Period=End of Neonatal Period to week four
Socialization Period=Week four through week twelve
Juvenile Period=Week ten until sexual maturity

A newborn puppy doesn't look much like a dog and goes through different stages of puppy development during his first twelve weeks. Dogs are considered puppies from birth to one year of age and go through several puppy stages and development periods. However, each dog develops differently, with smaller dogs tending to mature earlier and some large breeds not physically mature before they are two years old.

Newborn puppies vary in size depending on the breed; tiny dogs like the Chihuahua produce puppies sized about four inches long, while giant breed newborns like Great Dane puppies may be twice that size.

Rate of puppy development also varies from breed to breed. For instance, Cocker Spaniel puppies open their eyes sooner than Fox Terrier puppies, and Basenji puppies develop teeth earlier than Shetland Sheepdog puppies.

However, no matter the breed, all puppies are born totally dependent on the momma dog, technically called the bitch.

Tube Feeding

Sometimes newborn puppies are so sick and weak, they aren't able to suck or swallow, and will starve without being helped to eat. Experienced breeders often tube feed these puppies. It only takes a couple minutes to do—a huge time-saver when feeding several babies—and you know each baby gets the correct amount. A flexible hollow tube is threaded down the baby's throat into the stomach and food injected with a syringe. It's easy to do once you've been shown how by the veterinarian. Here's how breeders and veterinarians recommend tube feeding be done.

1. Buy a Number 5 French catheter with a 6 or 12 cc syringe from your drugstore. It's a good idea to lubricate the inside of the syringe and plunger with cooking oil before you begin, so there's no sticking. And after each use, be sure to wash everything in hot soapy water, rinse, and keep clean in a plastic bag.
2. Measure the distance between the puppy's mouth and her stomach, so the tube doesn't fall short of the target or go too far. Place the end of the tube at the baby's last rib—that's where the stomach lies—and measure from there to her mouth for the proper length. Mark the place on the tube with a piece of tape that can be moved as the baby grows.
3. Fill the syringe with the proper amount of commercial puppy formula. Warm it to body temperature—about 100 degrees—by floating in a bowl of warm water while you place the feeding tube.
4. Hold the baby in an upright position to make it easier to pass the tube. Put the open end of the tube against the roof of her mouth, and thread it down the esophagus into the stomach. This tends to trigger the gag reflex, but that should stop once the tube has gone beyond the back of the throat, and the puppy will swallow to help it along. Don't force the tube, it should slide down easily and if it doesn't, you may be in the airway by mistake—so withdraw the tube and start over.
5. Some puppies are so weak they may not cough or struggle even if the tube goes into the lungs, so check your placement before giving any food or you could drowned them. Put the end of the outside portion of the tube straight down in about an inch of water, so that no water runs into the tube—if you see a stream of air bubbles escape from the tube, that means you're in the lungs. Remove the tube and try again. Usually this isn't a problem because typically the tube is too large to pass through the windpipe and most easily goes down the esophagus as it should.

6. Connect the formula-filled syringe to the tube and slowly inject the puppy formula down the tube into the stomach. Then quickly remove the tube, and cuddle the baby for a moment to settle any bruised feelings. Usually, healthy puppies older than two weeks become strong enough to nurse on their own, and begin to struggle against the feeding tube.

At Birth

At birth, puppies are blind, deaf and toothless, unable to regulate body temperature, or even urinate or defecate on their own. Puppies depend on their mother and littermates for warmth, huddling in cozy piles to conserve body temperature. A puppy separated from this warm furry nest can quickly die from hypothermia—low body temperature. Cold, lonely puppies cry loudly to alert Mom to their predicament.

Puppies first experience the sensation of being petted when washed by their mother's stroking tongue. The bitch licks her babies all over to keep them and the nest clean, and also to stimulate them to defecate and urinate.

Neonatal Period: Birth to Two Weeks

From birth, puppies are able to use their sense of smell and touch, which helps them root about the nest to find their mother's scent-marked breasts. The first milk the mother produces, called colostrum, is rich in antibodies that provide passive immunity and help protect the babies from disease during these early weeks of life.

For the first two weeks of life, puppies sleep nearly 90 percent of the time, spending their awake time nursing. All their energy is funneled into growing, and birth weight doubles the first week. Newborns aren't able to support their weight, and crawl about with paddling motions of their front legs. The limited locomotion provides the exercise that develops muscles and coordination, and soon the puppies are crawling over and around each other and their mother.

Transitional Period: Week Two-to-Four

The second week of life brings great changes for the puppy. Ears and eyes sealed since birth begin to open during this period, ears at about two weeks and eyelids between ten to 16 days. This gives the furry babies a new sense of their world. They learn what their mother and other dogs look and sound like, and begin to expand their own vocabulary from grunts and mews to yelps, whines and barks. Puppies generally stand by day 15 and take their first wobbly walk by day 21.

By age three weeks, puppy development advances from the neonatal period to the transitional period. This is a time of rapid physical and sensory development, during which the puppies go from total dependence on Mom to a bit of independence. They begin to play with their littermates, learn about their environment and canine society, and begin sampling food from Mom's bowl. Puppy teeth begin to erupt until all the baby teeth are in by about five to six weeks of age. Puppies can control their need to potty by this age, and begin moving away from sleeping quarters to eliminate.

Socialization Period: Week Four-to-Twelve

Following the transitional phase, puppies enter the socialization period at the end of the third week of life; it lasts until about week ten. It is during this socialization period that interaction with others increases, and puppies form attachments they will remember the rest of their life. The most critical period—age six to eight weeks—is when puppies most easily learn to accept others as a part of their family.

Beginning at four weeks of age, the bitch's milk production begins to slow down just as the puppies' energy needs increase. As the mother dog slowly weans her babies from nursing, they begin sampling solid food in earnest.

The environmental stimulation impacts your puppy's rate of mental development during this time. The puppy brain waves look that of an adult dog by about the 50th day, but he's not yet programmed--that's your job, and the job of his mom and siblings. Weaning typically is complete by week eight.

Fear Period: Week Eight-to-Twelve

Puppies often go through a "fear period" during this time. Instead of meeting new or familiar people and objects with curiosity, they react with fearfulness. Anything that frightens them at this age may have a lasting impact so take care that the baby isn't overstimulated with too many changes or challenges at one time. That doesn't mean your pup will grow up to be a scaredy-cat; it's simply a normal part of development where pups learn to be more cautious. Careful socialization during this period helps counter fear reactions.

Puppies may be placed in new homes once they are eating well on their own. However, they will be better adjusted and make better pets by staying and interacting with littermates and the Mom-dog until they are at least eight weeks old—older generally is better. Interacting with siblings and Mom help teach bite inhibition, how to understand and react to normal canine communication, and their place in doggy society. Puppies tend to make transitions from one environment to another more easily at this age, too.

Juvenile Period: Week Ten to Puberty

Even though he may look grown up, the stages of puppy development last from birth to a year or even two before he's considered an adult dog. The greatest puppy development changes happen from birth to twelve weeks of age. But from twelve weeks on, your fur-kid still has lots of growing up to do.

The juvenile puppy period generally begins at age ten weeks, and lasts until puberty and the onset of sexual maturity. It is during this period that puppies begin to learn the consequences of behavior, and determine what is most appropriate to certain circumstances.

Puppies at this age have boundless curiosity, exasperating stubbornness, and enthusiastic affection. Expect your puppy to get into everything, and you won't be disappointed. This is an ideal time to begin training.

Nearly every waking moment is spent in play, which is not only great fun for the babies, but is great practice for canine life. Puppies learn how to do important dog activities like chasing and running, pawing, biting and fighting. Social skills and canine etiquette are learned by interaction with littermates and Mom. Puppies learn to inhibit their bite when they are bitten by each other, and learn canine language. Through play, they practice dominant and submissive postures, and prepare for life in the world.

Juvenile Delinquent Pups: Week ten-to-sixteen

Puppies test their boundaries during this period that lasts anywhere from a few days to several weeks. These dogs challenge owners to see who calls the shots, seem to "forget" any training they've learned, and act like rebellious teenagers.

Some of this has to do with teething. Pups lose baby teeth starting about three months of age. There can be discomfort as the permanent teeth erupt and puppies tend to chew more on anything and everything to relieve the pain.

Delinquent behavior also may be influenced by hormones. But even pups that have been spayed and neutered prior to this can develop the "oh yeah, MAKE me!" attitude. Owners who have done everything right may still experience this difficult, frustrating phase. Grit your teeth, keep him on leash and under control, offer consistent, patient and humane training, and tell yourself, "He's testing me, it'll get better." Because it will.

Four to Six Months

Pups grow so quickly during this period you may notice changes every single day. Not only may your pup test and challenge you, this is the time frame puppies also figure out where they stand with other pets in the group. Some squabbling and play fighting is expected. It's a dog rule that older animals teach the pup limits, which is normal and usually sounds more scary than it is.

In fact, an un-neutered male puppy's testosterone level increases at around four to five months of age. This is one way adult dogs recognize that even big puppies are still babies and they must be taught proper dog etiquette.

Puppies can also sometimes experience another fear phase during this period. It may last up to a month, and their maybe more than one especially in large breed dogs. This is normal and nothing to worry about. It tends to correspond with growth spurts, and you may notice some "flaky" behavior or unwarranted aggression, become protective of toys or territory. Just ensure you don't reward the fearful behavior with more attention, and know how to talk to puppies and not use baby talk. It's best to ignore the fear rather than risk rewarding it. Build confidence through training and the pup should transition out of it with no further problems.

Adolescence: Six to Twelve Months

Most of your pup's growth in height finishes by this period but he may continue to fill out and gain muscle mass and body weight. Puppy coat starts to be replaced by the adult coat.

While the baby may still be emotionally immature, during this period the boy pups begin to leg-lift and mark with urine. The testosterone level in male puppies increases to 5-7 times higher than in an adult dog by age 10 months, and then gradually falls to a normal adult level by about 18 months of age. This helps signal the senior male dogs that the youngster must be put in his place so you may notice more adult-pup squabbles during this period. Girl pups may go into heat (estrus) as early as five to six months, and boys begin to be interested in sex during this period.

Puppies at this age seem to explode with high energy and will do well with structured play and exercise. Training and continued socialization is vital to ensure your youngster knows how to behave politely with other dogs, other animals like cats, and other people including children and strangers of all sizes, ages, and looks.

Social Maturity: Between One and Two Years

Depending on the breed, your dog will be physically mature at this age. Small dogs mature much earlier and larger ones take more time. Your pup's social maturity also can depend on his or her experience with other animals. Socialization and training continues throughout your pet's lifetime, because there are always new things to learn—or old lessons to revisit and practice. After all, the joy of your puppy's first year or two predicts a lifetime of love to come.

Matching Your Lifestyle

The puppy is only half the equation necessary to make this match work. Before you settle on your final choice, it's important to evaluate your personal situation because not every puppy is right for each circumstance. Living with the baby will be much easier by choosing a puppy that fits your lifestyle, instead of choosing a puppy whose needs you can't meet. By knowing what to expect, you can avoid major heartache down the road.

Apartment or House? City or Country?

Where do you live? And where will the puppy stay? Take into consideration the amount of space you have available, not only for a tiny puppy—but for the adult-size dog he'll become in 12 months or so. Dogs can be quite territorial and do best when they can "claim" some of the real estate as their own property. This is especially important if you consider adopting more than one puppy and want to avoid future squabbles. A good rule of thumb is to have no more dogs than you have rooms—so a one-bedroom apartment is perfect for one puppy, depending on his size. But don't be surprised if the little Greyhound puppy claims the sofa!

A small apartment can be a perfect home. Medium and small dogs adapt well to being apartment and city pets. In fact, we shared our two-bedroom apartment with our first German Shepherd for nine years, and he fit in perfectly.

City dogs, though, are not safe outside so keep in mind your puppy should be safely homebound whether you're there to supervise his antics, or not. If you rent your apartment or home, your landlord likely will have something to say about pets so be sure to clear things first so there are no surprises. Landlords very often have both a size and sometimes breed restrictions in place, and insurance companies may also restrict various breeds.

Owning your own home eliminates the landlord question (but not necessarily the insurance issues), and gives you more room to satisfy an active puppy—or even several. A home with an enclosed garden or yard may also offer some flexibility about offering safe outdoor excursions.

But don't forget to take a look at your décor as well. Puppies and lots of fragile, expensive breakables within mouth reach or tail wags able to sweep tables are a recipe for disaster. All puppies play like non-stop whirl-i-gigs, but some are more active than others and may retain their high-octane energy even as adults. Decide whether you prefer a countertop-cruising climbing fanatic, like a Basenji or if a more placid Cavalier King Charles Spaniel suits you better.

WARNING!

Are you sure the resident dog really wants a companion? While dogs typically love companionship of the furry persuasion, an additional pet rarely solves an existing dog behavior problem and may actually prompt new ones. Statistically, single dog households have the fewest behavior problems. The potential for wrangling increases with each dog added to the household.

When a resident pet is involved, careful introductions are important to help them become part of one big happy family. That can take a great deal of patience, energy, and time. When you have a cat, it's certainly possible for the puppy and kitty to become fast friends. There will be safety issues, though, because some dog breeds have tendencies to be aggressive toward small animals. Detailed information about how best to introduce your new puppy to children, dogs, cats and other pets can be found in Chapter 6.

Time Constraints

Every puppy takes time. That's part of the fun, cuddling and playing with your new baby, and building an unbreakable bond that lasts a lifetime. Besides available space in your home, you must consider how a young puppy may fit into your daily routine.

Do you work outside of the home for long hours, when the puppy must be left alone unattended? If you're lucky (like me!) you can take your puppy to work with you, or work at home. Even then he'll need a safe place to sleep, eat, use the bathroom and play while you're distracted by business.

Kids and puppies go together like peanut butter and jelly. But parents are ultimately responsible, so be sure everyone is in agreement to add a "fur kid" to the family.

You'll also have to add training time, potty breaks, and routine maintenance care to your schedule. All puppies need basic care like nail trims, but some like the lovely Cocker Spaniel breed require more attention to ear care. Puppies with flat faces and big eyes, like the Pug, need help keeping their eyes clean and healthy.

While short coated dogs like Labradors need only a lick and a promise for coat care, Maltese and Yorkies and other puppies with luxurious long hair may need grooming every day. Before you choose your ideal puppy, be sure you'll have time to devote to keeping that fluffy big-eyed beauty in perfect condition.

Other Roommates?

Unless you live alone and own your own residence, you will need to consult with other people—like the landlord or family members—and consider their concerns before choosing your puppy. Will your spouse or roommate support the decision to acquire a puppy? Are your children responsible enough to take part in the care of the new family member?

Discuss plans with your roommate or spouse and be sure you have his or her support. After all, they'll have to make adjustments to the new family member, too. The new puppy deserves to have a happy and stress-free environment to bloom, with support from all the people he'll live with. It's not fair to him to be the target of tension or resentment.

Very young children can be taught to properly handle and respect a pet as a living creature—and not a stuffed toy to be dragged about by a leg or tail. Depending on age, children can also become involved in the care responsibilities of the puppy by filling the food or water bowl, and playing with the baby. But make no mistake—no matter what age your children may be, the ultimate responsibility for the puppy always falls to the child's parent. Always.

So if you choose to adopt a puppy and you have a toddler, a pet several months old is the best choice. Very young puppies are incredibly fragile and can be injured unintentionally by your youngster simply by being dropped or held incorrectly. An older puppy is better able to stay out of the child's way and avoid being "loved" too hard—and that also protects your child from an inadvertent nip when the puppy tries to defend himself. Young children beyond the toddler stage will also need supervision, but can help with some care responsibilities. Having a pet can, indeed, be a great way to teach a child responsibility—but just be sure it's not at the expense of the puppy.

You must also consider the impact a new puppy may have on other pets. I often talk with people who already have an adult dog and want to adopt a puppy as a "gift" to their pet for a playmate or companion. Age and gender of the new puppy can impact how well he'll be accepted by resident pets. A good rule of thumb is to introduce a younger animal of the opposite sex to the resident pet, because there's less chance for territorial challenges or threats to the older animal's social position.

When the Heart Rules

Even when we know how to pick the healthiest and best socialized puppy from the ideal source, our heart may not listen to our head. Instead, it's that sickly puppy with bald spots, covered with fleas, and eyes barely open that captures your soul. These "challenged" puppies need lots of help and will require much time and energy.

It's important to remember several things. Will you have time to medicate a sick baby, or get up throughout the night for puppy feedings if he's an orphan? Special needs puppies can require your attention and help 24 hours a day. Be sure you can address these needs either yourself or with help, before committing to such an adoption.

When the puppy starts out with strikes against him, it's a good idea to have your veterinarian evaluate his health so you know what to expect. Sadly, there are puppy illnesses like parvo and distemper that may not be curable. Rather than invest lots of time, money, and heartache you'll both be better served by making the baby's life as happy and comfortable as possible. And perhaps, with the caring help of a veterinarian, humanely end the suffering.

Other times, puppies have a rocky start but with dedicated nursing and medication can survive, and even thrive. It may require weeks of added expense and time. When the condition is contagious (like ringworm) you'll need to consider how to protect other pets or your children.

I can't make that decision for you. Just be informed before you embark on your puppy-saving crusade. Success will forge a strong, unbreakable loving bond between you that can last all the years of his life.

PART TWO

BRINGING HOME BABY

4: Putting Your

Best Paw Forward

Puppy Central

Every puppy deserves a room of her own. A private room offers several advantages, and more than anything else, helps your puppy more easily make the transition into becoming a part of your family.

Some puppies are so small they can become lost in a large home or apartment. Above all, you need to keep an eye on the baby, especially during the critical first several weeks. Because frankly, if there's trouble to be found, your new puppy will be in the middle of it.

By turning one room into *puppy central*, you help divide the puppy's territory up into manageable chunks for her to explore and learn. A whole house overwhelms the new baby, but a single room allows her time to explore, find familiar smells, and scope out all the really good nap spots. This room becomes her safe-haven, a place that's comforting, familiar, and stress-free for her to retreat when the world becomes too much. This should be a place she can go to nap, play quietly by herself, or escape the hectic pestering of children or other pets.

It's easy to create your own puppy central. Choose a room that has the least amount of foot-traffic. I chose the kitchen when Magical-Dawg was a puppy, and blocked off each entry with a doggy gate. A laundry room or a small second bathroom or guest bedroom could also work. Even a walk-in closet might be appropriate depending on the size of the pup.

On one side of the room, place the puppy's food and water dishes. Include a puppy bed—a dog carrier with a soft blanket works well—and a few chew toys for her to use. Your puppy will spend many hours in her safe haven, and it should be the most pleasant room in the house for her.

Puppy-Proofing 101

You'll need to make the house safe for your puppy just like you would for your human baby. Puppies dig at objects with their paws. They pick up and bite and taste everything, and squirm into interesting dark empty places. They have no experience what's safe and what's not, and may not survive a mistake.

For your new puppy, everything is a potential game. He uses his mouth the way infants reach out and grab. So tug-games with the curtains, keep-away when he steals your wallet, un-planting the potted palm or eating poisonous plants, and nosey sniffs of the candle flame get him in trouble.

During teething, he'll want to chew even more to relieve the discomfort, but most dogs love to chew their whole life. Puppies not only damage your property, he could hurt himself or die from munching dangerous objects. Be sure to check toy safety, too, and remove anything he could chew off and swallow.

Besides protecting the baby, puppy-proofing also protects your valuables. For instance, puppies clear tabletops with tail wags, help you by digging up freshly potted plants, or chew the leaves to pieces, what fun! You want to *prevent* problems like these, so you can enjoy the baby and build on the bonding experience instead of yearning to retaliate.

Before anything else, puppy-proof "Puppy Central" and make sure that her safe haven really is safe. Then move on to the rest of the house, anywhere that she'll have the opportunity to explore. Start first with puppy-level; invest in knee-pads and get down on all fours to see the house from her perspective. Then take into account the second-level areas because as she grows, you can be sure she'll graduate to vaulting onto the sofa to check out what treasures can be found on tabletops.

Once you've puppy-proofed the house, don't relax your vigilance, though. For the first couple of weeks, whenever she's not safely confined in her room, it's a good idea to follow her around. Puppies find danger you never imagined, so running after her will ensure her safety and ease your mind. Here are some common household hazards to address.

Puppies will find their own entertainment if you don't supervise them. Be warned!

Electrical Cords, Remotes and Paper

Puppies are very mouth-oriented. Like all babies, young dogs explore their world by mouthing and biting. Find a safe place out of puppy tooth range to store cell phone, TV remote, iPads, Ereaders or other such objects. These items are the right size for puppies to pick up and carry and (BONUS!) they smell like you, so are very attractive to chew.

If you're paper training the puppy, remember that the newspaper, books, magazines or music left on the floor may invite puppy potty attention you don't want. My first dog managed to chew up a lot of my music books. He also enjoyed sleeping in my closet among my shoes—all the clothing must have smelled like me—but he also gnawed the heel off several shoes.

Some of these chew targets cause aggravation but others could kill you puppy. For instance, chewing electrical cords is very dangerous. A bite can cause terrible burns or even death when the puppy stops breathing from the shock.

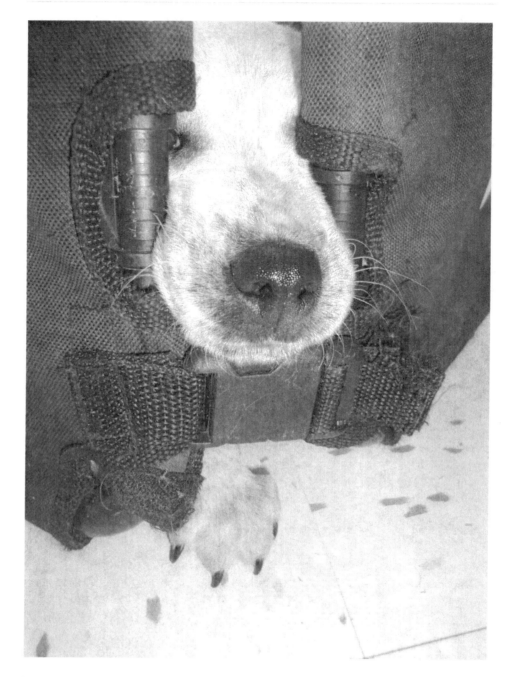

Puppies will stick their noses into everything, so be sure the illegal items are safely out of reach.

Eliminate as many electrical cords as you can and remove temptation. For those that are left, immobilize them with tape or run them through a length of PVC pipe to make them less attractive or accessible.

For a few puppies, a commercial spray called Bitter Apple that tastes nasty may deter mouthing and biting. An offensive smell also can work well as a puppy deterrent. A smell that works great to repel dogs is menthol, so you can try smearing a bit of Vicks VapoRub on exposed cords to keep the puppy far away.

If the worst happens and your puppy is shocked, be sure to turn off the electricity before you try to help her, or you may be injured, too. More details on first aid for electrocution are found in Chapter 11.

Hidey-Holes

Puppies adore finding hiding places and cubbyholes to sleep, or to lay in wait and leap out at unsuspecting human feet. Small pups can get trapped inside little used rooms when they door-dash without you noticing and get locked away. If you don't hear the baby's cry and rescue her, a day or more without food or water can spell disaster. Make sure you check for a puppy inside before you shut doors.

More lethal places include appliances like dishwashers the puppy may explore to lick soiled plates, or the warm clothes dryer. Even the open oven door can be attractive to a heat-seeking baby. Puppies die every day when trapped inside an appliance that's turned on.

Block off dangerous puppy-size openings. Check every appliance before turning it on. Make it a habit to bang on the tops or sides of the clothes dryer as a safety check. And if you see your puppy venture into one of these deadly places, it might be worthwhile to temporarily shut the door and then bang like crazy on the thing before letting her out. That may be enough to scare the puppy away from the danger permanently.

Plants

To your puppy, a plant offers an invitation to chew, dig, and climb through the leaves to play "jungle beast." Depending on the kind of plant, your puppy's exploration could prove lethal. Dieffenbachia, philodendron, and English ivy are some of the most common houseplants that can cause toxic reactions when eaten.

Make sure all plants are removed from the puppy's room, and either place toxic plants out of reach—or better, get them out of the house. Give them to a pet-less friend. Puppy-safe houseplants like coleus, piggyback, jade plant or others should be placed out of reach on high shelves, or hung from hooks.

Bathrooms

Toilet paper is a popular puppy toy. Drinking out of the toilet is another nasty habit that could be dangerous if a small pup falls in and drowns or ingests chemical cleaners. The easy fix is—shut the bathroom door, and/or always put the lid down.

Pay particular attention to human medicines, especially if the puppy's safe-room is a bathroom. Pills are great fun to bat and chase, but most pet poisonings come from swallowed medicine not meant for them. Keep your medication secure and out of reach in the cabinet.

Dirty laundry must smell like heaven to puppies. Concentrated beloved human scents found on worn socks and underwear or shoes can be very appealing. The pillow your head rests on when you sleep also smells like you. So protect the laundry basket, and close the closet door to keep puppy marauders from stealing and chewing shoes, purses or brief cases left on the floor. Puppies may confuse throw pillows with legal chew toys so make it easy for them to tell the difference and put forbidden objects out of reach.

Cleaning supplies under the sink can also pose a hazard for puppies if they are spilled on them, or the baby walks through something and then licks it off. Some pups learn to open cupboard doors. In these instances, childproof latches on cabinets that contain dangers are an excellent investment.

Puppies put everything in their mouths, including sticks, acorns and even rocks. Be alert that they don't inadvertently swallow something dangerous.

Windows and Screens

Puppies want to see out. They can push out window or storm door screens and get hung or escape. Jumping up to look out windows may tempt them to grab curtains or blind cords. They may play tug or can strangle if hung up in curtain cords, or choke on swallowed pieces of cord. When these materials reach the tummy or intestines, they can block the digestive system or cause cuts on the inside. That can require emergency surgery to remove the string and repair the damage.

Tie up curtain cords out of reach, or buy the child-safe kind that have a breakaway feature. Keep sewing supplies and fishing tackle boxes in secure cupboards.

Swallowed Objects

There are no safety standards for dog toys, so it's up to you to ensure no small objects—like eyes or tails on stuffed toys—can come off and be swallowed. Like all babies, puppies tend to swallow lots of nonfood objects. Besides the string-type hazards, sharp items like pins, paperclips and needles are common targets. Coins, rubber bands, and rubber baby nipples can also cause problems because they react with the digestive acids.

Even objects you wouldn't think dangerous can stop up the puppy's innards and cause life-threatening blockages. Anything that the puppy can put in her mouth could potentially be swallowed. Having a puppy around has forced me to become neat and keep the floor picked up.

Growing puppies can have voracious appetites and may eat any food scraps left within reach. They may even eat through food containers and grocery sacks left within reach to get to something yummy. That can not only interfere with nutritional balance, but could also upset tender tummies.

Waste baskets can be incredibly rewarding for a puppy to pillage. Table scraps to old used tissues can be found so invest in waste baskets with lids, hide them behind latching doors, or set them on countertops out of reach. Keep garbage covered and beyond puppy reach. Refer to the first aid tips in Chapter 11 if your puppy swallows something he shouldn't.

WARNING!

If you see a string-type object hanging from your puppy's mouth—or coming out the anus—DO NOT PULL IT! Chances are, it's attached somewhere on the inside of the body and you could do irreparable harm. Get your puppy to the emergency veterinarian as soon as possible.

Pet Potty Concerns

If you have cats, be sure the litter box is out of reach. Puppies like to snack on poop, especially kitty potty deposits and aside from the unsanitary issue, this will hiss off the cat and cause potential inter-pet problems. Most cats can leap onto a countertop to find their litter box, which keeps it out of dog range.

Puppies also spend time in the yard to do their own business. Don't think a fence makes him safe. Puppies can wiggle out of tiny openings or get caught and injured trying to escape. Anything that can be turned into a toy should be put out of reach. Lawn and garden chemicals should be shut in puppy-proof rooms or boxes.

Holiday Hazards

Many holidays throughout the year pose hazards to curious puppies. Halloween candy and scary strangers at the door (puppies can dash out) cause dangerous disruptions. Thanksgiving with lots of rich food and friends and family also offer risks. But the Christmas and Chanukah season are the most dangerous of all, because often the holiday decorations offer hard-to-resist canine temptations.

The menorah, fireplaces, and other holiday candles can burn puppy noses when they sniff the flame, gift ribbons can be chewed, and Christmas decorations from plants to tree ornaments can prove deadly if swallowed or the cord from twinkling lights is bitten. Spray-on artificial snow that's lead-based is toxic if swallowed, and icicles or tinsel are especially hazardous when swallowed.

Tree water doctored with aspirin or other preservatives can kill the puppy that drinks from the reservoir. Even tree needles can hurt when swallowed. Holiday plants like Easter lilies, and Christmas mistletoe are particularly toxic.

Less dangerous, but no less irritating, the tree seems designed for puppy-chewing tug-playing enjoyment. Older pups may decide to "water" the tree as practice of their urine marking skills. A toppled tree won't make your holiday particularly merry.

In most instances, you can apply the puppy-proofing tips to the holiday season. Keep candles out of reach. Secure electrical cords, hang breakable ornaments out of reach, and use only yarn or ribbon rather than wire hangers for ornaments. Avoid tinsel and snow-type decorations, and secure the tree so it won't topple. Some folks have luck placing the tree inside a baby playpen to keep the puppy out, or simply put it in a room blocked off from impetuous pets.

Look for the tacky sheets available at Home Depot and other stores designed to keep throw rugs from scooting around. Place these beneath the tree branches—dogs hate the sticky feel and avoid walking on the surface. Alternately, purchase sections of the clear carpet runners that have the nubs, and place them nub-side-up beneath and around the tree. That makes it uncomfortable for puppy lounging. Be sure to offer the baby dog a legal (and more comfy) resting spot.

You might want to invest in a second, small tree that's decorated with puppy-safe ornaments like treats or dried flowers. That might satisfy the puppy's urge to play, and save your formal tree.

Crossing the Threshold

Welcome home, Baby! There's nothing more exciting than bringing your new puppy home. The first few days—and especially the first night—can be a stressful time for both of you. After all, this budding partnership will change your lives. If at all possible, plan to bring her home at the beginning of a weekend, or take a few days off, so you have the time to devote to getting the relationship off to a good start.

It's a good idea to bring something familiar with the puppy from her first home. Dogs identify safe places and things by the way they smell, and the baby will certainly miss the scent of her mother and siblings. Plan ahead to scent a small hand towel or baby blanket with the signature smell of Mom-dog and the babies. Simply rub or pet the mother and other puppies with the fabric, then bring it home with your puppy as a friendly reminder. Place the scented fabric in the puppy's new bed.

Of course, you'll transport your new puppy in a dog carrier—or if you don't have that, a cardboard "pet caddy" available from shelters. When you are in the car, driving is your priority. The puppy must be confined not only for the driver's peace of mind, but for her own safety. An accident with a loose puppy in the car turns the baby into a furry projectile that probably won't survive.

PUPPY WAGS.

Dog pheromone products as sprays, plug-ins and collars are now available that help ease canine fear. Comfort Zone with D.A.P. (dog appeasing pheromone) is one of the better known products that mimics the "no fear" calming pheromone mom-dogs produce from their breasts while nursing, and it works with any age dog. It's especially effective with puppies going to new homes. It can be sprayed on the puppy bed, or worn as a collar.

Bring the baby into her safe-room. It should be ready with food and water, bed, and toys available. Set down the carrier, and open the door, and let the puppy come out on her own. Some shy puppies may prefer to stay hidden from sight and won't want to come out until you leave the room. That's fine. You can try sitting on the floor, which is less threatening to the baby. Give her ten minutes to come out on her own—if she doesn't, leave the room and come back in thirty minutes to check on her. Some puppies can't wait to explore their new home. That's fine, too.

She should not leave her room (except for potty breaks) for at least the first day or so. That gives her time to build an allegiance to her new room. Confining your new puppy also eliminates the opportunity for mistakes. She's not a mind reader and should be given every opportunity to do the right thing. This way you can control when to take her out for potty breaks, rather than allowing her to roam the whole house and leave you "surprises" to find later.

After the first few days, you can open the door and allow her to explore the rest of the house, at her own pace. One room at a time works best, and usually it's best to let the puppy make her own way from *puppy central* rather than carrying her. That way, she knows the way back to find her food and bed or crate.

When you aren't able to supervise puppy antics, the best and safest place for her is her room. If the area isn't easily cleaned, an even better location is her puppy crate—that will help with potty training as well. It takes only a few seconds for her to get into trouble. By the time you take the cookies out of the oven, or finish up that important phone conversation, she could be chewing up your new Kindle or pulling the tablecloth off the dining room table along with Grandma's antique dishes, or leaving you a little fragrant pile under the piano bench.

Magic hasn't been a puppy for quite some time. He's now almost eleven years old. And I still confine him in the kitchen to keep him comfortable when I'm out of the house, and keep him (and the two cats) from plotting mayhem. That's peace of mind for me and all the pets.

Choosing a Name

Finding a proper name is serious business. Puppy names come to us in flashes of inspiration, and often seem to be chosen by the pet herself. For instance, my dog's name—Magic—speaks to how it felt when we finally got him. Magical, indeed!

When you adopt a purebred puppy from a breeder, she will likely already have her name decided, at least in part. The "registered name" is the official identification for a purebred puppy, and can be a long tongue-twister that describes her ancestry. In the case of Magic, his breeder told us he came from the "M" litter (a way European German Shepherd breeders keep track) and so we were encouraged to name him something, beginning with the letter M.

Parts of the registered names are usually the breeder's kennel where the puppy was born. Magic comes from Fernheim German Shepherds, and so his registered name is Magic von Fernheim. Different breeds may have other requirements. The registered name also must be approved by the registering body so that no other dog of that name has exactly the same name. You can sometimes accomplish this by using unique spellings. For instance, my dog's name could instead have been spelled Magick, or Majik or other varieties. Your breeder will help you with choosing a registered name.

But your registered name may be different than the "call name" that the baby goes by for every day. After all, it's a bit of a mouthful to refer to "Magic von Fernheim" and other pups may have even more of a mouthful of a name. The call name is what the baby is called on a routine basis.

Puppies need not be registered to sport glorious, exotic, and imaginative names. Dogs are named for appearance (Spot), location where they were adopted (Win Dixie), for personality (Sweety), and even for famous people (Elvis). They may have descriptive names, like Re-Run who was a second-chance rescue pup. Mooch got his name by hogging his owner's pillow at night.

Choose a one- or two-syllable name that's unique to your puppy. Names that start with a hard consonant may be easier for youngsters to learn. Find a name that you like, too, since the new baby will wear the tag for the next decade or longer.

There's really only one rule to follow when it comes to naming your puppy. Make sure the name is a positive one. Puppies have egos, and she may not know the verbatim meaning of the word but the emotional intent comes through loud and clear. That's why negative names all too often foster poor behavior, while a positive one promotes self-esteem. It's a wonderful and amazing thing to see a puppy that's less than gorgeous respond to and blossom into a real show-stopper when named something like "Beauty."

Once you've found a name for your baby, try it on for size to be sure it fits. Puppies have a way of responding to and accepting the perfect name and it may take you a while to find it. Take your time. Puppy christening celebrates the canine spirit, and should complement the individual soul of your special friend.

Puppy Socialization

To be good pets, puppies require early-age socialization. That's a fancy way of describing how they learn to interact in a positive way with the world around them.

Dogs can be trained at any age, and continue to learn throughout their lives. But the prime socialization period is a narrow window during babyhood when learning the "wrong" lessons can emotionally cripple the puppy. Dogs not exposed to positive experiences with humans, other pets, important places and situations during this period may become fearful and bite out of fright.

Proper socialization develops canine social and communication skills. Socialization also teaches puppies what's safe, normal and acceptable. Anything the puppy doesn't learn about during socialization could potentially be considered dangerous, to be feared or even attacked.

Puppies are most receptive during a six-to-eight week window, but your dog benefits from socialization exercises for the first year. During the early weeks, mother animals teach many lessons by example. For instance, if Mom-Dog becomes hysterical around men, her pups pay attention and copy her behavior.

People raising litters must begin positive lessons before the babies go to new homes. Consider this kindergarten for pups. Youngsters have an increased capacity for learning when they're young, so it's helpful for new owners to continue these lessons after adopting a pup. Even after your little guy becomes a grown-up dog, regular practice sessions help remind him that the mailman is actually a good guy even if he wears a funny hat.

Puppy Kindergarten

How do you create kindergarten for pups? Create a checklist of all the experiences your puppy will face during the first several months living with you. And then systematically introduce her to each situation, while associating it with fun, happy benefits for the puppy. For example, handle her paws to help her learn to accept nail trims. Ring the doorbell, and offer a squeaky toy so she associates the sound and guests with rewards. Here are 10 broad categories of situations you can expect your new puppy to deal with.

1. **Handling** the puppy's paws, ears, mouth, eyes, and tail simply feels good. It's also a great way to prepare your pup to calmly accept vet exams.
2. **Owner's homes** are different so add your specifics to the list. In most cases, puppies will live with occasional delivery or repair people entering the house, the phone and doorbell ringing, guests (strangers) arriving, sweeping/mopping/vacuuming, the noise of the washer/dryer and dishwasher, and loud TV shows or music.
3. **People** come in different ages, genders, and ethnicities. Puppies won't necessarily accept all humans in the same way. Those raised in shelters by only women need help accepting men. Children—especially babies and toddlers—look, smell, sound and move differently.
4. What people **wear, carry or how they move** also changes a puppy's perceptions, so socialize the baby to uniforms, raincoats, hats, sunglasses, bearded men and even people shaved heads, or strong perfume if that's appropriate. What people carry or how they move also can surprise and frighten pups. Those destined for therapy work especially benefit from being socialized to people using canes, crutches, legs in cast, walkers, wheelchairs, baby carriages, back packs, or erratic body movement. Don't neglect athletes and their equipment, including joggers, skate boarders, bicyclists, tricycles, or roller bladers.
5. **Animals** also can frighten, intrigue, or prompt attacks. Even if your puppy will be an only pet, it's important to socialize him to other puppies and adult dogs, kittens and cats especially if he'll be living with

them. Do you live in the country? Socialize to the livestock so you won't have a pestering pup chasing the cows or chickens.

6. **Vehicles** either enrapture or terrify dogs. Your pup will need to make trips in the car, but don't neglect other experiences. Let him get used to trucks backing up, garbage trucks, motorcycles, or any other vehicle he might encounter.

7. **Noises and weather** can upset many pups. You can counteract much of this with socialization. Associate sirens, thunder/lightening, snow blowers, snow, rain, fireworks, people yelling and other unexpected noises with a favorite treat, toy, or attention.

8. **Yard equipment** can be scary, too. Pups not used to a garden rake might think you plan to hit with the stick. Get your baby used to shovels, the garden hose, sweeping with broom, wheelbarrows, lawn mowers or other yard equipment.

9. **New surfaces** can seem scary if a pup has never before seen ice, for instance. Dogs raised in kennels may not know how to pee on grass, or act frightened of dirt or gravel. Be sure your pup has practice walking on all kinds of surfaces including cement, sand, wooden decks, carpet, and learns how to climb up and down stairs.

10. **Environments** come in all shapes and sizes. Each new place could potentially be scary, so take your time but be sure your pup has experience with the important ones. That may include car rides, the vet clinic, boarding kennel, groomers, gas station, the bank, friend's homes, pet supply store, school grounds, car wash, walks after dark, crossing a bridge or busy intersection, drive-thru, crowd of people, the beach, hiking trails, or the office.

5: Puppy Equipment

A-Shopping You Must Go

What a world we live in, where all the proper puppy paraphernalia can be found nearly anywhere you look. In the past, only pet specialty stores carried certain kinds of puppy equipment, like leashes and dog beds. But today, you'll find a selection in most department stores like WalMart or Kmart, and even the neighborhood grocery store may have a pet supply area.

The smaller independent mom and pop pet supply stores often offer a range of products that satisfy puppy needs. Retail chains like Petco and PetsMart offer one-stop walk-in or online shopping with a variety of choices. Some of these stores even allow you to bring your pet along, and also provide care or training services like staff veterinarians, groomers and puppy classes.

Besides traditional walk-in stores, there are also huge numbers of mail order catalogues and websites that have unique puppy equipment, from inexpensive and plain to fancy high-dollar items. Of course, your puppy won't care how much you spend, nor will he have an opinion about the color of his leash or bed. He'll be satisfied with simple, utilitarian equipment.

Suppertime! Bowls and Dishes

Your puppy will need at least two bowls, one for water and another for food. If you offer him canned food, a third bowl or dish for the puppy is a good idea.

A variety of dish styles are available. Before making a fashion statement, it's most important to plan for the puppy's preferences, and care requirements. Just like people utensils, the bowls and dishes will need to be cleaned and so above all, choose something that's easy to keep clean. Puppies won't care what the bowl looks like.

Plastic bowls are inexpensive but can hold the odor of old food, and be difficult to clean. Some pets seem to develop allergic reactions to plastic dishes, too. Stainless steel bowls are the veterinarian's choice because they don't chip or break, and are easy to keep clean. They may also be too lightweight, so the puppy scoots them around the floor as he tries to eat. Larger pups could chew them, particularly during teething when the pup targets everything. I like the glass or ceramic choices because they are usually dishwasher safe and convenient to wash.

Puppies with long fur like Old English Sheepdogs or who have rather flat faces, like Pug babies, do better eating from a saucer rather than a bowl. One economical choice that some puppies prefer is to eat from a small paper plate. Rather than washing it when through, you can simply throw it away.

Once you've narrowed the practical choices, go wild. Goofy, whimsical, colorful, and elegant food dishes and water fountains can be found. Have your puppy's name inscribed so there's no question who they belong to.

Puppies tend to do best when meal fed. Their tummies are so small they aren't physically able to eat a huge meal at one time. Smaller portions throughout the day work better. When you feed a dry commercial food, you can "free feed" and leave a quantity in the bowl available all day. But for wet foods that spoil if left out too long, an "automatic food dish" might be something to consider. There are several kinds, but all have a series of small, sometimes refrigerated compartments that hold the meal, and open on a timer, so the food stays fresh.

Dog Nappers and Beds

Nothing looks sweeter than a puppy curled up fast asleep in a bed of his choice. Puppies sleep a lot, and they tend to have specific preferences. A tired pup will crash anywhere, but a warm, cozy and soft surface is best.

Lots of commercial dog beds, from pillow-like stuffed poofs to hammocks, will please the most persnickety puppy. I've seen the best selection at dog shows, where you can color-coordinate a bed to match or highlight your puppy's markings. They even have miniature human-style sofas for the diva puppy!

Most puppies, though, are perfectly happy to cuddle up on a soft blanket. A washable blanket is best. A great idea is to let the dog carrier play double-duty and serve as the baby's bed. Take off the door or leave it open, put the blanket inside, and it makes a wonderful puppy cave for sleeping. That also gets your puppy accustomed to being in the carrier, so there's less stress when he must ride there for a trip to the vet.

A tired puppy will crash and nap nearly anywhere. It's so much more comforting, too, when they have a nap buddy to use as a pillow.

Dog Toys, Cheap Thrills and More

Puppy play inspires people to create wonderful, fun toys for their enjoyment. It's hard to say who has more fun—the puppy, or the person watching their antics. Your puppy will tell you there's no such thing as too many toys. Playtime keeps the puppy brain stimulated, prompts exercise to keep him physically healthy, and keeps him emotionally engaged and happy. A bored puppy will seek out entertainment, and you may not like his choices.

There are two basic categories of toys: solo-toys where Puppy can keep himself occupied and interactive toys where you are part of the game. Make sure you have some of both. Also look into "indoor" toys and "outside" toys. Soft, smaller size toys won't do as much damage in the living room if your puppy misses catching them, while larger ones are less likely to be lost in the back yard.

The best solo toys are lightweight and easily bitten and carried, or moved with a paw-swat, and have an interesting texture or make an intriguing noise. You'll need to experiment to see what your puppy likes best. As a puppy, Magic adored stuffed squeaky toys to grab, toss and shake to "kill" and he also loved balls that roll and bounce. He's still a toy fanatic. Other puppies may have different tastes.

Any toy can become interactive, when you're involved. A toy on a rope tug toy works great to exercise energetic puppies. Balls, Frisbees and other toss toys inspire fun games of fetch. Terrier breeds enjoy lure toys similar to the cat's fishing pole toys with a "lure" toy on the end of a long string. You can sit in a chair and play with the baby from a distance. Please remember, though, to never leave string-type toys out unattended. Puppies may inadvertently swallow the ribbon or string, and end up in the emergency room when it causes problems.

There are also puzzle toys that can be filled with treats for the pup to maneuver for a tasty tidbit. Scenting breeds may prefer a scented toy that smell great and allow him to use his sniffing to find hidden toys. Modular fabric or plastic puppy gyms and tunnels can be designed for hideaways and play zones. Puppies have loads of fun chasing the beam of a flashlight—and you'll never have to leave your chair to fish it out from under the sofa. Just be cautious your pup doesn't become obsessed with the light.

Some of the best toys are homemade or found items your puppy discovers. I call these "cheap thrills" and some of the best include empty boxes or paper bags for hiding, wads of paper for playing chase and fetch, and hair "scrunchies" swiped by the baby.

Dog Carriers and Crates

Many styles are available, from disposable cardboard to hard plastic or zippered fabric totes designed for airline travel, as well as large condo-style wire crates. Dog carriers and crates are widely available, and have doors that open on the front or top, and come in several sizes.

Dogs prefer carriers that offer enough room, but are snug enough they feel secure and don't rattle around inside. Inexpensive cardboard carriers are available from pet stores, shelters, and veterinary offices. Crates and carriers can double as the puppy's bed, as well. Refer to Chapter 14 for tips on crate training your puppy.

Soft-sided duffel-styles with zippers are also widely available and quite popular, especially with people who travel a great deal with their dogs. They can be slung over your shoulder, and tend to fit easily under the airplane seat so the small size pet can accompany you as carry-on luggage.

Puppy Identification

Collars are more than a fashion statement for your puppy. They provide identification should he ever stray from home. Even indoor puppies sometimes slip out the door, and a tag may be the only thing that brings him home. It's a sad truth that many puppies and dogs picked up by shelters lose their lives because their owner can't be found. A collar is life insurance for your dog. Once you've found the collar, either order or make an identification tag to attach to it.

TAGS: Include your address, and a couple of phone numbers to make it as easy as possible for someone to contact you about your missing puppy. The rabies tag your veterinarian gives you often doubles not only as notice he's current on this important vaccination, but also as an ID, because the clinic is required by law to keep a record of that tag number.

There are many styles of identification tags, from fancy to plain. The best provide the necessary information, and don't bother the dog. If he's irked by the jingle of the tag he's more likely to try and remove the collar. Some collars have plastic windows where you can insert identification information, and there's no dangling irritation.

High-tech tags also include a tiny USB computer chip—sort of like a flash drive—that attaches to your puppy's collar. It holds reams of information you can download directly from your own computer. The drawback on collar tags, though, is that they can be lost.

There are many online database services that allow you to register collar tag number, USB, tattoo or microchip information. These systems can be accessed from any computer, and track down your lost puppy information no matter how far he's roamed.

TATOOS: Magic has a tattoo in his ear that identifies him, and my first dog had a tattoo on the inside of his thigh. The number is included on registration papers for purebred dogs. Often, puppies from reputable breeders receive a tattoo while just a tiny pup. Tattoos also may also be placed on the puppy's tummy.

Tattoos can be a good way to permanently mark your puppy to identify him. However, if your baby gets lost and is found by strangers, they must know to look for a tattoo. And they must also know what to do with the numbers. Unfortunately, tattoos fade over time or may be hidden by the pet's fur.

MICROCHIPS: Many shelter-adopted puppies are microchipped so if your puppy is ever lost and returned to the shelter and scanned, he'll be identified as your lost waif, and returned. Microchips are the gold standard for identification. Microchips can't be lost, they never wear out, and are engineered to last a lifetime. They're also easy to find and to trace.

The microchip, embedded in surgical glass about the size of a grain of rice, is injected beneath the pet's skin in the shoulder region. Even tiny pups won't react any worse to this procedure than when they're vaccinated. Owners provide the information that goes into the microchip, and it's stored on a pet recovery database.

The microchips are read using a hand-held scanner over the shoulder region. Microchips transmit specific frequencies like a small radio station, and the scanner must be "tuned" correctly to read the information. It's important that shelters and veterinary hospitals in your locale have scanners able to read the specific microchip implanted in your pet, so ask before you 'chip.

The most popular pet microchip companies also offer microchips in bulk for rescue or shelter organizations, recovery database systems, and other benefits like pet health insurance in case a pet is injured while AWOL. Local veterinarians and shelters provide the microchipping service using one or more

WARNING!
Don't rely on microchipping alone. Usually a lost dog is found by neighbors who may not turn him into the shelter. A tag on the collar remains one of the best ways to protect your puppy.

of these products, and the cost varies. Typically, shelters offer lower cost "deals" and microchipping may even be covered by the adoption fee along with spay or neuter when you acquire your pet.

Collars

Collars come in every color and size, with metal studs, rhinestones, plaid, with bows, or plain and simple. Keep in mind that your puppy, depending on his age, likely will outgrow his first collar. Puppies grow very quickly and your dog will need two or three (or more) before fully grown. Choose one that fits him now. It does no good if he can wiggle out of it. Flat buckle collars work well and can be purchased in a variety of colors and materials, from nylon woven to leather with silver studs.

The ideal collar fits snug around the pup's neck while allowing you to easily slip two fingers underneath. A size that initially fits him when snugged to the smallest fitting could be adjusted while he grows.

The old-style "choke" and prong collars used for training have no place anywhere near a puppy. A youngster's neck can be quite fragile. Although savvy professionals often claim they can train humanely with these tools, a puppy owner can accidentally severely injure a puppy with misuse, as well as risking damage to your loving relationship.

A martingale collar also works well for around the house or as a training collar. It has a limited tightening to give better control but with more safety than old-style chain "choke" collars.

Halters

Halters are a great choice for puppies. When a leash is attached, the halter distributes the pressure more evenly rather than focusing on the pup's fragile neck. Some puppies learn how to pull against the leash so that a collar slips off over his head, and when properly fitted, halters are much less likely to peel off the dog.

There are different halter styles now available. The standard H-harness may work fine. The harness is built like the letter H, and the top and bottom "feet" of the letter join to form two circles connected by the middle bridge portion. One circle goes around the chest behind Puppy's front legs, and the second fits around the base of his neck. The "bridge" of the H joins the two circles over his shoulders.

Harness styles include dog "jacket" and "vest" styles with soft webbing and Velcro fastenings that fit snuggly around his upper torso. These can be more difficult to fit correctly, and since puppies grow so quickly, it can be pricy to replace. If you'd like to invest in one of the jacket-style walk you may wish to wait until he's more mature.

For puppies that tend to pull, look into the variety of "no-pull" harnesses that help with training. These typically position the D-ring leash attachment to the front of the dog's chest, rather the standard spot over the shoulders. When the puppy pulls, the front-chest position turns him back to the person who holds the leash, which is a humane self-correction that teaches him not to pull. In order to move forward, Puppy must keep the leash loose and not tug. When Magic was young, I trained him using the Pet Safe Easy-Walk Harness, which is quite popular and effective. Others often recommended include Sporn Pet Halter and Sense-ation No-Pull Harness.

Finally, there are "head halters/collars" that do much the same thing as the no-pull harnesses. These are used as training tools and fit over the puppy's face and around his mouth, to gently guide him in the same fashion as a horse wearing a halter. Gentle Leader and Halti are two popular brands.

Most harnesses are adjustable and can be enlarged as the puppy grows. Go for quality with your halter choice; be sure the catches are secure and won't come loose in the middle of a jaunt across the back yard. A good harness will last the dog his whole life.

Cute picture, right? But do be careful about leaving leashes within reach, since these are not toys—and puppies are likely to chew them up. You don't want Junior Dog getting in the habit of chewing and destroying training equipment.

Leash

Once the halter is fitted onto the puppy, the leash attaches to the metal or plastic ring set into the material at his shoulders (for standard harnesses). Look for a lightweight leash that won't weigh him down or be too cumbersome for a small puppy.

A leash offers a way to control your puppy from a short distance away. It can be a great training tool, but more than that, could be considered a safety net for your dog. He should be on the leash anytime he's outside and not within a fenced area. In some locals, the law requires your dog to be on leash whenever off your property.

Leashes are made from flat nylon mesh, chains, leather, braided rope or cable and come in designer colors as well as plain-Jane practical models. You may not need a heavy leash for your eight-pound puppy, and a light weight style can be fine for first obedience lessons. But heavier versions will be needed as he grows.

For control, your puppy needs to be near you. A six-foot leash offers more than enough ranging room. Avoid the retractable cable leashes for two reasons. First, they give your dog too much ranging room and you'll not be able to intercede in time when the puppy's 25 feet away. Second, these leashes teach your puppy to pull the leash, rather than follow your lead. If he learns to pull as a youngster, he'll tug you all over the world as an adult.

Nylon and chain leashes won't be particularly comfortable for your bare hands, should the adolescent pup decide to challenge your control. And while designer colors may be stylish, your dog won't care. A versatile, rugged soft six-foot leather leash works well for general dog walking and obedience training.

Some puppies never bat an eye when presented with the halter and leash, and others throw a hissy fit. Learning to accept leash-training opens up the world and allows your baby to accompany you—safely escorted—beyond the walls of your house. Learn all about how to introduce your puppy to the halter and leash in Chapter 14.

The Ins and Outs of Dog Doors

The dog flap—a small pet door—may be an option you want to consider. These doors can help keep your puppy's private space protected. That keeps nosy adult dogs away from puppy food, and gives your baby dog potty access even when you're not there to supervise.

Pet doors can be installed in interior or exterior walls, doors, and or even sliding panels to give access to a room, or safe outdoor area. The simplest offer a finished opening that's too small for other pets, and is used for access into interior rooms. The next level provides a vinyl flap that covers the opening, for the puppy to push through, and protects against wind and wet. More expensive models provide a hinged screen or window, which keeps the opening free from buggy intruders or seals air conditioning inside. Most of these can be "locked" so that the puppy stays safely inside when you're not there to keep an eye on his antics.

The ultimate in pet doors offer "keyed" access that lock so that only the pet wearing the magnetic collar or microchip ID can get into the house. That prevents strays or wild animals from invading your home, and keeps the cat inside while giving the dogs freedom to play in the yard.

Measure the pet's height at his shoulders to determine the size door needed. Remember that your puppy may have some growing yet to do. If you have other pets, decide if you want them to have access too, before deciding on the size of the door. You can find a large selection of dog doors from pet products stores.

A safety harness and seat belt can keep puppies safely confined in moving cars.

Traveling Puppies

Every puppy must travel during his lifetime, if only to visit the veterinarian for preventative care. Confinement in a carrier keeps the baby safe while he's in the car, halters and a leash control him when he's out of the safety of your house. Should the worst happen, identification will allow your puppy to be returned to you if he gets lost.

On The Road

Unless dogs have happy travel experiences as babies, they may not be happy campers when you hit the road. Show dogs travel all the time, of course. And these dogs do well because they've learned to accept being in their carrier for long periods of time—four to six hours or more at a stretch.

You probably won't need any special preparations to drive your puppy an hour or so away to visit friends or family. Most states require that pets have a health certificate from a veterinarian accompany them if they cross state lines. It's a good idea to bring his health records with you.

He'll be in his familiar, safe carrier, of course, strapped safely in the back seat. Take along a bottle of water from home to be sure strange water doesn't upset his digestion. Include his food bowls and food, favorite toys and blanket. Bring clean up material to pick up his puppy waste along the way. If the trip is longer than a couple of hours, stop in a rest area, and give him a break. Be sure he's safely on leash before you open the car doors.

Why Puppies Hate Cars

The first ride in the car takes your baby dog away from the only family he's ever known. The next several car rides end up at the veterinarian for needle pokes for vaccinations and rude cold thermometers inserted in uncomfortable places.

New owners want to comfort the frightened, fussy baby. But whining back at your cry-puppy can backfire. That tells the puppy that you agree that there's a good reason to fuss, and that car rides ARE horrible!

Instead, associate cars with fun, happy experiences instead of just trips to the vet. The process, called desensitization, takes patience and time, but works whether a pet acts scared, sick, or just hyper. And once your puppy realizes a car ride means wonderful things she'll look forward to every trip.

1. Make meal time car time. For very frightened pups just set the bowl next to the car. After several days when she's used to that, feed her in the back seat while leaving the car door open.
2. In between times, throw treats in the open car door for the pup to find, and play fun games near the car. She should learn that only these good things in life happen when you're near the car.
3. Next, when your pup's eating or otherwise distracted in the back seat, get in the front seat behind the steering wheel. Just sit for a while, no big deal, then get out, so she understands nothing scary happens when you're in the car too. Do this for one day.
4. The next day, when you're behind the wheel and your puppy's munching treats in the back seat, start the car. Then turn off the motor

and get out without going anywhere. Do this three or four times during the day until the pet takes it as a matter of course.

5. Finally, after you start the car, back the car to the end of the driveway and stop—do this two or three times in a row, always letting the pet out after you return. If the puppy whines or paces or shows stress, you may be moving too fast for him. The process takes forever! but it works.

6. Continue increasing the car-time by increments—a trip around the block and then home, then a trip to the nearest fun place like the park before returning home. Go somewhere you know your dog will enjoy— get him French fries at the nearest fast food restaurant, or a doggy treat from the tellers at the bank or dry cleaner. Make every car trip upbeat and positive so the experience makes the dog look forward to the next trip.

WARNING!

Puppies and dogs should always be confined during transportation in a car. Some pets become upset and interfere with the driver by getting underneath the pedals. Others become carsick and containment helps prevent a mess. Even well behaved pets should be confined, for their own safety. If you are in an accident, a loose pet inside the car could injure you or be hurt or killed himself from the impact, or he could get lost. Place carriers on the back seat and secure with a seatbelt, or use a puppy safety harness that connects to the seatbelt. Puppies riding on the passenger front seat (even inside a carrier) may be crushed if the airbag deploys.

Puppy Hotel Manners

Doggy delinquents can improve their conduct and become great roommates. And once they feel at home and understand what's expected, they'll have a great time and do you proud whether you stay at a budget motel or a high-dollar ritzy establishment.

1. Some dogs make a fuss when you leave them alone in a strange room. These tend to be the same puppies that get upset and suffer separation anxiety when you go to work and leave them at the house. So use the

same tips for leaving them in the hotel room that you use to train puppies to relieve separation anxiety found in Chapter 15.

2. A crate or carrier teaches dogs they can't be with you all the time, but that you do always come back. And dogs that use crates as beds identify them as a familiar and comforting island in a strange place. In fact, most hoteliers prefer your dog be crated when he must be left alone in the room. Kenneling dogs virtually eliminates the chance of room damage, and also reassures the housekeeping folks who may be afraid of dogs.

3. Strange sights, smells, and sounds are exciting and will keep dogs occupied for quite a while. But once the new wears off, dogs tend to get bored pretty easily especially when left alone with nothing to do. All too often, dogs relieve boredom by chewing. Although chewing is a natural behavior, it can make him an unfit companion when he targets the hotel room's television remote control while you're at breakfast. Provide chew toys to relieve his boredom and keep his teeth on legal targets.

4. Put a do not disturb sign on the door when dogs are left alone in the room. Otherwise, housekeeping could come in and upset your pup, or even worse, he could slip out the door and get lost.

5. The best time to walk dogs at hotels is very early in the morning, before 7 a.m. so you avoid running into other hotel guests who may not care for your puppy. Ask about the doggy potty spot and be sure to clean up after your pet. You may be asked to use the service elevator so other guests don't have to share a ride with a strange dog.

6. Just getting to the toilet area without baptizing the wall may be tricky for dogs not used to hotels. They may simply need to "go" or more likely want to leave their Pee-Mail message as a marking behavior. Pausing for even 10 seconds tempts pups to sniff and lift. Keep him moving until you reach the designated area. Practice "sit" and "down" to give him something to do while you're at the front desk, for instance. Dogs with a job rarely have an accident when they're "working." One helpful trick is to give your pup a ball or other toy to carry, to help keep him focused on that rather than sniffing and leg-lifting.

7. If he sleeps in a crate at home, use the crate. But don't banish your pup to the bathroom, unless you fear he'll be sick. That only increases his stress level. I sleep with my dog—yes, I'm that fond of him!—but in a hotel situation he sleeps on a blanket spread across the sheet. They should change the sheets between guests anyway. And when your dog is well mannered, nobody will know the difference or complain.

Plane Travel and Puppies

If you plan to travel by plane with your puppy, plan on spending an extra $100 or more each way for his fare. Depending on the airline, small pets may be allowed to travel in the cabin of the plane with you as "carry-on" luggage, but the carrier must be able to fit under the seat ahead of you. Call the airline ahead of time to find out the latest requirements for plane travel, as it can vary from carrier to carrier. Most of the soft sided pet carriers work well for plane travel.

You'll want to feed and water the puppy only small amounts before the flight, and give him an opportunity to use the bathroom. Most babies settle down and sleep during the trip. You must make a reservation and arrive early if you wish to carry-on your puppy because they usually only allow two animals per cabin at a time and as first come, first served. Otherwise he'll have to travel as cargo with the other luggage.

Most airlines have restrictions on the time of year animals can travel as cargo, and disallow them if it's too hot or too cold. Frankly, it may not be safe and certainly can be scary or uncomfortable for the baby. To travel as cargo he must have a hard plastic airline approved crate. New pet-friendly airline options such as Air Animal, Animal Airlines and others may specialize in pet flights.

Be sure to check him as "excess baggage"—don't send him "freight" because freight may not travel on the same plane. Ask the flight crew to watch out for your puppy during the flight by monitoring the atmosphere in the cargo hold.

Leaving Him Behind

Many puppies and dogs dislike traveling or spending time away from their familiar home surroundings. There are also times, like business trips or vacations, where it's not possible to take Puppy along with you. What are your options?

HOME ALONE: Make arrangements to have a friend, a neighbor, or a professional pet sitter to stay with your puppy (preferred) or to visit several times a day to take the pup outside for potty breaks, and check food and water. The puppy will appreciate some playtime and cuddles, too, while you're gone. Ask a friend to be on call during this period, in case your plane is cancelled and return is delayed. Be sure they know where his food, veterinarian's phone number, and medical history are located—just in case.

PET SITTER: If twisting a friend's arm doesn't work, the best option is hiring a professional pet sitter. You can get a referral from Pet Sitters International or from the National Association of Professional Pet Sitters. These folks are bonded and come to your home to care for your puppy several times a day, as requested. Rover.com is another option where you can find a variety of pet care professionals in your neck of the woods, set up interviews and figure out the best fit for you and your puppy.

BOARDING KENNEL: The last choice is to board your puppy. This may be a fine solution for confident babies, but very shy ones handle the stress of your absence more easily if they can stay in familiar surroundings. We're fortunate that our dog Magic's breeder has room for him in her home and kennel the few times we've had to be gone. It's like doggy vacation for him, where he gets to play with the other dogs.

Ask your veterinarian for options, too. Some vet clinics offer a boarding service for their clients. Reputable kennels require proof of adequate health care, so get vaccination proof from your veterinarian in advance. Some state-of-the-art facilities now provide pets with sofas, play times with other dogs, and even close-circuit television monitors owners can access over the Internet while on vacation, to keep an eye on their furry friends. Doggy Daycare facilities may offer longer term boarding for regular clients, too.

Visit the kennel yourself, ask for recommendations from other clients or veterinarians, and satisfy yourself Puppy will be happy and any special needs can be met. For instance, if he needs a particular food, or medication at certain times of the day, ensure the staff are aware and can manage this.

6: Com*pet*ability:

Puppy Society Explained

Imagine that an explorer searching the most hidden places on earth stumbles upon an unknown civilization, never touched by the outside world. The inhabitants have never experienced strangers before. The Explorer—a human being—is shocked at the strangeness of the other's language, culture, and social structure.

Science fiction? No, this is reality when it comes to understanding canine society.

The social structure of dogs is similar to people but there are enough differences that cause confusion. Human social system is based on a "group" mentality and held together by vocal communication. Dog ancestors—wolves—evolved to live in social groups, too, but dogs are not wolves and mistakes are made when we think of them in terms of their ancestors. Also, dog communication relies on a combination of vocalizations, and silent communication through body posture and scent signals. Each system works well for that particular group, but when you put the two together, there are bound to be misunderstandings. Unless you understand where your puppy is coming from, there will be a culture clash.

Human Society

To understand dog culture, you must first take a close look at the human equivalent to see how different they are. Social groups provide a greater benefit than one individual could get by themselves. Early people banded together to hunt and bring down big game that one person couldn't tackle alone. They built communities for safety, raised children together, and shared responsibility. Working together offered great rewards in terms of food, safety, and companionship.

In order to work together, people needed to communicate. When disputes arose, people created ways to settle arguments so that the group didn't suffer and fall apart.

In broad terms, human society chooses a leader to arbitrate decisions for the entire group and settles disputes. The followers who bow to the leader's wise council benefit from this situation by gaining the protection of the group. When the leader is absent, a second in command takes over until the boss returns.

A modern-day example happens every day when you report to work. A boss makes the decisions for you and your co-workers. When you follow the rules (i.e., do your job correctly), you receive your colleague's approval and respect, the boss' loyalty, and a paycheck reward. Well, that's the way it's supposed to work, anyway.

In communal animal societies, a single wolf can't easily bring down a deer, but the pack can. The group also offers better protection—they can take turns guarding their territory and den, and communally raise the young. A wolf cub that follows the rules gets to eat with the group, and has earned their affection and loyalty and protection.

Dog Culture

To be efficient and harmonious, the doggy social structure depends on a hierarchy of dominant and subordinate individuals. Social ranking decides which dogs get the preferred or prime access to valued resources: resting spots, food pans, water, toys, bones, your attention, and so on. However, dominance has nothing to do with bullying or aggression, nor does submission necessarily correlate with fear or shyness. In years' past, much has been made of the "canine alpha" dominance hierarchy of dogs, whereas today behaviorists describe it as a subordinance hierarchy.

Relentless, active appeasement and deference of subordinate animals allows for harmony in social groups. The canine communication often described as submissive behavior could more accurately be translated as signaling *non-contest*, or *let me be your friend*.

Dog society consists of a linear hierarchy, often with both a male hierarchy and a female hierarchy. Males tend to be more dominance-oriented around territory (the yard and house), while females are more likely to be territorial about toys, food, and other belongings.

This happens from puppyhood on, with a "top dog" and "bottom dog" usually established in a litter by eight weeks of age. Boys are usually bigger than girls, so the male often is the top dog. The top and bottom pups (and adult dogs) have the easiest time dealing with canine society since everyone is either above or below them, so they know how to act and react.

Middle pups have a harder time establishing rank and won't have a firm sense of social position until about three months or so, when rank usually correlates pretty strongly with sex and weight. But in non-related pups of different ages, once they all socialize to each other, the most important determinant of rank is age and sex. Pups that grow up with other dogs quickly learn that exaggerated appeasement gestures can cut short the harassment with a preemptive apology characterized by a low-slung, wriggly approach with ears back, a submissive grin, and tail and hindquarters wagging.

Older males usually rank higher, and size/strength help determine ranking as pups grow. Once they've grown up, though, and take their places within an already established adult hierarchy, there may be no correlation between rank and weight. Among adult male dogs, an individual's relative rank decides nearly everything in advance, such as who gets the toy, where dogs sleep, and which one gets to greet the owner first. Relationship between males and females can vary from day to day.

Girl dogs have a linear but less rigid hierarchy, with day-to-day success depending on the individual circumstances. The top bitch always gets the preferred toy or treat first, and if she's not there, the second-ranking bitch likely will score the trophy. However, the girls seem to respect ownership a bit more than the boys. While the highest ranking male might challenge a subordinate and take away his bone, the highest ranking female often allows a lower-ranking girl to enjoy the treat when it's already in her possession—dogs signaling possession by keeping a paw or two on the toy or just looking at it. And while a subordinate boy dog typically gives up the bone if a higher-ranking male tells him to, a lower-ranking girl may defend her ownership of the goodies. Think of this as a sort of "finders/keepers" mentality. Once a dog relinquishes possession, though, any lower-ranking dog of either gender can have at it with impunity.

Maintaining the existing social structure relies on the lowest-ranking dogs to express respect for the dogs of higher rank. The major function of the hierarchical structure is to lessen the need for fighting. For example, if two dogs see one toy, but the "owner" is predetermined by rank, there's no need to fight. Fights or noisy disputes are rare because top dogs have no reason to fight, and low-ranking dogs know they'd be foolish to try. Excess growling and repeat fighting are symptoms of insecurity and uncertainty about social rank compared to other dogs, and are the hallmark of middle-ranking males.

Crowning the "Ruler"

How do dogs decide who will be the boss, and who will be the follower in a particular territory? There are several factors that influence positions. There are exceptions to these rules, but basically four categories decide the status of a dog.

Sexual status plays a major role in the canine community. Dogs that have not been spayed or neutered typically rank higher than sterilized ones. The Mom-dog with puppies has the most power of all. Neutering all the dogs helps level the playing field, and eliminates the potential for many squabbles.

Personality impacts the way the puppy perceives herself, the world around her, and other pets. Every puppy is an individual and early socialization—exposing puppies to positive experiences during their formative weeks of life—will prevent many dog hierarchy disputes later in life.

Shy insecure puppies may feel the need to squabble to keep "danger" away out of fear. Brash in-your-face youngsters are more likely to become problem dogs because they like to pester even the boss-dogs, or may not be satisfied with a lower-ranking position. Confident puppies, those with the middle-of-the-road calm personalities, seem destined for leadership and handle it well.

Age defines who rules to a great extent. Puppies almost always bow to the rule of adult dogs. A mature dog usually will be dominant over an elderly pooch.

Health status throws out everything else. A sick dog loses any status she has, and becomes subordinate to healthy ones. Even a young puppy may bully a sickly elder-statesman dog.

Most dogs get along very well together especially when all are spayed and neutered and they have been properly introduced. Puppies raised in litters of four or more and that remain together until they are 12 to 16 weeks old usually get along best with other dogs.

Nose-to-Nose at Last:

Introductions

Often we are so excited about the new family member, we want to share our joy—immediately!—with everybody in the household. The new puppy is brought into the living room, dumped on the carpet, and everybody crowds around to get a look at the newcomer.

In the best of all worlds, the rest of your family (furred and otherwise) will accept the baby with no problem. It's love at first sight, and a peaceable kingdom is born. But more often, such an introduction backfires—everybody (including the new puppy) gets upset, and it can take days, weeks, or even months to smooth out the relationship.

The key to successful introductions is patience. One step at a time gets the job done, with the least trauma to everybody involved. Once your new puppy becomes a part of your human and pet family, she'll have a lifetime to get to know them better. Make sure everybody gets off on the right foot—er, paw—from the start. That not only prevents misunderstandings and potential behavior problems, but can increase the chances the new baby and your existing family will fall in love, permanently.

Resident pets—be they dogs, cats, or other animals—also have feelings that need to be considered. After all, how would you feel if a stranger suddenly appeared and wanted to share your food, your bed, and your favorite belongings—even the affections of your loved one?

Whether your puppy is 10 weeks old or 10 months old, she still is a stranger in a strange land, and may be frightened of the change. Confident dogs of any age seem to love new things, but may fear being startled with the unexpected. Familiarity with a known territory increases their feelings of security. It's important to create a happy, safe environment so the puppy feels confident enough to explore and enjoy new experiences.

That's why creating a room of her own is the first and most important step when introducing a new puppy into your home. This does a couple of things: First, it breaks up the enormous territory of a new home into a smaller, more manageable puppy-size real estate. She can become familiar with her room first, and use that as a safe retreat and home base. That's important if she's an "only" pet, too, but becomes vital when she will share the house with other animals.

Second, this segregation keeps the new puppy quarantined until her health is assessed by your veterinarian. The last thing you want to do is to expose your resident canine to an illness from the new baby.

Finally, segregating the puppy tells your resident pet that only a part of her territory is invaded. And the closed door may pique the resident pet's curiosity, rather than raise her hackles. Segregating the pets early on lets you control the introductions.

Some pets require more time than others to become used to the idea of meeting new animals. Resident pets that already get along well with other animals may accept the new puppy more quickly. A shy puppy may take days to weeks to feel comfortable in the new environment. You must also be prepared, though, for some pets to simply dislike each other. Cats are notorious for hating change and may take a long time to accept a new pet, if ever. In these cases, you can at least help them learn to tolerate each other.

Meeting Other Dogs

All else being equal, adult dogs tend to more readily accept pets that are younger and of the opposite sex. That means, if you have a resident neutered adult male dog, a female puppy would make a good choice; a resident spayed female dog would likely do well with a boy puppy. Of course, pairs of girls or boys can also become lifelong buddies with the right introductions.

Remember to spay or neuter your puppy as early as possible. That will eliminate many of the behavior problems that could potentially develop, and also helps smooth the pet relationships as the puppy reaches maturity.

The adult dog will also much more quickly learn to accept a new dog if exposed to them during early socialization. Be warned that a four-plus-year-old canine who has never before lived with another dog may strenuously object to a newcomer. He may either become antagonistic, or hide. Oftentimes, owners adopt another dog to keep the resident dog company—and the dog's reaction typically is, "Nobody asked me! I like having all the attention to myself!" A set-in-his-ways older dog may take a long time to accept a new pet, so again, patience is key.

Just remember that a resident dog naturally protects his turf. Your puppy may either feel uncertain in strange surroundings, or act like a clueless bozo clown-dawg who hisses off the mature canines. Proper introductions help ensure both pets start off on the same positive paw.

Neutral Ground

First meetings should take place on neutral ground, such as a neighbor's yard, training center, or tennis court. That way, King doesn't feel fearful, threatened, or protective of your house or yard, and can get down to the business of making friends with puppy. If neutral ground isn't available, visit a park where many dogs visit so your resident dog has less territorial claims and feels more willing to meet the new guy.

Fence Meetings

Dogs read your tension if you're the least bit wary. When this elevated excitement combines with a leash restraint ("I can't get away from that scary other dog!"), fearful aggression could develop. That's why first dog-to-dog meetings should take place between unleashed dogs.

For safety's sake, though, let them meet through a chain link fence or tennis net, so they can sniff but the barrier keeps them separated. That helps the novelty of "new dog" wear off before a true nose-to-nose meeting. It's also important when there's great size difference between the resident dog and new pup. Even friendly adult dogs could accidently injure the youngster with over-exuberant greetings.

Parallel Walking

Alternatively, take both dogs for a walk, parallel to each other, with a different person handling each dog—keep the leashes loose and give them room to move to reduce the potential for tension. At first keep them out of nose-sniffing range, and use a treat or toy to keep doggy eyes on the human (no challenge-staring at the other dog allowed!). Walk them together for five or ten minutes before allowing a head-to-head meeting.

Sniffing Opportunities

Once the dogs show happy interest in meeting, let them—keeping the leashes loose. Choose an area with open space to reduce tension. They'll be rude and sniff each other in unmentionable places, since that's proper canine meeting etiquette. First greetings should be kept to only ten minutes or so, to keep the dogs from tiring. Make a point of calling each dog away from time to time to give a treat or toy, to prevent any tension from escalating and to keep the mood happy.

Positive Signs

If they want to play bow, bravo! Watch for the doggy language that signals good intentions. A classic canine invitation to a game is the "play bow" in which the tail end goes up, and front end goes down. Doggy yawning also signals, "I am no threat" and can be a very positive sign from either dog. Whines, barks and growls are used in both play and threat so pay attention to other body language to judge what the dogs mean. Licking the mouth and face of the other dog and rolling on the back in dog language signals submission. The puppy should display these behaviors, which should tell the older dog he's just a baby and cut the youngster some slack. Allow play for only a few minutes during the first meeting, though, then stop and end the introduction on a good note.

Meeting On Home Ground
Once they've met off territory, repeat the introduction in your home yard— off leash if it's fenced. Call the dog and puppy apart every few minutes to ensure they don't become too excited. Remember, the new pup should only meet one resident dog at a time, not the whole gang at once.

Meeting In the House
Finally, arrange to have all of your resident dogs OUTSIDE of the house when you first bring the new pup indoors. Do this out of sight of the other canines. For instance, have your resident dogs in the fenced back yard playing while you bring the new puppy in the front door. For the least potential problems, the resident dogs should enter the house and find the new dog already there. Most dogs quickly work out their social ranking and decide how to interact in a positive way. It's best for the new puppy to be segregated in a room alone with a baby gait barrier when you are not there to directly supervise.

Meeting Cats

Dogs and cats living together? Getting along? Even liking each other? Of course! Your puppy and the family cat can, with the right introductions, become fast friends. In fact, nearly 30 percent of US Households share their hearts and homes with both dogs and cats together.

There are inherent safety concerns when the puppy and the cat vary a great deal in size. After all, a well-meaning but bumbling big dog could squash a tiny kitten just by stepping on her. Besides this, certain cats may view a scampering puppy as a tasty morsel. Fair play requires mention of the dangers of cat claws to canine eyes as well, particularly in some of the dog breeds with more prominent eyes. In spite of these concerns, the vast majority of dog/cat relationships are positive ones. Many of the same puppy-to-dog techniques work just as well with puppy-to-cat introductions.

It's important to recognize, too, that dogs and cats are very different creatures. They have different languages, different social systems, and want different things out of life. It's up to you, the owner, to understand them both and help them adjust to each other with proper introductions.

Understanding Feline Concerns

In terms of puppy and cat safety issues, as well as predicting if the pets will get along, canine personality is even more important than dog size. To a great degree, the dog's breed can offer clues as to what to expect. There are always exceptions, though, and because you live with your dog, you will be the best judge of his personality.

Just like dogs, feline society is defined by leaders and followers. However, most cats are driven to be the top cat and in charge, while dogs typically are simply happy to be part of the group and don't care who's the boss— (preferably the human!). Many dogs are perfectly happy to pledge allegiance to a human—or even a feline—leader. And when your puppy looks to you for guidance, it may be enough that you like the cat and expect him to accept her.

Arguments over turf that characterize feline disputes rarely happen to the same extent between dogs and cats, though. That's because they have very different social needs. Your dog is satisfied as long as he knows his place in the family group, while the cat's first priority is to own territory. They don't even value real estate the same way. Dogs can only lay claim to floor-level property. Meanwhile, the kitty prefers high perches the dog can't reach. Both the puppy and the cat will think they have won the contest, and will be happy ruling their own little kingdoms.

WARNING!

Predatory behavior is very important when judging safety issues. All dogs and cats have predators inside their brains, waiting to pounce. That's what drives cats to chase the fluttering ribbon, or the dog to fetch the ball—or to chase the cat. Certain dog breeds, like terriers and sight hounds, were developed to chase and kill prey. The instinct is hard wired into them, and the dog may not be able to control the urge to chase and catch a cat. Extra care must be taken when introducing a puppy of that heritage into a home with a resident cat.

When introducing the new puppy to a feline companion, have someone else bring the baby into the house so the cat does not associate you with that new scary "interloper." If possible, do this without the cat seeing the puppy's arrival.

As with the puppy-to-dog introductions, the new pup should remain in her own room for the first several days, only leaving the room for potty breaks to the yard. Cats that have been well-socialized to dogs when they were kittens will likely display some curiosity and want to sniff at the door. Meows and paw pats under the door are fine. Be sure to watch the cat and puppy's whole body to "read" each's true intent.

Be alert for raised kitty fur, hisses and growls. The pup also may display raised hackles—the fur along the neck and shoulders stands up with excitement and potential aggression. He may growl, or wag his high-held tail with excitement.

Let the cat sniff your hands and clothes after you've spent time with the puppy. The cat also can watch her "do her thing" in the yard from the window perch. That way he should have a good idea of what's inside the room long before a face-to-face introduction takes place. Cats often consider you to be the most important part of their territory, and so take care that he doesn't feel neglected. Try to spend extra time with your cat, and interact with the puppy in her room when the cat is otherwise engaged.

Once the puppy room has become old stuff, and any hisses or fluffed fur have subsided, it's time to let the puppy explore the house. Swap out the two pets—let the cat explore the puppy room (with the door closed) while the puppy gets a chance to run around the rest of the house.

With a puppy-to-dog introduction, even when you are positive the dog wouldn't hurt a fly, it's important that you place the puppy under leash control. Only then should the puppy be allowed out of her room, to meet the cat at her own pace. The leash is a safety precaution in case the cat proves irresistible to your new puppy and he tries to chase the cat. It also reminds him that you are in charge of the interaction.

Just as with the resident dog introductions, your goal is to have the cat associate the puppy's presence with good things for him. Talk to the cat, give him treats, have a feather wand interactive toy handy for him to play with, and praise him when he reacts favorably to the puppy. In future, you can reinforce the notion that having a puppy around is a good thing by having a treat or toy handy each time your cat acts "nice" to the new baby.

WARNING!
Dog eyes can be damaged by a frightened cat that lashes out in reaction to a nosy sniff. Before face-to-face meetings, be sure to clip the cat's claws.

Be sure to segregate the puppy in her room whenever you are not there to supervise the two pets. Even friendly play can turn dangerous, if either pet becomes over-excited or frightened. Cats should always have available a "safe place" they can climb—like a chair back, or cat tree—that keeps them beyond the reach of the dog. Likewise, the pup must have a private place, like a crate, where he can go to escape unwanted feline attention.

Meeting Other Pets

Puppies can become best friends with a wide range of animals. Remember, though, that puppies grow into dogs and will have a predatory interest in creatures smaller than themselves.

For instance, an aquarium filled with fish or reptiles offers great canine entertainment. So do cages with birds or pocket pets like gerbils or hamsters.

Remember, though, that small pets—especially birds—may suffer severe stress and develop behavior problems if pestered by an inquisitive puppy, even when they remain safely sequestered inside a cage. If you have these types of pets, the cage or aquarium should be set out of puppy reach, and doors or lids must be absolutely secure. You'd be surprised what puppy gnawing can open.

The larger, more confident birds like parrots are at less risk for being traumatized by the presence of a puppy or dog. In fact, parrots often are so assertive they scare the puppy or dog, so she gives them a wide berth. Other times, the parrot learns to tease or treat the puppy by dropping toys or food within reach, or by calling to the puppy in a human "voice."

Direct contact between your puppy and any bird, or smaller-than-puppy pets, is not recommended because the risk is just too great. Let them be friends from a distance, and with the benefit of bars or glass between them.

PUPPY WAGS.

Use a baby gate to keep the cat and puppy segregated. There are pet gates that bar the larger pup from getting through while allowing the cat to leap over the gate or go through an inset smaller opening. That keeps your new baby in a safe puppy-proofed room and away from pestering the cat. But it allows the two to safely interact through the barrier and learn to like each other.

Always supervise interaction between children and puppies. That protects them from accidentally injuring each other.

Meeting Children

Children seem to have an affinity for puppies. You should know, however, that puppies may not see it that way—at least, at first. That's because even though the puppy may trust adult humans, children are so very different she may not recognize them as safe. Depending on their age, a child has a much higher-pitched voice, often screams or cries, and moves very differently than adult people. Is it any wonder your puppy thinks the grandkids are from Mars?

Children need to understand that they can be scary to a tiny puppy—why from a puppy's vantage, even a toddler looks like a giant! Running after her, reaching out with waving hands that might pull a tail or ear, making loud high-pitched squeals, will send a puppy diving under the bed. Even the gentlest puppy will defend herself out of fear or anger if she's hurt or frightened.

When your children want to make friends with the new puppy, ask them to first sit on the floor. Chasing the puppy will at worst, scare her, and at best, force her to do something she doesn't like. The key here is to entice the puppy to come to the child on her own. Do that by making the experience positive and rewarding for the dog.

Sitting on the floor puts the child on the same level as the dog. That's much less threatening or frightening to the new pet. During the first session, just let the puppy wander around the room, exploring, and have the children pretend to be part of the furniture. This way, the puppy learns that having them there is a normal part of her environment--ask them to please not pick her up yet, at this point. But if she comes near enough, and lets them, a quick gentle stroke along her back is fine.

Is My Child Old Enough?

Pet owners are often anxious to share their affection for animals with their children. I'm often told by a parent that they want to get a pet to teach their kids about responsibility. Certainly, children raised to appreciate and properly care for pets will carry that love with them for the rest of their lives. But what age is best? And how much can you expect from your children—or a new puppy?

Obviously, an infant is in no position to care for a puppy, although babies certainly may appreciate watching the puppy play, or touching her soft fur. Both infants and toddlers may aggravate a puppy to death, poking fingers into her eyes or pulling fists full of fur. You will need to supervise all interactions between the new puppy and your infant or toddler. After all, when babies get together, anything can happen. You don't want the puppy dragged about like a stuffed toy and injured, nor do you want your child bitten when he corners the

PUPPY WAGS.

The best way to pick up a puppy is with one hand beneath her chest, and the other cupping her furry bottom. That supports the whole dog so no feet dangle. And it also makes her feel more secure and less likely to struggle.

frightened pet. Puppies old enough to outrun a toddler soon learn to avoid them.

By the time your children are six to seven years old, they can start to become a part of the puppy care team. Perhaps they can make sure the puppy always has fresh water, or can help "exercise" the baby each evening by playing with her. Young children will need direction in how to properly hold or pet a puppy—no poking, or tail-pulling allowed! Of course, the ultimate responsibility will be yours, and so be sure to supervise and follow-up to make sure the puppy's needs are never overlooked.

For very small children, ask them to first practice petting on their own arm, so they know the best way to stroke the puppy without making her uncomfortable. Perhaps you and your child can take turns "pretending" to be the puppy.

Another great way for children to interact with the new puppy is playing with a ball or other interactive toy that can be tossed for the baby dog to chase. This is particularly helpful with shy puppies who fear getting too close—they can play safely from a distance, and learn that your child is fun to be around!

Also, once the puppy has been worn out with play, she'll be much more likely to want to cuddle on a lap.

Whenever the children want to interact with the puppy, make it a rule that they should sit down on the floor, nearby, and let her approach them. That will also help them control excited loud voices. Explain that a puppy prefers soft-pitched talk, and that yells and screams and high-pitched voices are scary to dogs. Make it a game and a contest to see which child can speak in the best "puppy friendly" voice.

After several successful sessions of play with the toy, your puppy should learn that the children are fun, and they don't grab at her and make her feel scared. Once she starts to venture closer, make sure the children have a couple of scrumptious dog treats ready to offer her. If she can learn to associate your child with playtime and treats, she'll more readily accept them.

WARNING!

Never let your puppy play with fingers, hands, or feet. It's great fun for her to bite and pounce on these moving objects, but she can hurt or frighten you (or your children) if she gets too excited. A puppy grabbing your ankles or tugging shoelaces as you walk could, in fact, be dangerous. Instead, give her suitable toys to bite and wrestle, like stuffed animals.

PART THREE

PUPPY CARE 101

7: Feeding For Health

Good nutrition is the foundation of puppy health. A shiny coat, strong bones, boundless energy, and a loving personality all begin with the proper diet.

A mother dog produces nutrient-rich milk especially designed for the needs of puppies. Mom-dog takes care of the puppy's hunger pangs from birth to about six to eight weeks of age. A good diet for Mom ensures her milk will also provide optimum nutrition for her growing babies. The first milk that puppies nurse, called *colostrum*, contains protective antibodies from the mother that help keep them healthy until their own immune system matures.

As the puppy grows, he becomes interested in what Mom eats and will sample food from her dish. That's fine, but puppies shouldn't eat adult dog food. They grow so fast, puppies need a very different formulation than Mom does, and that can vary depending on the age and breed of the puppy.

An eight-week-old puppy needs about twice as many calories per day compared to an adult dog. Puppies require more protein, fat, calcium and phosphorus. These nutrients must be in the proper balance because too much or too little can cause problems. Commercial foods make this easy for you by preparing formulations specific to the needs of a growing puppy.

Some foods specify they're for "toy breed" or "large breed puppies" for example. The tiny mouths of some little dogs may require smaller kibble to be more easily chewed. And growing too fast can result in obesity or joint problems later in life for big breed dogs. Foods designed specifically for a large-breed puppy adjust the calcium and phosphorus ratio, calories and protein to slow the growth rate. Your puppy ends up just as big, but slowed growth lets joints develop and stabilized. Growing too fast could put too much weight strain on immature bones and joints.

Part of your responsibility is choosing the proper diet for the puppy. Today, there are literally hundreds of commercial puppy foods available. There also are some do-it-yourself pet food recipes you can make at home that can be very good (or very bad). That makes feeding puppies simpler—and more confusing—than ever before.

Some of that is because nutrition is an evolving science. We know more about canine nutrition today than we did yesterday, and brand-new information will be uncovered tomorrow. There are also differences of opinion even among the experts. On top of that, puppies are not identical. There are individual differences between them that make one food better for this puppy, and another food ideal for that one.

Commercial Food Categories

There are three broad categories for commercial pet food: super premium, premium, and low-cost products. These are generic terms with no legal definition. But some generalities apply.

Super premium foods tend to have the most bang for the buck. They have the highest nutrient density—the pup won't need to eat as much—as well as highest digestibility. To accomplish this, these foods use the costliest and highest quality ingredients.

More fat makes foods very tasty so puppies willingly eat the diet. High digestibility means you clean up less poo because more of the food is used by the body. Super premium foods are marketed primarily through specialty pet stores or veterinary clinics. Picky puppy eaters that have difficulty gaining a healthy amount of weight can benefit from super premium foods.

Premium name brand products can be found at many grocery stores. They aren't as expensive as super premiums, but have solid quality ingredients. These products may work fine for the average puppy.

Specialty brands often are super-premium or premium. They vary in quality and usually cost more because the manufacturer makes smaller quantities and distributes often only regionally. Specialty brands may be more difficult to find.

Store brand generic foods are the least expensive foods are typically sold in grocery stores or discount outlets as the "store brand." Cheap ingredients result in less tasty food and lower digestibility. These foods increase dog poo because they contain fillers that end up on the lawn instead of being digested. House-brand products claim nutritional value equal to national name brand products, but at a lower cost. In fact, these "private label" foods often are produced by quality pet food companies, and some adult dogs may do fine on these foods.

"Store brand" foods ARE NOT APPROPRIATE for puppies. Stick to the super premium and premium foods.

How do you choose the best food for your new baby? First, ask for advice from a puppy expert you know and trust. Talk with the puppy's breeder or the shelter staff to learn what he's used to eating. Consult with his veterinarian for a recommendation. And read the rest of this chapter, so you know what to expect, what questions to ask, and how to evaluate your choices.

Puppy Food Ingredient List

Every food label you look at will be different. There are some generalities that apply to all, though. The food label must, by law, include a list of all ingredients used in the food. They are listed in decreasing order of the amount present, by weight. That is, the first listed ingredients are present in the greatest amount, and the last listed ingredients are the tiniest amounts. In general, the ingredient list for your puppy's food should have:

1. ONE OR MORE PROTEIN SOURCES, which should be one of the first two ingredients in canned dog food, and one of the first three in dry dog food. High-quality protein is essential for muscle tone and development, and healthy skin. Commonly you'll see fresh meat and/or chicken/meat by-product meal, meat by-products, soybean meal, and egg listed here. NOTE: a "by-product" just means it was produced while making something else, and a "meat by-product" includes organ meats that have high nutritional value.
2. CARBOHYDRATE SOURCE, such as cereals, are needed for energy. Common carbohydrate sources in dog food include corn, rice, barley and sorghum.
3. FIBER SOURCE promotes intestinal tract health as well as weight management. Common fiber sources include cellulose, soybean mill run and beet pulp.
4. FAT SOURCE includes essential fatty acids and provide energy, improve taste (palatability), and aid in healthy skin and coat. Frequently you'll see these listed as animal fat, fish oil and vegetable oil; and
5. LARGE NUMBERS OF TRACE MINERALS AND VITAMIN SUPPLEMENTS, which will be toward the bottom of the list.

Unfortunately, the label won't tell you anything about quality of the ingredients. Also, pet food manufacturers may get "creative" when listing ingredients, and include "fractions" of a food type rather than calculate the total amount. For instance, they may list corn, corn gluten meal, and corn byproducts separately which places them further down the list—when, if listed together, they would be noted nearer the top of the ingredient list because of the total volume. All pet foods involved in interstate commerce must, by law, disclose on their labels very specific information. These include:

- **Product name and brand name.** The label includes the principle display panel which identifies the product by brand and/or product name.

- **Species name.** Many times, a picture identifying the species (dog) is on the display panel along with the words dog food or a similar designation.

- **Quantity statement** that includes a net weight

- **Guaranteed analysis.** The information panel contains a guaranteed analysis statement listing minimum levels of crude protein and fat, and maximum levels of crude fiber and moisture. "Crude" refers to the amount measurable by laboratory equipment, not the amount that can be used by the dog. PLEASE NOTE: This is NOT an accurate assessment of nutrient levels, and is designed primarily to meet the regulator's need to test and assess the food.

- **Statement of purpose** and/or **validation of nutritional adequacy** (for puppies or adults, for example). Nutrient profiles have been established for dog foods intended for growth and reproduction, or for adult maintenance and pet foods formulated to meet these standards may claim to provide complete and balanced nutrition. Alternatively, pet food manufacturers may use their own standards, which may be more stringent than the AAFCO standards.

- **Feeding directions.** For instance, it can tell you how much or how often to feed your puppy. Manufacturers generally err on the side of recommending too much rather too little food, so be prepared to adjust up or (more likely) down for your puppy.

- **Name/address of manufacturer.** Any questions concerning a dog food product should be directed to the manufacturer. Many reputable manufacturers include a toll-free telephone number on the label for consumer questions.

- **Ingredient statement.** Knowing the ingredients in a puppy food may be important to help you avoid cases of food allergies. The dog food label must also list ingredients in the food in decreasing order of the amount present by weight before manufacture. Therefore, ingredients listed first are present in the greatest amounts, while smallest amounts are listed last.

Comparing Foods on Dry Matter Basis (DMB)

Water content varies depending on the form of food: dry foods contain a maximum of 12 percent moisture, soft-moist foods contain a maximum of 33 percent moisture, and canned foods contain 78 percent moisture. Here's how to convert a food from the "as fed" details listed on the package to dry matter basis (DMB):

1. First subtract 100 by the moisture content you'll find on the Guaranteed Analysis panel. So if the guaranteed analysis states the food contains 75 percent moisture, you'll be left with 25 percent DMB (100-75=25).

2. Then divide the nutrient by the DMB. So for instance if the guaranteed analysis says the food contains 10 percent protein on an as fed basis (above), you'll divide 10 by 25 DMB and determine that on a DMB (dry matter basis) the food content actually is 40 percent protein.

3. In addition, several types of "corn" may be listed (or split and cited separately) and therefore fall to lower in the list, when if combined they instead might weigh more and be listed toward the top of the ingredient list. It's more difficult to determine the reality of nutrient percentages when splitting is used, because ingredients like corn may provide several different nutrients—corn supplies protein, carbohydrate, fatty acids and antioxidants, for example. In these cases, relying on the label comes down to how much you trust the reputation of the manufacturer as well as recommendations from your veterinarian and your pet's health when eating the food.

Puppy Nutritional Needs

Food scientists spend years researching the specific nutritional needs of puppies. Because your new pet is a baby and growing so quickly, he has very different requirements compared to adult dogs. It's important that you choose a food designed to support and promote puppy growth and health.

Puppies need a food that's "complete" and that's "balanced." That means the food contains all the necessary components, called nutrients, in the proper amounts that are balanced one to another. Nutrients benefit the puppy both individually, and by interacting with each other in the proper ratios. Puppies need a combination of six different classes of nutrients for good health: proteins, carbohydrates, fats, vitamins, minerals and water.

Protein: When we talk about protein, most times our first thoughts turn to meat. In fact, proteins are made up of twenty-three different chemical compounds called amino acids—some are available in non-meat sources, like corn or soy. That's why many commercial puppy foods include a large percentage of cereal grains in the formulation. Dogs by definition are omnivores which means they can do well on a balance of vegetables, grains and meat. Protein builds and maintains bone, blood, tissue and even the puppy's immune system.

Carbohydrates: Carbohydrates provide energy, and the fiber helps regulates the bowels and can help the body absorb some of the other nutrients.

Fats: Fat may be one of your puppy's favorite things about his food, because it provides the flavor he loves. That's important if the puppy is to eat the food. After all, the best diet in the world is worthless if you can't get your puppy to eat it.

Fats also are the number one energy source in foods. They provide two and a quarter times as much energy as a comparable amount of carbohydrates or proteins. That's important when the puppy has high-energy needs for play and growth.

Certain vitamins can only be used in conjunction with fatty acids. Fats and fatty acids give your puppy's fur coat that healthy sheen. A deficiency causes a wide range of symptoms, from greasy fur and dandruff, to weight loss and slow-to-heal sores.

Minerals: Minerals are needed in relatively tiny amounts, but in the proper balances. Minerals are essential for nerve conduction, muscle contraction, fluid stability inside the cells, and a wide range of other functions.

Minerals work together, and the balance is as important as the amount. Too much is as dangerous as too little. Necessary minerals include calcium, phosphorus, magnesium, potassium, sodium, chloride, and the trace minerals cobalt, copper, iodine, iron, manganese, selenium, and zinc. An imbalance of minerals can cause bone deformities, anemia, muscle weakness, heart or kidney disease, and countless other problems.

Vitamins: Vitamins are used in biochemical processes inside the cells. They are divided into two groups. B-complex vitamins are water soluble and not stored in the body and so must be replaced every day. Fat-soluble vitamins are stored in the body and include vitamins A, D, E, and K. Only small amounts, in the right combinations, are necessary for good health. Too much or too little of certain vitamins could cause health problems from skin disease and rickets, to bleeding or nervous system disorders.

Water: I've saved the most important nutrient for last. Sixty percent of a dog's body weight is water. Water is necessary for the body to run smoothly. It lubricates the tissues, and makes it possible for the blood to carry nutrients throughout the body. Water is vital to keeping the puppy's body temperature regulated. It is used in digestion of the food, and carries away waste products in the urine and feces. Water is so important to health that only a 15 percent loss of body water causes dehydration that can kill the puppy.

When a commercial food is complete and balanced, all the nutrients have been calculated to the proper proportions. Special therapeutic diets are available from veterinarians for specific health problems. Every puppy is different, but most healthy puppies do well when they eat a quality brand commercial puppy food. The growth rate and overall health of a puppy is carefully evaluated during feeding trials, to make sure the food supports normal puppy development.

Reading Food Labels

The labels on commercial diets will tell you everything you need to know— once you learn how to read them. They can be misleading when the manufacturer gets creative in describing the ingredients and benefits. To simplify the confusion, here are some basics to look for.

Puppy Food. That sounds like a no-brainer, right? But seriously, the manufacturer should have the product labeled for use in puppies, not just in "dogs." After all, your puppy has very different nutritional needs than an adult. Typically, commercial pet foods are formulated for "life stages" of the pet. You want the one designed for "puppies," not for adult dogs, senior dogs, or other designations.

Complete and Balanced. Some foods, believe it or not, are designed just for snacking or for supplemental feeding. Those may be fine for an adult that isn't growing so fast, and gets the rest of his nutrition in another form. But puppies can only eat tiny bits at a time, so whatever they eat should be complete and balanced to ensure they're getting enough of everything. So, if the food does not say it is complete and balanced for growing puppies, choose another food.

Feeding Trials. Look for a statement on the label that tells you the food has been tested by feeding it to other puppies. That's the only way you'll know that your baby will actually benefit from the food.

WARNING!

Some labels may say the food was tested/formulated to meet established nutrient profiles—but it has not been tested in feeding trials. This means a chemical analysis or calculation method was used to validate the food. It's perfectly legal—but it does not actually prove the food can be digested or used in a real-live puppy.

AAFCO Guidelines. The Association of Animal Feed Control Officials (AAFCO) has established dog/puppy food nutrient profiles, and feeding trial protocols, that are used as the industry standard.

Recognizable Company. There are countless pet food companies and even more brands available. The really good ones have been around for many years, and their reputation has stood the test of time. Reputable companies spend millions of dollars on research and feeding trials, and include information on the label for you to contact them with questions. Look for a familiar name or ask your veterinarian to recommend one.

A Matter of Taste

What is it that makes your puppy say, "Mmmmmm, yum!" The technical word for it is "palatability." With puppies—and dogs in general—taste of the food is only a small part of what tickles their fancy. Pet food manufactures go to extremes to make their brands palatable so that puppies beg to eat it, and return to the bowl time after time.

Palatability not only means taste, but also smell. Puppies care much more about the smell of a food, the more pungent the better. Texture of the food also is a deciding factor. Puppy food is available in several different forms—dry, canned, dehydrated, semi-moist. Each has advantages and disadvantages, and every puppy has his own preferences.

Canned Varieties

Canned puppy foods are extremely tasty and most puppies readily accept them. That's because the moisture releases the odor that puppies love. Canned diets may be perfect for youngsters just learning to eat solid food. They come in a variety of flavors, and are packed with calories so puppies don't have to eat a lot. Because of the high water content, a canned diet partially fulfills the puppy's water requirement.

Canned puppy food is processed exactly the same way as human canned foods. Canning preserves the food, and as long as the can remains closed, it will stay fresh nearly indefinitely.

Canned foods are the most expensive, though, because they are up to 70 percent water. That also means puppies fed canned food may have a softer stool than those that are fed dry food. Also, once the can has been opened, the food must be refrigerated or it will spoil. When feeding a canned product, you must pick up the leftovers after about 30 minutes. That can mean some waste if your puppy refuses to eat leftovers.

Soft diets tend to stick to the teeth and can predispose the puppy to dental problems. For large breed puppies, a canned diet may be cost prohibitive, but may still work well for occasional treats.

Dry Diets

Dry foods are relatively inexpensive. They come in bags, boxes, or plastic jugs, can be purchased in larger quantities, and do not require refrigeration. Because of that, they are considered the most convenient diet for owners to feed, and can be left out at all times for free-feeding for the puppy to snack on at leisure. They are thought to help reduce the chance of tartar buildup and dental problems by about 10 percent.

Some puppies prefer crunchy diets. But very young puppies may not be able to chew the food until they grow enough teeth. Dry foods also tend to rely more heavily on grain-source protein rather than meat, because of the processing constraints. Called extrusion, this high-pressure cooking process dries the kibble and gelatinizes the starches in the grain ingredients to make them more digestible. Dry foods are typically preserved with additives that keep them fresh for several months.

Semi-Moist Meals

Semi moist foods are often packaged as individual servings. They are kept moist by ingredients like corn syrup that keep the food from drying out. These foods are convenient to use, especially for travel, because they don't need refrigeration. They tend to be more expensive than dry foods.

Remember, no matter which type of food you serve, puppies need something to drink along with their food. Keep a bowl of water available for your puppy at all times. Set the water bowl next to his food, so he always knows where to find it.

Dehydrated Foods

In recent years, a number of dehydrated pet food rations have become available. These store very well, and typically advertise high quality or even human grade ingredients. Because they are dry, dehydrated foods can be mixed with warm water for each meal, insuring less waste and that the food is always fresh. As with the canned diets, dehydrated pet foods may be costly for large breed dogs but can work well as supplemental feeding, as treats, or mixed with other less pricy forms of food.

TECHNICAL STUFF. Fats added to dry food makes them taste good. However, fats tend to spoil—oxidize—which is a kind of biological rust process. Antioxidants help preserve the dry food and keep it tasting fresh and the nutrients viable. Common antioxidants include chemicals like BHA and BHT; or additives like mixed tocopherals (a kind of vitamin E mixture), vitamin C, and vitamin E.

"Quality" Categories

As more and more pet foods find their way to the store shelves, companies look for new ways to make their brand stand out of the crowd. Category designations have long been a way to differentiate products, but today the lines tend to blur.

First there were plain old "pet foods." They were typically quite inexpensive, and often available in grocery stores. Some actually were labeled as the "store brand." In the past these diets used less-expensive ingredients, and the pet needed to eat more volume of the product to obtain the nutrition he needed. Consequently, these diets typically filled up the litter box more quickly, when the output increased with input.

Next, "premium" foods came onto the market. They used higher quality ingredients that were more expensive, and so the product cost more. Often, they were sold only through licensed dealers—like pet products stores or veterinary offices. The better ingredients meant pets needed to eat less volume, so although the foods were more expensive, there was also more bang for the buck. The volume of doggy poop in the back yard decrease as well.

"Super" premium foods claim to use the best quality ingredients, and command the highest prices. They tend to be calorie-dense foods so the pet requires a small amount to fill his nutritional requirements. They are so highly palatable, though, they can be very easy to over-feed. Super premium diets used to only be offered through veterinarians but can now easily be found through pet products stores and online specialty outlets. Today, this category includes small niche companies that create formulations that claim to use only "human grade" ingredients, low-to-no-carb/grain foods, commercial raw diets and more, while they market them as "natural" and healthier for the dog.

It may be true that you get what you pay for. Certainly, the cheapest no-name food out there isn't a smart choice. Conversely, not every puppy will require the equivalent of rocket-fuel, if he spends his life playing quietly in your living room. Choose foods to support you and your pet's lifestyle, health demands and activity level. The average puppy does quite well on the mid-range diets.

Feeding Your Puppy

Once you have figured out what kind of food to offer your puppy, you must set up a feeding schedule. How often you feed your little one depends to a degree on the form of the food, but more importantly, on your puppy's age.

Most pups should be fed at least three times a day until six months of age. Tiny puppies like Yorkies and Chihuahuas are prone to hypoglycemia—low blood sugar—if they don't eat often enough, so four meals daily may work best.

Feed three or four separate meals to young puppies during the first few months at home. Then gradually wean them to one or two meals daily by the time they are six months of age.

However, there are some puppies that either won't or aren't able to eat enough when fed once or twice a day. Their growth may suffer. Ask your veterinarian about feeding smaller servings several times a day.

Meal Feed on Your Schedule

It's tempting to simply fill up the bowl with dry food and let puppies snack all day. While convenient for you, that won't allow you to monitor the baby's intake, which also helps predict output—when she needs a potty break. Use meal schedules as part of your house training efforts.

Schedule meals also alert you to check with the vet if your puppy glutton one day refuses a meal. Scheduled meals have several benefits. Certainly, wet foods must be meal-fed anyway, to prevent your puppy from snacking on spoiled food. But meal-feeding a dry diet works well because it allows you to monitor the puppy's eating habits. Does he finish all of the meal? only part of it? or snub the bowl altogether? That can be an early warning for health problems.

Free feeding from an always full bowl can be dangerous for that reason. The amount you feed depends on your puppy's age and the type of food you offer. Directions on the food are only a starting guideline, so be ready to adjust the amount up or down if your baby is still hungry, or leaves food behind.

Routine is important so be consistent. The best way to do that is base the feeding times on your schedule. Dogs consider meals a social affair, so timing your own meals with the puppies can work well. Puppies thrive on routine, so feed your puppy in the same place every day, and at the same times. A low-traffic area works well, such as one end of the kitchen or the laundry room. A specific area of his private room is ideal. When you have more than one pet, feeding separately gives the puppy privacy to eat so that he isn't pestered. That also keeps older pets from swiping the baby's food—puppy formulas have more calories and adult pets can gain weight on these diets.

A first meal might coincide with your own breakfast, the second when the kids come home from school in the afternoon, and third coordinate with your evening meal. If you're not able to be there to feed at proscribed times, you can provide one of the puppy's meals in a treat-toy, and leave it with her in her crate or play area while you're gone.

Feeding puppy meals in the crate or carrier also associate "good things" with the crate. Scheduled meals not only are healthy for the puppy, they aid in house training and crate training, and can be a bonding experience with your puppy.

Remember, obesity is the number one nutritional problem of adult dogs, often due to the never-empty food bowl. Free-feeding dry food is more convenient, no doubt about that. But it's much healthier in the long run to start puppies out right, and continue meal feeding throughout their life.

PUPPY WAGS.
Meal feeding offers a great training advantage, too. It trains the puppy to expect when food is served, so he doesn't constantly pester you. Otherwise, puppies become very good at training the unknowing owner to jump to fill the bowl at each whimper.

How much should you feed? That depends on the individual puppy, his age, and the specific diet you choose. Usually, puppies will self-regulate the amount they need to eat—that is, they'll each just the right amount of a given food to fulfill their energy requirements. That could be more of one food, and less of another, depending on the calorie content.

Although obesity is a problem of adult dogs, don't worry about restricting the food for a growing puppy. He should be given as much food as he wants to eat. Use the guidelines on the package as a starting point. But every puppy is different, and some high-energy breeds may need more food than a placid puppy. Set out the food at mealtime, and give your puppy about 30 minutes to finish eating. Then pick up the food until the next meal.

Measure the amount of food you put in his bowl. Then measure the amount left after he finishes eating. Do this for two or three days to get an average amount he eats during the day to give you a ballpark range of how to divide up the amount he needs per meal.

Puppies younger than ten weeks old may have trouble eating dry food, and you'll need to soften the kibble or use a canned diet. To soften dry puppy formulas, use warm water (about an ounce to 1½ cups of food). The warm liquid also tends to unlock odor, which triggers canine appetite.

Once the baby is happily eating the softened kibble, begin to reduce the amount of liquid gradually. By ten weeks of age, puppies generally have enough teeth and the ability to eat dry diets, and won't need water added.

Puppy digestion can be delicate so once you find a food the baby likes, try not to change the diet. Sometimes, of course, you'll need to make a switch perhaps on the advice of your veterinarian. When changing his food, always do so a little bit at a time and start out by mixing the old food with the new in a 50/50 ratio. Gradually increase the percentage of the new diet over a week's time until finally he's eating only the new puppy formula.

When your baby is younger than three to four weeks old, you'll need to take over nursing duties and provide a commercial puppy milk replacer until Junior grows enough to eat solid food. Adopting an orphan is discussed in Chapter 3 and offers tips on feeding a tiny puppy.

Puppy Food Calories

Some dog food labels will include a statement of caloric content in the food. A calorie is a measure of energy produced by eating a specific food.

A single calorie is such a small unit of measure that often a unit of 1000 calories, termed a "kilocalorie" (or interchangeably as a Calorie) is a more useful measure. You won't always see a disclosure of calories on the dog food label, except in diets making "lite" claims for weight reduction. When it appears, it's stated as "kilocalories per Kg of food." For convenience sake, it's also often labeled as "Calories per cup" or "per unit" of food.

Dry rations generally contain 1400 to 2000 metabolizable kilocalories per pound of diet (3080 to 4400 Kcal/Kg); semi-moist have 1200 to 1350 metabolized kilocalories per pound of diet (2640 to 2970 Kcal/Kg); and canned rations only provide 375 to 950 metabolized kilocalories per pound of diet (825 to 2090 Kcal/Kg) because such a large percentage of canned foods is water (up to 70 percent!). That's why dogs must eat more canned foods than dry diets to obtain the same energy intake.

WARNING!
Cow's milk can be hard on puppy digestion and cause diarrhea. That's because puppies past the age of weaning often don't have enough of the enzyme lactase needed to properly process the milk sugar lactose. Use warm water to soften food, or a commercial puppy milk replacer.

The amount of calories a dog requires varies widely from puppy to puppy and dog to dog. Your pet's age, size, metabolism, and energy expended determine each dog's need. On average, large dog breeds need less food per pound of body weight than small breed dogs.

- Small breed dogs are those whose adult body weight is less than 20 pounds. Adult small breed dogs require about 50 kilocalories per pound of body weight each day.
- Medium breed adult dogs are those weighing 20 to 50 pounds. Adult medium breed dogs need approximately 30-40 kilocalories per pound of body weight each day.
- Large breed dogs weigh 50 to 100 pounds, while the giant breeds exceed 100 pounds as adults. They need 20 to 30 kilocalories per pound of body weight each day, or less.

Treats, Supplements and Homemade Diets

Today it has become popular to offer our pets the same kinds of "natural" foods and supplements that health-conscious people want to eat themselves. Some of these products are very good. Others are questionable at best. The difficulty arises in trying to tell the difference between the good and the bad.

Do puppies and dogs benefit from natural foods and nutritional supplements? Without a doubt, some benefit a great deal, particularly those that have less than ideal health status. In these instances, the puppy may actually need the extra nutritional help of a special kind of diet, or a therapeutic food supplement. For instance, a puppy suffering from anemia would benefit from extra B vitamins, or food sources like beef or organ meats because the extra protein builds red blood cells.

The vast majority of puppies that are otherwise healthy, though, will thrive on commercial puppy foods. Adding supplements, especially extra vitamins and minerals, to a complete and balanced commercial product can throw off the delicate formula. That can cause dangerous toxicities when too much or too little of certain nutrients end up in the puppy.

Making your own homemade puppy diet can be even more dangerous, again because of the necessity to carefully balance all those nutrients. Be very cautious about taking the advice of the self-proclaimed experts. Lately there has been an explosion of "natural" diets promoting everything from feeding raw diets to cooked recipes to bones. When it comes down to it, frankly, the most natural diet would be offering your puppy live varmints, with all the attendant parasite concerns and bone obstruction dangers—not to mention the mess!

Yes, home-prepared foods are possible. Many reputable holistic veterinarians recommend these diets, and will offer good advice on how to do it safely. Practically speaking, though, it takes a great deal of time and effort to cook for your puppy—and it's very easy to make mistakes. I personally don't have the time, the patience, or the confidence that I could do it right—consistently—to ensure good health for my dog. There are just too many things that can go wrong, even when the recipe comes from a true veterinary nutrition expert.

When your puppy's health is at stake, I believe it's best to take the safest road. Choose a complete and balanced commercial puppy formula—there are products touted to be "natural" and even pre-packaged commercial raw foods, and that may be an option you prefer. Use this as a base, and then with the advice of your holistic veterinarian, perhaps you can offer appropriate kinds and amounts of fresh foods as treats.

Supplements tend to be regarded as therapeutic—that is, they are designed to act on your puppy's physical health in a positive manner. However, by definition, anything fed to your puppy in addition to his regular diet is considered a supplement—and that would include treats.

Treats are legal. They are, in fact, a great benefit to the bonding process and can be instrumental when used as rewards to train your puppy to be good. They work best, though, if reserved for special times, like rewarding good behavior. They'll lose their punch if fed too often, or for no reason. Also remember that small puppies get filled up very quickly, so keep treats to a minimum so they don't take the place of the meal your puppy needs to eat. Commercial treats often will have the "complete and balanced" notice on the label, so you know they won't upset the baby's nutrition.

What about table scraps? I'll probably surprise you here, but I believe table food can be perfectly fine—it just depends on what's on your table! Junk food that's bad for people is no better for our pets; healthy foods like lean meats, fish, fruits, fresh vegetables, cheese, even yogurt often are relished as treats. My dog Magic adored oranges and banana when he was a pup, and still can't get enough of broccoli and asparagus. Again, any treating from your plate must be done within reason. Nutritionists typically tell you that such tidbits shouldn't make up more than 10 percent of the pet's total diet.

Eating Habits

Every puppy develops his own eating style. Many just crouch above the plate and munch. Others take one bite at a time, and carry it to another room to eat. Some want you there to watch—for dogs, mealtime is a social occasion. Both finicky puppies and gluttonous gorgers are extremes to avoid, but dogs come by the gorging instinct honestly.

Ancestors of the dog hunted in packs, enabling them to kill large prey animals, which supplied them with massive amounts of food. But it wasn't as if the pack could put left-overs in the deep freeze for later. There were other animals waiting in the wings to outright steal, or at least nibble and scavenge the remains. Anything the wolf/dogs didn't eat in one meal was up for grabs; the rule was use it or lose it.

Consequently, ancestors of our modern dogs became highly talented gorgers able to handle huge amounts of food at one time. After stuffing themselves to overflowing, the pack would settle down to digest, sometimes for days at a time. They didn't need to hunt as often, because when they were successful, the meal lasted them for days rather than hours.

Think about it—where do you think the term "wolfing down food" came from? There's a report of a wolf that went without food for seven days, then ate 1/5th of its body weight in one meal. That's like a 180-pound man polishing off a 35-pound steak.

Many modern dogs have retained this ability, particularly hound type dogs. They don't chew; they simply grab mouthfuls of food and swallow, and keep eating until the bowl is empty. Beagles and Labradors are also notorious gorgers.

In addition, dogs have a very distinct sweet tooth, just like people. It makes perfect sense because fruits and vegetables that are richest in calories are the sweetest, and that's why we choose to eat them.

Dogs still possess a number of flattened molars, designed specifically for mashing and

WARNING!

Dogs and puppies love bones. Cooked bones become soft and can splinter, be swallowed and cause potentially deadly blockages. Chewing raw bones may break teeth, and if handled inappropriately, may transmit bacteria that make puppies and people sick. Never offer your puppy cooked bones, and supervise if you choose to treat him with a raw bone. Puppies and adult dogs rarely chew food enough to scrub their teeth and gnawing bones can aid dental health, if used with care.

grinding vegetable matter. Wolves often eat grass or ripe berries, while foxes are said to relish grapes and sweet corn, and our domestic dogs are no different. This ability and willingness to eat a variety of foods is what made wolves such adaptable survivors. It's no wonder many dogs plant themselves under the dinner table, and inhale anything, from fruit to fish, that falls within snapping distance.

The dog's enthusiasm for food, though, can be problematic when Poochie shares dinner time and space with a cat. That's because cats tend not to finish a meal at one setting, but often leave food in the bowl for later.

The gluttons eat anything that doesn't move faster than they do. For these puppies, as they mature you'll need to keep an eye on their waistline, and ensure they exercise enough to burn off the calories. They may also be at risk for "garbage gut syndrome."

Such puppies may think anything left unattended is fair game, and even raid the garbage—and end up with predictable results (vomiting, diarrhea, or both). Oftentimes, it is the stray puppy, the waif you've rescued from the streets that turns into a bottomless pit. That's likely because these babies have truly known hunger when they were on their own. They remember. And they don't want to take the chance of ever being hungry again.

The other extreme, the finicky puppy, usually is a product of the way a puppy is fed early in life. In other words, most finicky dogs are taught to be finicky. Owners understandably grow concerned when the dog doesn't immediately eat the offered food—so they try another kind of flavor or brand. Puppies can be just like children, and hold out for a favorite flavor, especially when they know you will offer them a choice. Puppies (and especially adult dogs) may not be hungry for every meal. Just because they don't gobble it up all at once doesn't necessarily mean they dislike that food. Give them a bit of time.

In fact, puppies and dogs can have their appetite "worn out" by having food available too long. That can trigger the hunger centers in the brain to temporarily shut off. Appetite is better tempted by offering the food for 15 to 30 minutes—then removing the food for an hour or so before trying again.

Many dogs enjoy variety in their diet—and canned foods cater to this urge, as well as our own desire to treat and please our puppies. Many dog owners offer a different canned food every meal. Others may provide a dry diet for one meal, and offer a smorgasbord of canned varieties as treats for the second meal. This decision is up to you—puppies and dogs can do well on such a plan.

However, you should know that puppies and dogs do not *require* variety in the diet. People do—because we do not have available to us a complete and balanced "people ration."

As long as the puppy's diet is complete and balanced for a growing puppy, he will do fine on the same food every single day. After all, in the wild a dog eats the same critters every single day, if that's available to them. He won't know any different, and won't crave variety and become finicky, unless you teach him otherwise.

One last thing to remember is that pet food companies design puppy foods to tempt you first and your puppy second. After all, you are the one with the wallet. Puppies don't care about the color of the food, if it has gravy, or looks like luncheon meat—that's aimed to get you to buy the product. Commercial pet foods often develop products that appeal to human tastes first by looking like something we'd want to eat ourselves, or that mirrors human health food trends that may (or may not!) apply to canine health. To make the best choices, consider your puppy's nutritional needs above all else.

8: Grooming

Considerations

Oh, that soft, luxurious puppy coat—it feels so good to stroke, and to cuddle with your new furry wonder. The colors and patterns puppies sport are gloriously intricate, and help make them individuals as much as the unique way they beg for attention.

The puppy coat goes beyond turning your puppy into one of the most handsome creatures on the planet. Fur has very practical applications for the dog. All dogs have fur. Nature designed the fur coat to have very specific benefits.

The length of individual hairs has a wide range. A puppy may have hair up to four inches long. Even the so-called "bald" Chinese Crested has fur. She's covered in downy, velvet-like fuzz that grows about one-eighth of an inch. She may have a bit of longer fur on her lower legs or tail.

Fur—A Big Hairy Deal

The fur coat is made up of thousands of individual hairs. Each is a threadlike multi-colored filament made from keratin, a kind of fibrous horny protein that grows from the skin—this is the same material that makes up the puppy nails. Hair is 95 percent protein. That's why one sign of puppy malnutrition is a dull, lifeless coat.

Some puppies require more coat care than others. Thick, double coats characteristic of Northern breeds like Siberian Huskies and Alaskan Malamutes may be challenging for those with limited grooming time available.

The hair collectively serves as a protective barrier between your puppy's skin and the outside world. Fur shields the puppy from extremes in temperature. It keeps tender skin from burning in the sun and protects the body from cold weather. It even helps shed water to keep the baby dry.

Muscles in the skin near to where the hairs grow allow puppies to "fluff" fur to offer ventilation to the skin on hot days. On cold days, the fluffed fur traps warm air between the hairs, and creates an insulating blanket of warmth next to the skin.

Hair also acts like a candle "wick" to route scent-chemicals related to identification and sexual status from the skin into the air. Fur serves as a communication tool, especially the whiskers and hackles (over the pup's shoulders). Raised hackles signals fear or excitement, while whisker position signals a variety of emotions and intentions.

All healthy dogs have fur, but the amount and type of hair coat varies in individuals and from breed to breed. Even the hairless variety of Chinese Crested dog breed has hair on the face, feet and tail.

What Is Hair?

Hairs are composed of the hair shaft, which is the visible portion of the hair, and a root generated by a hair follicle within the skin. Dogs have compound follicles, which means as many as 20 hairs can grow from a single pore. People have simple follicles, which produce only one hair for each pore.

Dogs have three kinds of hairs characterized by length and diameter. Guard or primary hairs are the longest, coarsest hairs of the outer coat. Secondary hairs of various lengths make up the undercoat. Medium length awn hairs make up the intermediate coat, and undercoat is soft, short cotton-like fur that's curly or crimped. All three types may sprout from a single compound follicle.

The length of the hair shaft, and the ratio of guard to undercoat hairs varies from breed to breed. When the hair follicle that produces the hair is slightly twisted, the hair that grows is curly. These differences, as well as a variety of colors and patterns, produce each pup's distinctive coat.

Whiskers are the thick, long, wire-like hairs that protrude from the dog's face. Also called vibrissae or sinus hairs, whiskers are specialized hairs that are long, supple and thick, or groupings of short stiff bristles. Whiskers are much more developed in animals that hunt during the night or low-light times. They act as feelers, and are seated deep in the skin where they trigger nerve receptors at the slightest touch.

Dogs have whiskers in four places on each side of the head, and two on the lower jaw. The most obvious are those on each side of the dog's muzzle, where whiskers grow in four rows; they provide information when the dog is sticking his nose in and around objects.

Bristles of four to five whiskers above each eye act like extended eyelashes. They prompt a protective blink reflex if touched. A clump of whiskers is located on each cheek, and a smaller one near each corner of the mouth. Finally, the dog has a tuft beneath the chin, which probably serves to keep his head from scraping the ground during tracking behavior, or may even help digging puppies in food-burying activities.

Shedding

All dogs and puppies shed. That's because hair grows in cycles, from the root within the skin, outward in a continuous pattern of rapid growth, slower growth, and a resting period. When new hair begins to grow, it pushes out the old ones, which are shed.

Each hair grows from the root outward in a cycle of rapid growth called anagen; shrinkage called catagen in which the root detaches from the follicle; and a resting period , termed telogen. Old loose hairs in the telogen phase are pushed out—called shedding—by new hairs as the anagen cycle begins. Shed fur is composed of telogen hairs.

A single human hair may grow for up to six years before being shed and replaced by a new one. The growth cycle of your puppy's hair is much shorter and more synchronized, which accounts for the massive shed. While it varies from breed to breed, fur growth cycle averages about 130 days. The exception is the so-called "non-shedding" breeds like the Poodle and some terriers, whose coats actually grow for several years before being replaced.

Shedding can turn into a big hairy deal, but is a normal part of living with a puppy when you understand why dogs shed. All puppies shed, even the "non-shedding breeds." It's a dog rule that they leave dark fur on white clothes and furniture—and white fur on contrasting surfaces. You don't have to live with drifts of fur, and can keep your home and clothing relatively hair-free with simple tips.

The length of the hair growth period varies from breed to breed. Most dogs have a seasonal shed in the spring and/or during the fall. It's not the temperature that prompts shedding. Light exposure, either to sun or artificial light, determines the amount and timing. More hair is shed during the greatest exposure to light.

Outdoor dogs living in the northeastern United States shed every year with the most fur flying in late spring for the several weeks during which daylight increases. But house pets under constant exposure to artificial light may shed all year long.

Some breeds like Poodles and some terriers are referred to as "non-shedding" actually do shed. But instead of the anagen hair-growing phase lasting a short time, their hair grows for years before it's shed. It may grow quite long unless clipped.

WARNING!

Shedding does not mean hunks of fur pulling out that leave bald or sore spots on the skin. That might be a sign of a fungal infection of the skin called ringworm that needs veterinary treatment.

These types of coats don't tend to shed all at once. You won't notice clumps of fur being shed all at once because they only lose a few hairs at a time. Because these breeds also tend to have curly coats, lost hairs tangle alongside the growing hairs and don't always end up on the furniture. The fur may turn into long cords as with the Puli and Komondor breeds unless kept trimmed.

Depending on when your puppy was born, he may shed his puppy coat before the regular seasonal shed in the spring or fall. Most puppies lose their baby coat between six and twelve months of age as the new adult fur replaces it. This varies a bit from breed to breed.

You don't have to groom the whole puppy at one setting. Spread out grooming sessions over several hours or days to keep him happy. Follow each session with a favorite treat or game so your puppy identifies grooming with good things. Be sure to comb your puppy thoroughly before you bathe him, which will loosen even more shed fur.

What's the Mat-ter?

Breeds that have heavy double coats that shed in clumps are more prone to developing painful mats. Mats happen when fur is trapped next to the skin, especially in the groin and armpit regions. Mats can create bruises, and can lead to hot spots.

You can't stop shedding, but you can reduce the aggravation to yourself and your pet. Comb and brush him regularly. Thickly furred puppies need daily attention, but short haired pets also benefit. Pay particular attention to combing the mat-prone areas behind the pet's ears, beneath his tail, and in the creases of his legs.

Because mats are so painful, it can be difficult for a puppy to hold still while you untangle the mess. After all, pulling a comb through the mat just tugs at the bruised skin, and hurts even worse. Whatever you do, *don't* get the mat wet.

PUPPY WAGS

My favorite de-shedding tools work extremely well. The EZ-Groomer (EZ-groomer.com) is light weight, claw-shaped tool that works well to break up established mats and to pull off shed fur. Unlike most other combs or brushes, you can use the EZ-Groomer to comb backwards on the pet, for a beneficial effect. This product also is quite economical, in the $10-$15 range, and comes in two sizes for small to large pets.

The Furminator won't work on mats, but does an extraordinary job removing shed fur. Tiny shallow close-fitting teeth pull off 80-90 percent of loose fur. Try grooming your pet with a standard comb or brush, and you'll take off a bunch—then follow up with the Furminator, and you'll be shocked at the mountains of fuzz. This product also comes in different sizes to match your pet, but is quite pricey. Make sure you groom your pet outside, or in an area easy to clean, or you'll deal with a furry tornado inside the house.

The "Untangler" (TheUntangler.com) combs are designed with stainless steel rotating teeth that glide through tangles and remove loose hair. Combs and shedding "rakes" come in several sizes and cost around $10, and are available at pet supply stores or mail-order catalogues. Another great option is a rubber curry-style brush called the "Dog Zoom Groom." The tips are ultra-soft, and the brush is in a fun dog face shape and comes in different colors. Dog Zoom Groom costs about $6 at pet stores.

That simply sets the tangle like it was cement. The key to de-tangling mats is to work with them dry. Rub some dry cornstarch into the matted fur, before you begin to comb. That helps separate the individual hairs and makes it easier to unravel the mess.

Use a comb to help take some of that painful tension off puppy's skin. Thread the teeth of the comb through the mat, close to the skin. Then use another wide-toothed comb or a slicker brush, and brush on top of the buffer comb. That keeps the fur from being pulled as you work at the tangle. Start at the very ends of the mat, and comb it out a tiny bit at a time, layer by layer.

If your puppy will not hold still for being picked at, the mats likely will need to be shaved out with electric clippers. Your veterinarian or a groomer can do this for you. Usually, a number 10 clipper blade is best because it doesn't tend to cut the skin. Ask your veterinarian or groomer for a demonstration before you attempt to de-mat your puppy yourself with electric shavers. If you aren't able to manage grooming yourself, have it professionally done. Fur removed by grooming won't cause mats, or end up on your clothes or furniture.

It's best to prevent mats to begin with by grooming your puppy appropriately. Shaving or even combing out mats tends to leave bald patches that are unattractive. Turn grooming into an extension of petting so your puppy will welcome the attention—and prevent painful mats down the road.

While this Poodle is a "non-shedding" breed, the coat may require professional grooming.

A variety of trims and cuts are available for Poodles, to make coat care easier.

Grooming Supplies

Invest in some quality grooming tools. That way you'll have them for the lifetime of your dog, even after Baby has grown to adulthood. The higher quality products not only last longer, they tend to do a better job. For instance, cheaper nail trimmers tend to become dull more quickly—that means they end up crushing rather than snipping off the nail. And a Teflon-coated comb, or one with rolling teeth is more comfortable for the puppy with long fur because it glides more easily through fur and won't pull.

You don't need anything fancy for routine grooming. Basic grooming tools are available in most pet supply stores, your veterinarian's office, or over the Internet. If you have a purebred puppy and want to show her, there may be special grooming provisions you'll need to learn. Visit a couple of dog shows, and ask questions to get the answers you need for your special puppy. Your breeder is also a great resource for this information.

Puppy and adult dog skin is very sensitive. That means any comb or brush teeth must never be sharply pointed. They are designed to be smooth and rounded so the grooming experience is pleasant, and there's no chance of injury.

Types of Fur Coats

Whether you adopt a purebred puppy, a "designer breed" or the mutt-next-door, the first thing you'll notice is his fur coat. A puppy coat can change as the dog matures, so it's a good idea to know what to expect when Junior grows up. The color, pattern, and coat type varies between breeds, and impacts the amount of fur shedding and grooming care needed.

There are five basic coat types. "Long fur with undercoat" types include the Rough Collie and German Shepherd Dog; "silky coat" breeds include the Afghan Hound, Pekingese, setters and spaniels; "smooth coat" are the shorthaired dogs like Boxers, Chihuahuas and Labradors; "wiry" coats are found on most terriers and the Schnauzer; and the "non-shedding curly" type coat grows constantly but must be trimmed on such breeds as Poodles and the Bedlington Terrier.

Specific types of coats require different levels of fur care. Smooth coats require the least amount. The longer fur can demand combing or brushing on nearly a daily basis especially during shedding season. Wired coats require plucking, and the non-shedding curly coats need to be clipped and sometimes shaved. All coat types benefit from a bath now and then, but some dogs get dingier than others. Special grooming products are designed for specific coat colors, too, to make white fur dazzling and rich or dark colors striking.

Puppies come in Westie white, Kerry Blue blue, Weimaraner silver, Scottie black, and a range of browns from Wheaten tan to Golden Retriever gold, Irish Setter red, and Labrador chocolate. Dogs in solid colors are referred to as "self colored." Pattern is equally diverse.

- Ticked refers to small isolated areas of black or colored hairs over a white ground color.
- Sable is produced by black-tipped hairs on a background of silver, gold, grey, fawn or brown.
- Brindle is a pattern of black tiger-like stripes on a lighter background (usually tan).
- Parti-color (also pied or piebald) refers to patches of two or more colors on the coat.
- Harlequin is patches of color (usually black or grey) on a white background.
- Tricolor is a coat with three distinct colors, usually white, black and tan.
- Merle color pattern has dark blotches against a lighter background of the same color, while mottled pattern is characterized by round blotches of color on a lighter background.
- Points are the same color on the face, ears, legs and tail, and are usually white, black or tan.
- Grizzle is a mixture of black or red hairs with white (also called roan), and is often a bluish- to iron-gray color, or may be orange or lemon.

Grooming Tools

To take good care of your puppy's fur, you'll need at least one *comb*. The teeth of the comb will be set together in a fine, medium, or coarse fashion. The closer together, the finer the teeth are said to be. Medium to coarse combs are good for longer fur, while medium to fine combs work best for short fur. Some combs have one side with fine teeth and the other with medium or coarse teeth.

Puppies with short fur may do fine with regular sessions using *hound gloves*. These are special gloves with inset rubber nubs in the palm that smooth the fur and remove any loose hair. Hound gloves are a puppy favorite, because the action just seems like you are petting them.

You may also want to invest in a second fine-toothed comb to finish the coat once all the tangles are smoothed. A *flea comb* works great— it has ultra-close teeth designed to capture any stray bugs that set up housekeeping on your puppy. A flea comb also can remove caked or crusty material from the puppy's fur.

When looking for a brush, be sure the bristles or nubs are soft enough not to scratch tender puppy skin, but firm enough to reach through the fur and brush efficiently. A *pin brush* is

WARNING!
Use a slicker brush only after combing or currying out any tangles. A gentle touch works best. Be sure to only use sheers and clippers when you have someone to help you restrain your wiggly baby, so he won't accidentally be nicked.

WARNING!

Puppies are highly sensitive to substances put on their skin. Bathing products that are safe for adult dogs may be too harsh for your puppy. Human "baby shampoo" is designed to strip away oils in the hair and scalp and may dry out your puppy's skin, which needs these natural oils to remain healthy and supple. Be especially careful of flea products, or you may accidentally poison your pet. Look for the words "safe for puppies" before buying the product.

designed for brushing puppies with longer fur. Wire pins mounted in a soft, flexible rubber pad have protective round plastic tips on the end to ensure a comfortable brushing. A *curry brush* is rubber or plastic with short nubs that work great to smooth fur and remove loose hair on smooth coated puppies. A natural *bristle brush* can also work well. Some are designed to work on longhaired puppies, too.

A *slicker brush* is designed for the final finishing touch and works especially well on curly coated dogs like Poodles and Bichon Frise puppies. It is made up of closely-arranged fine wires that smooth the coat. You must be careful not to brush the skin, though, or you could cause "brush burns."

Thinning sheers can be used to trim out excess hair but won't leave an obvious cut line. And *electric clippers* with detachable blades and snap-on combs can keep your puppy trimmed and looking well groomed at home, and reduce the time spent at the groomers.

Shampoo

Besides a brush and comb, you need a quality shampoo. Unless you see a problem with fleas, there's no need to choose a flea product—a grooming shampoo works fine. Often you can find one that includes some sort of conditioner, or purchase a coat conditioner separately.

Conditioner helps reduce static, tangles, and helps prevent drying out the skin. I particularly like the dog bathing products that include oatmeal, which is a natural skin-soothing ingredient. There are "dry" shampoos available for dogs. These typically are wipe-on, foam, or spray products that are worked into the dingy fur, wiped off, and left on. They may do a good job in between the more thorough dunking.

For Puppy Nails

All pups benefit from a bit of manicure help. There are four options for nail trimmers. All work well, and the choice really is which style you are most comfortable with.

Tiny breed puppies have tiny claws. For them, human nail trimmers work very well. They may be easier for you to manipulate, too.

Scissors-style nippers are also a good choice. They may take the least getting-used-to, if you are new to pet nail trimming.

Guillotine-style nail trimmers are a popular choice. They come in a couple of sizes, with the smallest ones designated for puppies and cats. If your puppy will grow up to become a jumbo-size dog, choose one sized for the adult. These will work for baby dogs, and you won't have to upgrade to bigger ones when Junior Dog grows older.

Professional groomers have used Dremel nail grinding tools for many years. Commercial products now are available for pet owners. You'll need to get the puppy used to the idea, but this can be a good option and avoids the risk of "quicking" the claw—that is, cutting too close into the nail bed and making it bleed.

Two considerations are important when choosing a nail trimmer for your puppy. First, whatever the style, it must be very sharp so it cuts and doesn't crush or tear the claw. Second, you must be comfortable using it.

For Eyes and Ears

Puppies can develop small amounts of sleepy-crusts in their eyes, or a bit of light yellow wax in their ears. That's normal. Regular ear and eye checks are as much to monitor puppy health as to groom them. Any kind of discharge is an alert to check with your veterinarian.

Normal eye secretions are clear and liquid, just like human tears. And the inside of a puppy's normal ear is pink and clean. Dark crumbly gunk in the ears or thick discharge from the eyes can be signs of a health problem. The most common causes of these signs are discussed in Chapter 10.

Even normal tears can turn crusty in the fur and irritate the tender skin around the puppy's eyes. Flat-faced babies like Pekingese are particularly prone to this problem because their eyes are so large and prominent, and tend to water.

There are commercial preparations available at pet stores that help remove tear stains safely from the puppy's fur. But you don't really need any special supplies for eye and ear care—what you have in your own medicine chest works fine. Cotton balls, cotton swabs, mineral oil or baby oil, and plain water—or saline solution you use for your contact lenses--are more than adequate.

For Teeth

Why bother worrying about your puppy's teeth? Even if they're baby teeth she'll lose anyway, once she's six-months-old you'll need to take care of those adult choppers. They are the only ones your pup will ever have. They don't make dentures for dogs.

Unfortunately, we can't train puppies to brush their own teeth. That's something we must do for them. Veterinarians provide dentistry services, including routine teeth cleaning to scour away collected plaque. But puppies won't open wide and say, "Ahhhhhh," so veterinary dentists must first anesthetize pets to clean the teeth.

That's not necessary if you train your puppy from an early age to accept you brushing her teeth. You can greatly reduce or even eliminate the need for professional teeth cleaning simply by paying attention to tooth health with home dental care.

Head to Tail Grooming Tips

Grooming not only feels good to the dog, it doubles as a home health check. You can make sure your puppy is healthy, whiskers to tail, simply by paying attention to her skin, fur, eyes, nails, ears, and teeth on a regular basis.

Dogs groomed daily as puppies learn to expect and relish the experience. Combing and brushing become an extension of petting. Puppies thrive on routine, so decide on a regimen and stick to it. That's not only a time, but also a place such as a tabletop, your lap, the floor, or other platform that's convenient for you. The top of the washer and dryer works great for smaller pups, and gives you space to set out all your combs and brushes. As mentioned before, smooth coated puppies can get by on a weekly once-over with a comb or hound's glove. Pups with thick double coats like Chows or long silky tresses like Maltese need daily fur attention to prevent painful mats.

Several days before you begin the lifetime grooming schedule, help your puppy get used to the idea. She'll want to sniff and investigate these strange items. Leave the comb and brush out with her toys—make them part of the furniture, a normal part of her life that becomes familiar, so it's not scary. You may be surprised to see her play with the brush, or even pick it up and try to carry it around.

Always begin your grooming session with petting. Feel your puppy all over, from head to neck, under her chin, down her back, in her armpits, the length of her tail. That not only gets her tail wagging, it will tell you in advance if any problem areas have developed. That way you won't run the comb into a mat unexpectedly. Petting helps relax the puppy in preparation for the grooming.

Practice touching her all over—ears, down each leg, handle her paws, gently stroke her tummy—and find all the places she likes best to be petted. If she objects to any area it may be tender or feel odd to her. Take time and don't force the situation. Only touch briefly (don't hold the paw or ears!) and reward your pup with a "Good Girl!" and perhaps a treat for allowing this. Soon she'll identify your touches and even gentle restraint with a benefit for her.

Puppies have very tender skin. When using the comb or brush, start with a light touch, and let your baby "tell" you how to proceed. Think of grooming as gently scratching the puppy's skin rather than brushing. She'll often arch her back into the brush when she wants a heavier stroke.

Begin and end your combing or brushing session by paying attention to the puppy's *sweet spots*. These are her favorite places to be rubbed or gently scratched, and include her cheeks, chin and throat, perhaps her tummy or the itchy spot right above the base of her tail. Have a game ready to play for her bravery and calm acceptance of the grooming.

Begin grooming with the pup's head and face. Finger-comb first to determine if there are any mats to address. Then proceed with your comb or brush.

After carefully combing her face—pay particular attention to the mat-prone areas around her ears—progress down both sides of her neck, and under her throat. Most pups enjoy having their chest groomed, as it reminds them of a nice scratch session. For drop-eared pups with very furry ears like Cocker Spaniels, pay attention to carefully brushing the pinna (ear flap). Lay the flat of the inside of her ear on the palm of your hand, and gently brush the fur on the outside. Puppies tend to drag furry ears into food bowls, or catch burrs and dirt when they lower their heads to sniff, so the ears can act like furry dust mops to catch a lot of debris.

Next, groom each of her sides in turn. Be careful not to brush or comb too hard, especially against her spine or nipples. Then cover her flanks, inside and out. One trick is to gently lift a rear paw while you brush and comb the other side—the pup must maintain balance on that remaining paw and so has less inclination to pull away.

Pay attention to the feathers—that's the fluffy fur on the rear area of the flanks. Also check the area beneath the tail. Pups that haven't yet mastered squatting or leg lifting behavior can leave stains on their fur that may take more than comb and brush, and require a damp cloth to clean off. For several months, when Magic began his marking routine, his aim was so bad he nearly always ended up "marking" his own front paw!

The tummy can be tough for a few pups, although many enjoy a tummy rub. If she'd rather stand, you can simply brush her underneath as much as you can reach. If she'll show her tummy for you, start with petting, and alternate one hand-stroke with a brush stroke. There is no law that says you must groom the entire puppy at one setting. If your puppy becomes upset, stop and finish at a later time. Doing a little bit each evening while you watch TV will turn that into a nice expected routine for you both, and by the end of the week, you'll cover the entire pup nose-to-tail and be ready to start over.

Finish the grooming session as you began it—with the sweet spots. Also, offer your puppy a favorite game or a treat once you've finished. That will help her associate the grooming session with positive things for her, so she looks forward to the next time.

Bath Time

A bath stimulates the skin, removes excess oil and dander, and loose fur. It also gets rid of dingy spots your furry dust-mop has collected by playing under the bed. Bathing too often, though, can dry out the skin.

It's the nature of puppies to get dirty and need a puppy bath so make plans now to learn how to bathe a puppy. While some breeds need more bathing than others, excessive baths can strip natural oils from the coat and dry the skin. Unless they get quite grubby, have a close encounter with a skunk, or are dog show prospects that need frequent grooming, most puppies shouldn't need a bath more than one to four times a year.

Puppies shouldn't be bathed until they are at least four weeks old—six or eight weeks is better. The little guys have trouble regulating their body temperature at that age, and can become chilled. Puppies who get sick with diarrhea may need a dunking, but the stress of a bath can make the illness worse. They could even end up with pneumonia.

- Poodle-type coats require the most bath time. Plan on bathing your curly coated pups at the same time they get the coat trimmed, trim about every two months. Silky and wiry coats do well with four baths a year.

- Double-coated breeds like German Shepherds need a bath a couple of times a year. Aim for spring and fall after their normal shed.

- Smooth coated pets like Rottweilers may need a bath only once a year. Of course, if they get smelly or dingy between times—Dachshunds tend to get a wee bit pungent—additional baths may be needed. With smooth coats, though, often a damp wash cloth or dry bath product can take care of the between times.

13 Steps To Bathe Puppies

Be sure there are no mats by thoroughly combing and brushing your puppy before you hit him with water. Moisture cements mats into solid masses impossible to remove without electric clippers. Clip his nails first, too, or you may end up scratched if he tries to climb out of the tub or sink.

1. Assemble all the supplies you need beforehand. Puppies object to baths when they're frightened, so prepare ahead of time out of his sight. That includes puppy shampoo, cotton balls, mineral oil, wash cloth, old clothes—for you to wear because you WILL get wet!—and at least twice as many towels as you think you'll need.

2. Use only shampoos approved for puppies. People products–and especially human baby shampoo—is designed for oily scalp and can dry out your puppy's tender skin and possibly cause allergic reactions.

3. Bathe large to medium pups in the bathtub. If the day is warm, the garden hose in the back yard or patio may be appropriate. A waist-high sink works well for small dogs, and is easier on your knees. For little pups, you can use a series of buckets or even clean waste baskets filled with water and 'dunk' the baby to soak his fur, suds him up thorough, and then rinse.

4. Place everything near your sink, tub, or patio within easy reach. When bathing indoors, the area should be warm and draft-free. Be sure to push shower curtains and any breakables out of the way that could spook your puppy. If you're container-bathing, fill the tub, sink or bucket with dog-temperature water (about 102 degrees) before you bring in the victim—er, your pet. Making him watch isn't nice.

5. It's easier to bathe your dog when two hands are free. Bath tethers are available that have a suction cup that secures one end to the tub or sink while the other clips to the puppy's harness. When bathing outdoors, tether the puppy with a short lead to a fixed object. Place a rubber mat or towel in the bottom of the container to give the puppy better footing. Puppies are scared of slippery surfaces.

6. Before beginning, place cotton in the pet's ears to keep out the water. A drop of mineral oil or artificial tears in each eye helps protect them from errant suds.

7. Place the dog in the standing water. It doesn't need to cover him; level with his knees is fine, and lets him feel he can stand above it without risk of drowning.

8. Use a plastic cup or ladle to dip water over the pup, or use a hand-held sprayer. Many pups get scared by sprayed water, so use only a low force and keep it against the coat to soak the fur. Don't spray or dunk the puppy's face; that is very scary. Instead, use a washcloth to clean and rinse the face.

9. Once the fur is wet, apply a thin stream of pet shampoo along the back—or lather the shampoo in your own hands and then apply—and suds your pup thoroughly, then rinse. If you're using a flea product, suds the pup's neck first to create a flea barrier the bugs won't cross. Most shampoos, especially flea products, work best if left on for ten to fifteen minutes.

10. The most critical part of bathing your puppy is the rinse cycle. Leaving soap in the coat can cause an allergic reaction, can attract dirt, and makes the fur look dull and dingy. So after you've thoroughly rinsed the pup, do it once more before calling it quits.

11. Then allow your pup to do what he's been yearning for the whole time—shake off the water. If his shaking doesn't fling out the cotton, you remove it from his ears. Leaving the cotton in can cause ear infection.

12. Smooth coats air dry very quickly. Puppies with more fur require lots of towels. As much as pups may dislike the bath, they often relish the

toweling-off afterwards. It's a chance to steal the towel, and play puppy games of tug or keep away. The more you can make the bathing experience fun, the less you're your dog will dread the experience.

13. Some pups tolerate a blow-dryer on a low setting, which will help fluff up the fur. Be sure the dog is dry to the skin before allowing him outside if it's a cold day.

PUPPY WAGS.

If bathing for fleas, you don't need a flea shampoo. Any shampoo will work, and water will drown the bugs. Just lather up the suds around the puppy's neck the very first thing. That creates a barrier the fleas won't cross, so they won't try to climb onto her head to breathe.

Expressing Anal Glands

If puppy scooting across the carpet, ground or grass has become a problem, you need to learn how to express anal glands. Puppy scooting generally means the fur-kid's bottom is irritated and that can be caused by tapeworms, diarrhea or even fleas, but most often can be blamed on irritated anal glands. Taking care of the anal glands is best done during the bath, so you can clean away any smelly debris on the pup's fur.

Your puppy has two anal glands located beneath the skin on either side of the rectum. The pea-size glands function like a skunk's scent organs, but thank goodness our pets can't squirt the stink. Instead, anal glands give pet bathroom deposits sort of an individual smelly fingerprint. Pets sniff each other's bottoms as a way to communicate and "read" these scented name tags to identify each other.

Normal anal glands secrete a liquid, or a creamy brown-to-yellow substance that's expressed whenever the puppy has a bowel movement. Glands may also be expressed when the fur-kid is suddenly frightened or stressed and he contracts his anal sphincter—that's the circular muscle that controls his rectum. You'll notice a strong odor if this happens.

Overactive glands that cause an odor problem. Other times, soft stools or problems with diarrhea may not supply enough pressure to empty the glands. A few pups just have abnormally small anal gland openings. An affected puppy may lick the area to relieve the discomfort, or scoot—sit down and pull himself forward while dragging his bottom against the floor.

Small dog breeds like Toy Poodles are affected most often, and unexpressed glands can become clogged or impacted. You'll know your dog has a problem if the area on one or both sides of the rectum swells. When glands become infected the secretions contain blood or pus. In severe cases, a painful abscess may develop. The swelling will be red to purple on one or both sides of the rectum.

When the glands are infected or become abscessed they'll need veterinary attention. Infected anal glands usually heal without complications, but pups that suffer recurrences of impaction or infection will need the anal glands emptied at least once a week.

The treatment requires manual expression of the anal glands. Many puppies object to owners messing with them "down there" especially when they are very tender from anal gland distress. It's best to have your veterinarian perform this service for your pet when anal glands are infected so you don't accidentally force the matter deeper into the tissue. If you are a hardy soul willing to give your all for the well-being of your pet, ask for a demonstration before trying this yourself. For those who are NOT faint of heart—or nose—here's how it's done.

1. Anal gland secretions stink, and the best place to perform anal gland maintenance is during your puppy's bath. That way you can wash away any stray stuff that spills onto the fur.
2. Wear rubber gloves. That protects your hands and reduces the "yuck" factor.
3. Stand your puppy in the sink. If doing this outside of the bath, stand small pups on a tabletop or kneel on the floor beside larger puppies.
4. You may benefit from an extra pair of hands to steady the dog's face end while you pay attention to the tail. Alternately, attach the leash to the pup's halter or collar, and secure to the faucet or other stationary object to help limit the pup's movement.
5. Lift your pup's tail and find the glands on each side of the anus at about eight and four o'clock. They'll feel a bit like small marbles beneath the skin.
6. Once you've located the glands, cover the area with a tissue. This will catch the debris as it's expressed.
7. With your thumb and forefinger on each side of the gland, gently push in and upward, and squeeze as you would to express a pimple.
8. Use the tissue or a damp cloth to wipe away the smelly discharge as the sac empties.
9. Offer your puppy a toy or treat to reward for being such a good dog during this unpleasant business.

If your puppy has had a close encounter of the stinky kind with a SKUNK, use this chemistry cure to neutralize the odor. Mix one quart of 3% hydrogen peroxide with ¼ cup of baking soda, and one teaspoon of pet shampoo (any kind will work). Apply to the puppy's wet fur, allow the mix to bubble for three or four minutes, then rinse thoroughly. This recipe, created by chemist Paul Krebaum works better than anything on the market. You can't buy it, though, because the formula can't be bottled. It explodes if left in a closed container. So if your puppy gets skunked, mix only one application at a time. Otherwise you'll be cleaning up more than just the pet.

Trimming Nails

Puppy grooming includes clipping dog nails. Don't wait until Junior-Pup gets big and turns nail trims into wrestling matches. Teach puppies while small that nail trims are a normal part of life, and nothing to fear.

Over-grown nails can become caught in bedding and carpets. They may curl as they grow, and embed into the tender flesh of the paw pad. Claws can split or tear as in the picture, and need surgical repair that's pricy and painful. Overgrown nails cause the foot to spread or splay, and can change your puppy's gait. Dewclaws on the inside of the lower leg need particular attention since they never contact the ground. Keeping the toenails trimmed also helps reduce inappropriate digging that some terrier breeds of puppy adore.

Nails at their longest should just clear the ground when the puppy stands in place. If you hear him "clicking" over the linoleum like a tap-dancer, he needs a trim. Your groomer or veterinarian can trim your dog's nails at routine visits, but it's easy enough to do yourself. Choose a style trimmer that you feel comfortable using.

Many puppies hate having their paws touched. Handle your pup's feet routinely during play and petting, and reward him with petting and treats when he puts up with it. That helps socialize him to being handled by you and future handling by the vet. Begin simply by touching each paw, one after the other. When the puppy allows this without pulling away, gently hold a paw for five seconds and releasing—again with the reward for tolerance.

Next, hold a paw and touch the nail clipper to a nail—but DON'T trip. Do this several times, and reward him for not struggling or pulling away. Stop before he gets fussy so you leave him with a good memory of the experience.

Once he's used to the idea of you holding a paw and touching the nail, trim just the tip of the nails. All the nails don't have to be done in the same session. Rather than fight the puppy and make him upset by getting them done, trim a single nail every evening for two weeks. It gets the job done without scaring the baby and damaging your relationship.

It's helpful to have two pairs of hands during nail trimming, one to steady the paw while you handle the clippers. A wiggling dog makes it more likely you'll catch the hair in the trimmer (painful!) or "quick" the nails, cut into the living vessels that feed the nail bed, and cause them to bleed.

When the nails are white or clear, the pink quick is visible and makes it easy to avoid the danger zone. If your pup's nails are dark or opaque, clip off only the hook-like tip that turns down. Tipping the nails will prompt the quick to draw back up, so you can trim a little each week until reaching the proper length.

If you do happen to quick a nail, stop. Use a styptic pencil or corn starch and direct pressure to stop the bleeding, or rake the claw through a bar of soap. Give the pup extra attention or treats to show that even if something uncomfortable happens, he'll get compensated.

After the nail is trimmed, throw a puppy party! Tell him what a good dog he is, and play a favorite game to show how pleased you are. Reserve a special treat that the dog gets only after a successful nail trim, and soon you'll have your pooch begging for a pedicure.

Cleaning Eyes and Skin Folds

Most puppy eyes need minimal care, though Peke puppies and other flat-faced breeds require more eye attention. Pups with deep facial wrinkles—Shar Pei puppies, Bulldogs and similar breeds—also need "wrinkle care" because the skin folds can harbor bacteria and become sore and inflamed if not kept clean.

For both skin folds and puppy eyes, soak a cotton ball with warm water or with saline solution you use for your contact lenses. Soften the secretions at the corners of the puppy's eyes with the wet cotton, then wipe them away. Wipe out the skin folds and check daily to be sure there's no problem. Daily attention to her eyes will prevent skin irritation.

Grooming Ears

When you choose your new friend, take into consideration grooming needs and that you will need to learn how to clean puppy ears. Different dogs require various amounts of ear grooming care. Healthy ears are pink, and a small amount of amber wax is normal and helps protect the ear canal. A discharge, bad smell, and/or dark or crumbly material may indicate an ear infection, otitis or parasites such as ear mites. Check your puppy's ears at least once a week, and clean at least monthly unless oftener is recommended by your veterinarian.

Commercial ear cleaning solutions are available from veterinarians and pet stores, but a 50/50 vinegar and water solution is fine for general cleaning. Place a small amount of solution on a cotton ball, soft cloth or cotton swab, and gently wipe out only the visible portions of the ear. Never squirt cleaner or put any instrument down into the ear canal unless instructed to do so by your veterinarian. You may inadvertently damage your dog's ear.

When recommended by the veterinarian and/or demonstrated by the groomer, ears can be cleaned in this way. Grasp the outside (pinna) of the puppy's ears firmly, while applying the cleaner into the ear. Then gently massage the base of the puppy's ear--he may groan and "talk" about how good that feels and lean into your hand--and then let go of the ear so he can shake. You'll want to wear old clothes because it's likely the head-shake afterwards will spray you with cleaner and possibly ear debris.

The pendulous ears of breeds like Cocker Spaniels tend to trap moisture, and the poor air circulation provides a perfect environment for ear infections. If your dog has this type of ears, he'll benefit from a weekly cleaning with a drying agent (epiotic solution) or "airing out." Draw the ears up over his head or behind his neck, and tape them in place for a few hours. It looks funny, but can prevent ear problems down the road.

Ear Plucking

In Poodles, Cocker Spaniels, Schnauzers, Lhasa Apsos, Bouvier de Flanders, Old English Sheepdogs and some other breeds, hair actually grows inside the ear canal. This tends to block air circulation, holds moisture, and makes these dogs prone to ear infections. Every one to three months, use electric clippers to trim the hair around the ears, and pluck out the fur growing inside the ear.

Serum that oozes from the hair pores after plucking is an ideal medium for bacterial growth. Follow ear plucking with an antibiotic ointment as recommended by your veterinarian to prevent infection or inflammation. You may be able to perform plucking service for your dog once a veterinarian or professional groomer shows you how.

Brushing Teeth

Puppy breath can be a pleasant aroma when the baby is quite small, but when it begins to melt your glasses that's an indication of a problem. Stinky mouth odor means you won't welcome those up close and personal snuggles. But it also points to potentially painful, dangerous dental problems.

By the time dogs reach the age of three, 80 percent of them have some amount of dental disease. That makes sense because dogs don't brush their teeth, and they tend to gulp—not chew—their food. Just think what your teeth would look like in three years if you never brushed!

Adult dogs often object to tooth brushing. It's best to start puppies with a dental hygiene program while they're too little to argue and consider it a game or a treat.

Routine cleaning is available from most veterinarians, and involves ultrasonic scaling, polishing, and sometimes fluoride treatment or antibiotics, especially if teeth are pulled. But the best way to prevent dental disease as your puppy grows up is to provide home treatment. Here's 6 tips to keep your puppy's teeth clean and bright.

- Crunching dry food reduces dental problems by about 10 percent, compared to canned food that sticks to teeth. If you feed both, encourage your puppy to crunch dry after the wet appetizer.
- Many dogs relish healthy people foods like raw veggies or fruit, and chewing on these "detergent" foods can help scrub teeth clean. Offer your puppy carrots or apple slices for healthy natural dental snacks.
- Special "dental diets" and treats available in grocery stores or dispensed from the veterinarian can help especially with dog breeds that seem more prone to dental issues like Yorkshire Terriers. Look for sodium hexametaphosphate (sodium HMP) listed in the food, which helps prevent plaque from attaching to teeth.
- Most veterinary dentists dislike cow bones, pig hooves, and other hard chew objects that may break your puppy's teeth. Sterilized bones designed for doggy dental care, though, may be just the ticket.
- Puppies love to chew. Offer your dog a legal object that also has dental benefits, like the "dental toys" that contain a nubby surface designed to scrub the teeth.
- A wide range of commercial dental chews (rawhide, ropes, treats) available for dogs may also prevent doggy breath. Some are infused with special enzymes that kill bacteria and help prevent plaque. Also look for dental rinse products from your veterinarian.

When your dog struggles with tooth problems, the best way to maintain dental health is to brush your puppy's teeth. Here's how.

1. Over several weeks, get your puppy accustomed to having his mouth handled. You can get pups used to having something inserted into their mouth by flavoring your finger with low-salt chicken broth. Why not use clicker training to communicate to your puppy what you want him to do?
2. Offer doggy toothpaste as a treat. Special meat-flavored toothpaste is available from pet product stores or your veterinarian that gives pups the incentive to open wide. Never use human toothpaste. Puppies can't spit so they end up swallowing the foam, and swallowed fluoride can be dangerous and damage your puppy's internal organs.

3. Once they accept mouth handling and like the toothpaste, try propping the puppy's mouth open with a favorite toy. Simply encourage him to bite on a chew object, and wrap your hand around his muzzle to hold it in place. That gives you access to his open mouth and also gives him something to do with his teeth. Practice doing this several times and praising him while giving toothpaste treats before you introduce a toothbrush.

4. Special pet toothbrushes are smaller and may be designed to better fit the dog's mouth. A soft child's toothbrush works well.

5. Some puppies better accept your finger. Finger toothbrushes are available for brushing pet teeth, or simply wrap a damp cloth over your fingers and use that to scrub the outside of his teeth. Puppy tongues clean the inside surface of teeth so you won't have to worry about poking too far inside the mouth.

6. Brushing after every meal is recommended, but a two to three times a week is good. Always be sure to praise and throw a happy puppy party afterwards so your puppy is left with a good taste over the experience—literally!

9: Preventing Puppy Health Problems

A healthy puppy is happy and just plain fun to be around. Good health goes beyond physical considerations, and includes emotional status. Emotional and physical health are two sides of the same coin and cannot be separated. Each influences the other.

Physical illness impacts the baby's attitude, and a positive or negative personality influence physical health. Negative emotions, collectively referred to as "stress," can depress the puppy's immune system. Stress makes the dog more prone to physical illness, and can make it more difficult for the sick puppy to recover.

Body and Soul—Signs of Good Health

Your puppy shows he's healthy by the way looks and the way he acts, and reacts, to the world around him. He should literally be the "picture" of health. It's very easy to monitor your puppy's health simply by paying attention to him. In most cases, signs of good health are very obvious. Once you become familiar with what is normal, you'll be better able to recognize signs of problems, both physical and emotional.

Healthy Fur: The fur on a smooth coated puppy should be shiny, smooth, and feel like silk against your hand when you pet him. Pups with longer fur have fluffy, silky, or cotton-like texture depending on if it's a double coat, curly, wirehaired or combinations.

Fur Problems: Dry lifeless or brittle fur, bald patches, mats and tangles, and a dirty coat are all signs of a health problem. One of the first signs of illness shows up in the fur coat. It may point to problems with nutrition, or parasites like intestinal worms or fleas.

Healthy Skin: In normal puppies, you won't see much bare skin. The inside of the ears, the nose, and paw pads are bare. When you pet your puppy his skin underneath the fur should feel smooth and without blemish.

Skin Problems: Any lump, bump, scab or sore in the skin should alert you to a problem. Bald places, red or rough skin, or discoloration can be a warning sign of a variety of health problems. For instance, very pale skin on the inside of his ears may indicate anemia, while a yellow tinge, called jaundice, points to a liver problem.

Healthy Eyes: Healthy eyes are bright, clear, and have only a small amount of clear tear-like discharge (if at all). Puppies meet the world with their eyes wide-open.

Eye Problems: A squinting eye points to discomfort or pain. Puppies can scratch their eyes or get dust in them, and end up with a watery, squinty, or cloudy eye. Any discharge from the eyes, other than moderate clear tear-like secretions, is cause for concern. The cause ranges from simple irritation to a viral or bacterial infection like distemper that can be life-threatening to young puppies.

Healthy Ears: Normal puppy ears are clean. The visible skin is a healthy pink. There may be a bit of amber-colored waxy substance that's easily wiped out. Your new youngster will also be alert to interesting sounds.

Ear Problems: Shaking his head or pawing and scratching at his ears alert you to problems with your puppy's ears. Ear infections or parasite infestations can cause these symptoms and make your baby miserable. Any sort of discharge points to a health problem. For instance, a crumbly dark material inside puppy ears often is due to an infestation of ear mites.

Healthy Nose: Puppies are literally led around by the nose, so a healthy one is important to both physical and emotional health. The nose can be different colors, from light pink to black, or even freckled. Usually the nose stays moist, from the puppy licking his nose and from minimal clear discharge.

Nose Problems: Nasal discharge can be a sign of illness. A gummy, runny or crusty nose or sneezing are signs he needs help.

Healthy Gums: The gums above the teeth in your puppy's mouth are naturally pink. Some pups have a bit of pigment in the gums and can have darker gums. For instance Chows typically have black gums and tongue. Depending on his age, your pup may have a few teeth missing or new ones coming in. Those places can be a bit sore.

Gum Problems: A sore mouth could be due to teething, while sores on the gums, on the tongue, or roof of the mouth can be caused by chewing the wrong item that causes injury, or an infection, or even fungal or autoimmune disorder. The puppy may refuse to eat because his mouth is so sore.

Healthy Nails and Paws: Paw pads are soft and smooth, while the claws grow cleanly from the ends of each toe.

Problem Claws and Paws: Puppies often limp when a paw hurts. Torn or split claws are painful and need attention. Also, any crusty material at the base of the nail bed (where the claw grows out) could indicate a more serious whole-body health problem with the puppy's immune system. Infestation with hookworms (an intestinal parasite) can also affect the skin of the paw pads.

Healthy Elimination: The puppy's anus should be clean. Check the furry bottom area beneath his tail. Puppy elimination is a barometer of his health. The consistency of feces varies a bit depending on his diet, but should be well formed and not liquid. Normal urine is yellow to amber colored. Monitor your puppy's potty deposits to keep track of his normal bathroom habits.

Problem Elimination: An occasional soft stool probably isn't cause to worry, but diarrhea is serious especially with tiny puppies. They can become dehydrated very quickly. Diarrhea can be a sign of a wide range of health problems, from intestinal parasites to viral infections. Straining to "go" is just as serious, and may indicate constipation or cystitis—bladder inflammation that makes it hurt to urinate. Blood in the urine or feces is always a sign of a health problem.

Healthy Appetite: Since puppies can't always eat enough to sustain them through the day (their tummies are tiny!), your baby may not always gulp down his food when first presented. Meal feeding helps with this. As puppies get older, some individuals and breeds may turn into gulpers and gorgers, which is how dogs evolved to best survive. You'll want to monitor your puppy's food intake whether he's a nibbler or a gorger.

Problem Appetite: Refusing to eat (anorexia) can be a dangerous problem in dogs, and especially puppies. Loss of appetite can be gradual or sudden, and either can point to a health problem. Missing one meal probably won't hurt him if there are no other signs of health concerns, UNLESS he's a Toy breed or very young. Missing meals in these guys can cause low blood sugar (hypoglycemia) which can kill youngsters. Vomiting is another warning sign you should take very seriously. Like diarrhea, vomiting can dehydrate the puppy very quickly and make him even sicker.

Healthy Attitude: By nature, a puppy is non-stop energy, and loves to play. The emotionally-healthy puppy meets the world with in-your-face curiosity.

Problem Attitude: A red alert of a health problem in puppies is lethargy. Puppies that act depressed may be running a fever or have an illness brewing that makes them feel icky. Any kind of personality change or alternation in normal behavior could point to a health problem. In other words, an energetic puppy that acts depressed, a friendly puppy that becomes aggressive or shy, or a laid-back puppy that turns hyperactive all should be a cause for concern.

Picking The Best Veterinarian

Finding a veterinarian who meets your puppy's needs is an important consideration in the life of your pet. Like our pets, all veterinarians bark, purr, and growl (depending on their mood). They all have hair (more or less). And without exception, people become veterinarians because they like and care about animals. But the best vet for you also involves finding a vet with the personality, services, and convenience that meets your needs.

Unlike your new puppy, veterinarians come to you already well trained. There are twenty-seven schools and colleges of veterinary medicine in the United States where students study for eight to ten years before they receive their "doctor of veterinary medicine" degree (DVM) or veterinariae medicinae doctoris (VMD) degree.

While human medical doctors learn to care for a single species, veterinarians are expected to understand and care for all sorts of animals. Local veterinarians know how to recognize, prevent, and treat everything from routine puppy vaccinations and spay/neuter surgeries, to feline fatty liver disease, feather mites of birds, bacterial infections of reptiles, and nutritional disorders of the cow, horse, or hamster.

Most puppies receive optimum care their whole lives from general practice veterinarians. These professionals often are neighbors and become friends. In the best situations they come to know your pets almost as well as you do.

Of course, you live with Cutie-Pup and know her best—and can tell the doctor something's wrong if she suddenly has no interest in her squeaky toy the way she normally does. This partnership means you stay alert to any warnings, then your veterinarian deals with the medical issues specific to your pets. Hopefully your pets only need to see the veterinarian a couple of times a year for general checkups and preventive care.

What's right for you may not be for another person. But it's a good idea to ask other pet owners for recommendations to see what they like (or don't like) about a particular vet. Consider making an appointment to visit a potential veterinary clinic ahead of time. The doctor's office is a busy place, so avoid times when the staff must deal with regular appointments or surgery. Your ideal veterinarian should offer:

- Office hours and location convenient to your schedule
- Fee and payment structure you can afford
- Emergency services either through their clinic or shared with other facilities
- Knowledgeable and personable staff.
- Value added—some practices include boarding, grooming, or training facilities

Personality of the doctor certainly can be an issue. You should like or at least respect each other, and the doctor should care about your pets, and be willing to explain treatments and answer your questions. Conversely, you must be willing to provide necessary information, respect the doctor's time and expertise, and trust his or her judgment.

Take the time to develop a positive relationship with the people who care for your new puppy—and all the pets you love. After all, you're on the same team and want the same things—to create the pet of your dreams.

The veterinarian is your partner in health care for the lifetime of your puppy. In the best of situations, the veterinarian sees your pup only a couple of times a year.

Meanwhile, you live with him, and that means you know your puppy better than anybody. You are in the best position to sound the alarm if your puppy feels under the weather, and get him to the veterinarian for the proper care. That's a dynamic and effective health care partnership.

The Doctor's Role

Your veterinarian examines the puppy for general health, from head to tail. A technician usually takes the pup's temperature first and makes notes about the puppy's health history and any concerns you have.

Then the veterinarian listens to the baby's heart and breathing, feels him all over, and looks in his mouth, eyes, and ears for telltale signs of problems. She may ask the technician to run screening tests to diagnose, for instance, any intestinal parasites. It's up to the veterinarian to keep an accurate record of the puppy's preventative treatments such as vaccinations, the status of his health, and any prescribed therapies.

Your Responsibility

Since you live with your puppy and know him the best of all, it's up to you to learn what is "normal" puppy behavior and appearance. That way, you'll easily recognize something that's out of the ordinary, so you can get timely help from your veterinarian.

The veterinarian relies on your information about the puppy to provide the best care possible. Does your puppy eat well? Play with enthusiasm? Use the bathroom regularly, or have intermittent diarrhea where he misses the mark? Perhaps he pants or wheezes a bit after a game of chase-the-ball. Or maybe your Junior-Dog is the healthiest, best-behaved and prime example of puppyhood ever to grace the examining table.

When you take your puppy for his veterinary visit, be prepared to answer questions, offer information, and even ask pointed questions of your own. Don't wait to get home to wonder what the doctor meant by something she said—there are *no* stupid questions when it comes to caring for your puppy. Be sure to get all the information you need to make informed decisions about, and properly care for your puppy.

PUPPY WAGS.

When you call to make the appointment, ask what, if anything, you should bring along to the visit. For example, puppies are routinely checked for worms by testing a sample of their stool. It's much less upsetting for the puppy if you bring a fresh deposit from his potty duty rather than having the veterinary technician obtain one on the end of the thermometer (or in some other rude fashion).

Preventative Treatments

Veterinarians agree that preventing health problems is much easier to do than treating the puppy once he becomes sick. It's also much less expensive. Preventative care has made an incredible difference in the lives of puppies. In the past, a large percentage of furry babies never reached adulthood because they became ill and died while in infancy.

Puppies are much more susceptible to illness because their immune system is still maturing. That's why it is vital to not only have your new puppy examined right away, but also to protect him against the most common dog illnesses. These are caused by a variety of viruses, bacterium, and parasites.

Preventative veterinary care such as vaccinations has increased the lifespan of dogs. In the 1960s a dog could expect to live to reach seven to ten years of age. Not too long ago, 50 percent or more of dogs died of canine distemper or parvovirus before their first birthday. These little victims suffer through painful vomiting and diarrhea and too often must be humanely euthanized to end their suffering. These diseases today are entirely preventable.

VACCINATIONS

Puppies are susceptible to a variety of diseases caused by viruses and/or bacteria. To a large degree, they can be prevented with a series of preventative vaccinations—the shots every puppy should receive.

Vaccines contain harmless, but recognizable parts of the disease-causing virus or bacterium. By presenting these to the body with shots—or sometimes with nose or eye drops—the immune system learns to recognize them as foreign. In response, the body creates antibodies that circulate in the bloodstream, and other components that work at the cellular level, for instance, inside the puppy's nose.

WARNING!

Preventative vaccinations are important to protect your puppy from life-threatening illnesses. However, even the best vaccine will not provide 100 percent protection. Your vaccinated puppy will still be at risk for disease especially if repeatedly exposed.

These immune soldiers are like smart bombs, programmed to search out and destroy anything that looks like the disease-causing agent. Adult dogs have a mature immune system ready and able to create these immune-protectors.

Puppy immunity, though, takes a bit more coaxing for a couple of reasons. First, their immune system isn't quite up to speed until they're about eight weeks old—and every puppy is different, so it's hard to predict the timing. And second, all the good immune protection they got from nursing Mom-dog tends to sabotage vaccines by misrecognizing them as bad guys and making them ineffective. This "passive immunity" from their mother can last until the puppy is about 14 weeks old.

That's why it's so important for puppies to receive not just one, but a series of protective vaccinations over a period of time. This better ensures that as Mom's immunity fades and Junior's takes over, he'll be protected by some or most of the shots that he's given during that critical period.

In the past, shots were given every single year as a matter of course, even though no studies had been conducted to show the duration of vaccination protection. Also, puppies and adult dogs were often vaccinated against a wide range of illnesses, even when the risk for getting the disease was slim. Today, veterinarians agree that puppies should be protected against those conditions for which they are at risk.

Most puppies are inoculated with a series of protective shots as maternal protection fades away. First vaccinations are typically given between six to nine weeks of age, with boosters repeated every three to four weeks until the puppy reaches 14 to 16 weeks of age. The exception is the rabies shot, which typically is given at 12 to 16 weeks for the first time, and then either yearly or every three years depending on local law. Because rabies has human health risks, the law requires that dogs be vaccinated for this disease.

Today, a number of veterinarians also recommend that after the initial puppy shots and first year booster, dogs be re-vaccinated every three years rather than annually—follow your own veterinarian's recommendation. She'll know best what will work for your individual situation.

Remember, every puppy is different. Some are "only" puppies that live exclusively indoors with quick rambles into the back yard. Others share the house with many dogs or run outside, play at the dog park and are exposed to extra risk. Therefore, no one vaccination program works for every situation—it must be custom-designed for your baby, based on his individual needs. Your veterinarian will know what illnesses may be prevalent in your neck of the woods, and how the puppy's lifestyle may affect exposure risk.

Some puppies and dogs experience a vaccine reaction. Usually the pet acts a bit lethargic for a day or two, and sometimes has a small swollen or sore place at the shot spot. It's a good idea to monitor the site of the injection to make sure any swelling goes away within several days. If it doesn't, a trip back to the vet is in order.

The effectiveness of the shots depends on many things: age of the puppy, individual immune system, exposure risk, and other health problems. In the case of shelter adoptions and of back-door waifs, the puppy may look perfectly healthy but be incubating an illness he was exposed to before you found him. The stress of a visit to the veterinarian may prompt him to come down with something—it's rarely the shot that causes such a problem.

Just because a vaccination against sleeping sickness is available doesn't mean all people should get it. In the same way, veterinarians agree that just because a vaccine is available doesn't mean your puppy should automatically receive protection. Generally, it is recommended that all puppies receive protection with "core" vaccinations—that is, the most common and dangerous illnesses for which the puppy will likely have the greatest risk for exposure.

Distemper, parvovirus, hepatitis and rabies are designated "core" vaccinations. All puppies should receive these, and often they'll be combined into a single shot. "Noncore" vaccinations are recommended for puppies at specific risk for those conditions, such as Lyme disease, kennel cough and leptospirosis.

Your veterinarian determines when to start and how many boosters your pup should receive based on health status and exposure. Usually puppies receive a series of either three or four boosters three weeks apart, starting at either six weeks (6, 9, 12, 16 weeks of age) or starting at nine weeks(9, 12 and 16 weeks). Rabies is given at 16 weeks, and all of the core vaccinations are repeated a year later.

Most of the "core" vaccinations have been shown to provide protection for (on average) about five to seven years. Your puppy as he grows will need to see the vet more frequently anyway if only for well-dog exams. Veterinarians may recommend giving distemper vaccination one year, parvovirus the next, and so on. Usually either an annual or every three years revaccination provides the best insurance on the core vaccines.

The noncore vaccinations are best given more frequently prior to expected exposure. That's because most bacteria-protective vaccines give only about six months protection, which means the

WARNING!

Most vaccines are designed to prevent disease, but some will only reduce the severity of the illness but not keep the pup from getting sick.

leptospirosis, bordetella/kennel cough and Lyme vaccines for your dog are not suited for a three-year protocol. Because rabies is a zoonosis—disease that affects people—local laws dictate how often your dog needs revaccination. That's usually either every year or every three years.

Protect your new puppies and dogs by budgeting for these vital vaccinations. It's much easier, saver, and CHEAPER to prevent illness than to diagnose and treat once your furry love becomes sick.

WARNING!

Vaccination reactions like lethargy or soreness are much more likely to occur when multiple shots are given at the same time. Ask your veterinarian about spreading the vaccinations out over several visits instead. Rather than the combination shot, for instance, separate inoculations with one or two at a time may be more appropriate.

PARASITES

Puppies naturally attract all kinds of buggy freeloaders. They may be on the inside where you don't see them, like worms that wreak havoc in the tummy or heart. Others such as fleas, ticks and mange or ear mites live on the outside of the body.

The internal parasites are best addressed by your veterinarian. Sure, there are "worm medicines" you can buy at the supermarket, but these often are not effective against the particular kind of worm your puppy has. You'll waste your money or worse—make the puppy sick—by using home-remedies.

Today, a variety preventative therapies are available that keep puppies free of both external and internal parasites, some with a single product application. I use Revolution on my German Shepherd Magic, and it controls a host of intestinal works prevents fleas and ticks and even protects against heartworms.

In the past, flea control was complicated by the fact that the chemicals used to kill the bugs were often extremely toxic to puppies. It's also complicated because fleas lay eggs that mature into larvae, spin cocoons and emerge as adults—and not all products will kill each of these life stages. That means the flea war must be waged often year-round in many parts of the world.

One of the best ways to control fleas is a two-pronged attack that protects your home, and the pet. Adult fleas prefer to stay on your puppy, but the other life stages (eggs, cocoons larvae) end up in your carpet. For more information about puppy parasites, treatment and prevention see Chapter 10.

For treating premises, sprays and foggers cover every square inch of the home, creep into the crevices and delve into the carpet to treat hidden eggs and larvae. Choose one designed to kill the adult fleas on contact, which also contains an insect growth regulator (IGR) to stop immature fleas from developing. That zaps the babies as they emerge from the cocoon, or stops eggs from hatching.

Natural premise control products that may help include borate-containing powders that dry out the fleas and kill them by dehydration. Diatomaceous earth (pet grade) does the same thing. Both can be a bit messy. Mint-type sprays have some repellent effect, but they don't kill fleas.

The best natural technique for fighting fleas in the house is daily vacuuming that sucks up flea eggs, larvae and cocoons. Be sure to throw out the vacuum bag, though, or you'll risk having the bugs hatch inside and spread them the next time you sweep.

Just because a product is natural does not automatically mean it's effective, or safe. After all, poisonous mushrooms are natural, too! Puppies are incredibly sensitive to flea products, even natural ones like citronella, so follow your veterinarian's advice to avoid dangerous reactions.

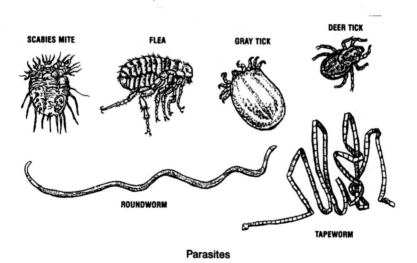

Parasites

WARNING!

Be sure to read and follow product directions very carefully. Many of the premise sprays and foggers are toxic to puppies and other pets (especially birds, cats and fish). It may be best to take your puppy for a weekend vacation, and have the house bug bombed while you are away. Flea products used on the pet also have the potential for harming your puppy, especially if the product directions aren't followed. Read the label. Be sure it's labeled safe for puppies—flea products designed for adult dogs are not always safe for pups. Never combine products unless advised to do so by your veterinarian. What's safe when used alone may become deadly when combined with another product.

BREEDING PUPPIES?

Take a look at the furry wonder sleeping on your lap. If he came from a shelter, consider that he is the lucky one who found a home. Four puppies out of every litter of five will draw the short straws and not survive to live the good life on some loving person's lap. There are just not enough good homes to go around.

Unless you are an experienced breeder and your puppy has the pedigree qualities that would benefit his breed, there is no reason to mate him—or her. Responsible professional dog breeders spend a great deal of time and money on their animals. They research and study family trees. They learn about genetics to better predict what type of puppies they can expect from a particular match-making. And when puppies are born, they celebrate the joys of a successful breeding, and suffer the agonies of disaster when babies die. In any case, they fund their hobby with love and money, and take responsibility for bringing puppies into the world.

Breeding purebred dogs can be incredibly rewarding. But it's not easy to do it right. If you are interested in this hobby, take time to learn about what's involved. There are some good books that provide guidance, but learning from a book alone isn't the best idea. A better place to start is your puppy's breeder. Ask him or her about the process, visit dog shows and become involved in these fun family events.

Realize that dog breeders do not make money. After the expense of proper puppy vaccinations, parasite treatments, Mom-dog's veterinary visits and prenatal care, and feeding the whole crew, they do well to break even. The best-known kennels that demand the highest prices for their puppies tend to be those who spend lots of time, money, and energy into campaigning their dogs to championships by traveling across the country and competing in many shows.

If you do decide to breed your puppy, be prepared for some behaviors you'll have to learn to live with as he—or she—matures. Girl dogs will go into "heat" about twice a year when they become receptive to the male's attention. Heat or "estrus" produces a blood discharge that can be messy.

Boy dogs want to meet all those lovely girl dogs. To make sure there's no mistake about their intentions, intact male dogs leg lift to leave urine as an advertisement. For some dogs, that can mean your walls, furniture, carpet, and other household landmarks are prime targets for this canine baptism. Intact male dogs are also more prone to health problems such as abscesses from fight wounds.

The Gift of Spay and Neuter

Neutering puppies is the responsible thing to do, and it's important to know when to neuter a puppy. When love is in the air, the dogs know it. Girl pups mature more quickly than you might think. They can become pregnant as early as five or six months of age, and most dogs can produce two litters a year. Don't be surprised when they pick window locks with their rabies tag to meet furry Romeos—and present you with their litter-ary creations.

The words *altering, sterilizing,* and *neutering* all refer to surgery performed by a veterinarian that removes the reproductive organs of either a male or female animal. Castration removes a boy dog's testicles. An ovariohysterectomy—or spay—removes the girl dog's ovaries and uterus.

Surgery prevents unwanted litters. It also eliminates obnoxious romantic behavior such as roaming, fighting, excessive urine marking, and mounting visitor's legs.

The surgeries help prevents fight wounds, messy canine vaginal discharges, and uterine infections. Castrating boy pets eliminates the chance of testicular cancer, and spaying your dog before her first breeding season reduces any risk of breast cancer by seven times.

Newer studies also indicate sterilized dogs live an average of a year and a half longer than intact dogs. However, there are also some recent concerns raised about sterilizing dogs, and new non-surgical sterilization options available.

What Is Zeuterin?

Zeuterin appears to answer many of these challenges. It neuters your puppy with less pain, no anesthesia (usually only sedation is necessary), he recovers more quickly, and it costs less than surgical techniques. Because it requires less time, that's a cost savings to the veterinarian, too.

Ark Sciences that owns the drug and procedure says its initial offer to nonprofits in the United States was 1/5th the average cost of surgical castration. That makes Zeuterin a good candidate for shelters and those dealing with stray and feral populations. Savings to the pet owner may potentially reduce the cost of sterilization by 30-50 percent compared to surgical castration.

Zeuterin is an injectable spermicide composed of Zinc Gluconate (a trace element), neutralized with L-Arginene (an amino acid), two natural and essential substances for the dog's body. It's actually been around since 2003 when it was called Neutersol, but the company and product went away after about three years. According to Ark Sciences, the parent company owning Neutersol created too much inventory which expired before it could be used, and the company had to shut down. In addition, not enough attention was paid to teaching proper administration of the product, which increased the potential for adverse reactions and gave Neutersol a bad name.

Ark Sciences bought the rights to the product in 2007, and renamed it. The company has since conducted clinical trials starting in 1999 on 270 dogs. They have followed 40 of these dogs for over two years, and collected information on many of the study cases for over five years. Since 1999, the company has not received any reports of long-term side effects.

In addition, Ark Sciences has embarked on a veterinary education and training program targeted primarily to shelter medicine practices. Veterinarians or vet techs (under supervision of a licensed veterinarian) must be trained and certified to qualify to perform the procedure. Only those trained by Ark Sciences may administer Zeuterin, and by doing this, errors and adverse reactions are uncommon. That protects your puppy to ensure the best possible outcome.

Esterilsol™ is Ark Sciences' product for international markets and is registered in four countries, and pending approval in several others around the world. It is approved for all dogs over three months of age in Mexico.

How Does Zeuterin Work?

Zeuterin is injected in the testicles. Ouch! Wait—nope, your pup or older dog isn't likely to notice at all. There are no pain sensors inside the testes, only pressure sensors. So when properly administered by your trained veterinarian, little to no sensation will be experienced by your sedated dog.

When injected into the testicles, the compound diffuses throughout the testis, and the Zinc acts as a spermicide and destroys all stages of sperm maturation. The tubules that were filled with sperm are emptied, and collapse.

In response, blood flow increases to the testicles to heal, and this causes inflammation resulting in scar tissue (fibrosis) within days. These block the "feeder" conduits permanently, and causes irreversible sterility. The Zinc Gluconate and Arginine are ultimately absorbed and metabolized by the dog's body.

Sperm stops being manufactured within three days, but sperm may reside in the organ for up to 30 days. Because sperm maturation lasts 60 days, the company recommends keeping your Zinc-neutered adult dog away from a female for at least that period. Over time the interior structures of the testicles including the prostate all atrophy, and shrink in size.

Unlike castration that removes 100 percent of testosterone from the body, "Zeutering" removes only about 50 percent. Leydig cells that are responsible for the endocrine function of the testis are not affected and in test dogs, overall testosterone levels were reduced by 41-52 percent. The testis continue to produce the hormones at a level that recent research shows is protective and beneficial.

There's a low incidence of severe side effects in surgical castrations, with discomfort and swelling, licking and occasional infection noted. Similar adverse reactions may occur with Zeuterin, and most do not require medical care.

Minor local reactions include testicular swelling, which is a normal reaction to the inflammation from the injection. Pain may be demonstrated by the dog not wanting to sit, or sitting with hind legs open, or licking/biting the area. More rarely, systemic reactions include vomiting, loss of appetite, lethargy and diarrhea.

Most reactions in the clinical trial group of 270 dogs were seen with the first week after the injection treatment, and more than 93 percent didn't show any painful signs. When discomfort was noted, it usually happened within the first two days and then went away.

Long-term observations have shown no increase in risk for testicular cancer in dogs neutered with Zeuterin. But to date, no studies have been performed to see if there might be a decreased risk of testicular cancer.

What Else Should I Know About Zeuterin?

If your puppy has undescended testicles, surgical castration is still the best option. Not all dogs are the best candidates and your veterinarian will know if he has a history of allergic reactions to any of the components in the drug, for example.

Zeutering may or may not eliminate the behaviors associated with mating, although anecdotal reports from owners of dogs indicate the effects are similar to those expected from surgical castration. Of course, surgical castration doesn't guarantee to totally suppress mounting, roaming, marking or aggression, either.

Puppies and dogs sterilized with Zeuterin will still appear to be intact. For dogs and pet parents getting the "hairy eyeball" at dog parks and gatherings, you may want to invest in a bandana or other way to show off your pet's special Zeutered status.

Because he'll still look intact, it's recommended that you document the dog's sterilized status on his microchip and/or a tattoo (a "Z" near the scrotum) be placed. That way if the worst happens and your dog becomes lost, he won't be castrated at a later date if found by a rescue organization.

Will It Change My Dog's Personality?

Spayed and neutered pets are just as affectionate, protective, and trainable as intact dogs—perhaps more so because they aren't distracted when love is in the air. Reduced interest in roaming often means pets should eat less food, though, or they can get pudgy. Be sure to adjust the amount and frequency of meals. Removing the sexual organs can alter the pet's metabolism, which also can change as the pup matures.

Dogs continue to be just as playful, protective, loyal, and smart whether they can reproduce or not. Unless a puppy is an ideal example of his breed and in a professional breeding program, is a conformation show and/or performance prospect, or there are medical reasons to delay the surgery, spaying and neutering is highly recommended.

What's The Best Age?

Adult dogs can be neutered at any age, but the best time is before sexual maturity. For many years, the recommended spay/neuter age was six to nine months. When a puppy's future involves performance competition, ask your veterinarian and breeder about timing. Delaying for a couple of months may allow the pup to attain better physical development important to these demands.

However, since dogs can become pregnant prior to six months old, for most pets an earlier timeframe makes better sense. The American Veterinary Medical Association recommends that shelter pets be sterilized by four months. Many shelters neuter puppies when they reach eight weeks of age—or two pounds in weight—before they are placed for adoption. These babies recover more quickly from the surgery than adult animals. They will grow just as much, and sometimes a bit taller, than if fixed later in life.

The Surgery

Puppies are completely anesthetized during the surgery, and won't feel any discomfort. Anesthetic may be injected or inhaled. Sometimes heart and breathing monitors or EKG machines are used. Doctors may prefer absorbable stitches, surgical staples, or even skin glue to close the incision. The specific routine depends on the size and age of the pet, and what your veterinarian prefers.

The surgical incision for male puppies usually is made in the scrotal sac, while an older dog's incision is often at the base of the penis in front of the scrotum. If one or both testicles have not yet dropped into the scrotum, a tummy incision may be necessary. Girl pups also have an abdominal incision for the spay surgery.

Pets act a bit woozy until anesthesia wears off. Some will be ready to go home the same day, while others must spend the night at the clinic. Most animals are up and running within hours.

Limit your pet's activity for at least a couple of days. Keep the puppy inside to allow healing to begin. The surgery site should be watched for swelling, redness, or pulled stitches, but such problems are rare. If stitches are used, your pup will need to return to the clinic to have them removed in about a week.

Puppies usually spend the night in the hospital. They may be admitted the evening before, have the surgery the next morning, and then be released later that afternoon or evening.

Every puppy reacts differently to the surgery. Many may want to sleep and lay around for a day or two, but most bounce

TECHNICAL STUFF. Occasionally a boy puppy's testicles do not descend. That is, they remain in his abdomen, rather than normally moving into the scrotal sac. In these cases, called "cryptorchid" for both and "monorchid" for one retained testicle, it's even more important to neuter. Retained testicles are more prone to developing cancer. The veterinarian will need to make a small incision in the puppy's abdomen in these cases to find and remove the testicle(s). Stitches and recovery are similar to a spay procedure.

back very quickly and act as though nothing has happened. Your veterinarian may ask you to restrict the puppy's activity until the incision heals and stitches are removed.

Spay and neuter surgeries offer several health benefits to puppies and dogs. First, it eliminates the sex-related objectionable behaviors. That can prevent abscesses or injuries from bite wounds, and roaming behavior that puts dogs at risk for being hit by a car. It also eliminates or reduces the possibility of some kinds of cancer, such as testicular or breast tumors.

These surgeries also relieve your puppy of the bother, nuisance, and stress of worrying about breeding issues. It frees them to become pets. Dogs do not yearn to be "fulfilled" by parenthood—they simply won't miss what they've never experienced. Spayed and neutered puppies get to enjoy life concentrating on bonding with you and your family.

Finally—and perhaps most importantly—spay and neuter prevents the births of unwanted puppies otherwise destined to die. It is simply the right thing to do.

CROPPING & DOCKING

Cropping puppy ears—otoplasty—refers to the practice of surgically altering the shape of the dog's external ear. The procedure may be done to correct congenital defects or damage from injury or disease.

Historically, ears were cropped on protection and "varmint" dogs to prevent ears from being mauled during fights with prey or each other. Also, erect "prick" ears are said to be healthier because they allow air flow that's blocked in hanging or "drop" ear conformation of dogs like Beagles.

Truthfully, the procedure rarely is required for the puppy's health. Usually it's done purely for cosmetic reasons to change a folded or hanging ear conformation to an erect look favored by dog show fanciers.

In the United States, ear cropping is historically performed on more than fifty breeds. These include Boston Terriers, Boxers, Doberman Pinschers, Great Danes, and Schnauzers to conform to the specific look of each breed standard.

The surgery is performed on eight to ten week old puppies (Boston Terriers more typically at four to six months of age). These early age surgeries create stress that can predispose at risk puppies to health problems like parvo or even distemper. Ear cropping requires general anesthesia and the expertise of a veterinary surgeon familiar with individual breed standards.

Various breeds standards dictate the preferred shape of the ear. A "show trim" often looks longer and more extreme on a Great Dane destined for the show ring than for a pet. And breeds like the Bull Terrier or American Pit Bull Terrier calls for shorter ear cropping.

Splinting and other specialized ear-bandaging techniques help form the puppy's ears for a week or more following the surgery, and will need to be monitored and changed as the ears heal. Discomfort from the bandaging and wound can make healing a challenge since pups paw at bandages and shake heads to relieve the discomfort. Pain medicine is recommended.

In recent years, the ethics of cosmetic ear cropping has been called into question both in the United States and abroad. The American Kennel Club breed club standards for

TECHNICAL STUFF.
November 2008, and later revised July 1999, the American Veterinary Medical Association passed the following policy: "The AVMA opposes ear cropping and tail docking of dogs when done solely for cosmetic purposes. The AVMA encourages the elimination of ear cropping and tail docking from breed standards." Shortly thereafter, a number of veterinary clinics including Banfield Pet Hospitals stopped tail docking and ear cropping altogether.

these breeds generally include descriptions of both the ideal cropped, as well as a natural ear conformation. Some dog show fanciers believe cropped dogs do more favorably in competition and continue to crop in order to succeed in the show ring. Show dogs in some other countries may be disqualified if the ears are cropped.

The practice of surgically altering the conformation of a dog's ears is expensive, painful, requires tedious owner follow up, and is not always successful. Changing the way ears look may also interfere with the dog's body language. If conformation dog shows are not in your plans, there's no reason to put your puppy through ear cropping. Please consult with your veterinarian—and consider your own motives—before putting your puppy through this elective procedure.

Docking refers to the amputation of all or a portion of the puppy's tail. Docked tails can done for medical reasons, such as damage from frostbite or fracture if the pup's tail gets shut in the door. Some dogs like Labradors retrievers are "tail beaters" in a constant state of bloody injury from flailing their tails against objects. Sometimes a puppy is born with a "crook" in the tail that may catch on objects and cause injury, and so this is removed for safety reasons.

But most puppy tail docking happens for cosmetic reasons, so that the dog will look a certain way. Hunting dogs and terrier breeds most typically have docked tails. Historically, tails were docked (or "curtailed") to prevent injury to them during work. Centuries ago when only nobility were allowed to own certain kinds of dogs, a commoner's "cur" dog had his tail docked to easily tell him apart from purebred dogs owned by the aristocracy. Today the American Kennel Club member dog breed clubs includes docked tails in more than forty breed standards.

The length of the docked tail varies depending on the specific breed. Some are docked quite short and close to the body. The Pembroke Welsh Corgi standard calls for tails to be "docked as short as possible without being indented." Other breeds are kept rather long—the Wire Fox Terrier standard calls for a three-quarter dock. If a puppy of a normally "tailless" breed is born with a tail this may be corrected with docking. Typically, the surgery is performed on three to five day old puppies often without anesthesia. Yes, puppies feel pain and cry when the procedure is done.

The puppy tail is measured, and the amputation made between the appropriate vertebrae. Absorbable stitches or tissue glue ensure a more cosmetic healed tail with skin closed over the stump of the bone, rather than just lopping off a portion of the tail. It should be done under sterile conditions by a veterinarian familiar with breed standards.

As with ear cropping, today, the practice is more a tradition than a health consideration. In fact, dog registries in Europe forbid tail docking as inhumane. The practice is controversial, even in the United States.

When you adopt at a conventional age of 8 to 12 weeks, your puppy likely already had his tail docked. While the majority of puppies may never suffer known physical problems, some veterinarians believe docking may predispose dogs to urinary incontinence later in life. Docking a dog's tail also cuts off tail talk to a great extent, which potentially could cause communication problems between dogs. Purebred and mixed breed puppies with natural tails and ears are no less loveable, trainable, or beautiful.

10: Recognize & Treat Sick Puppies

You are the most important person in your puppy's life. Not only are you the source of all her favorite food, attention, and play. You are the guardian of her health. Of course your veterinarian is a vital part of puppy care. The doctor you choose provides important advice, preventative care to keep her healthy, and expertise to diagnose and treat problems when they arise. But it's up to you to recognize there's a problem in the first place, so you can get that veterinary care. That means you must become intimately familiar with "normal" puppy behavior and appearance, so that a deviation from the norm sounds an alert.

Remember, you are an important part of the health care team, and a partner—with your veterinarian—in ensuring your puppy stays well. In the best of all possible worlds, you'll only need to call on your veterinarian for routine preventative care three or four times during her first year of life and only once or twice a year thereafter. But you live with your baby dog all year long. You know her best, you are most familiar with all her special quirks. So you are in the best position to know when something isn't right.

People often tell me they enjoy a close, almost mystical bond with their special puppies, so much so that their "intuition" tells them when there's a problem. For instance, you may wake up in the morning and simply "know" your puppy feels bad, even before you see that she's had an accident under the piano bench. The closer your bond, the more likely this special closeness may become. Holistic veterinarians encourage pet owners to "listen" to that little voice inside, the intuition that offers warnings. Our subconscious often may recognize clues we otherwise might miss.

The Home Health Exam

Make a habit of giving your puppy a home health check on a routine basis. That helps familiarize you with what's normal for your puppy, so you can promptly recognize a problem. It's easy to do, and can double as a bonding experience. Your puppy will just love all the petting.

A good time to give your pup a thorough once-over is in the evenings, during the television news program, or whenever she's winding down for the day. Place her on your lap, and begin at her head and face. Check her eyes, peek into both ears, and be sure her nose is clean. You'll want to make sure there is no abnormal discharge forming. If she'll let you without fussing too much, take a look inside her mouth, too, to make sure her gums are a healthy pink.

Finally, pet your puppy all over her body, starting at her head and running fingers gently down both her sides, under her tummy, and her flanks. She'll think it's a love-fest, when you're actually checking to be sure her skin is healthy and there are no scabs, sores, or ticks. You can finger-comb her at the same time, to check for telltale mats that tend to form in the creases of her legs, or behind her ears. Don't forget to check under her tail to be sure there's no sign of diarrhea, or worm debris.

This home health check not only feels good to your puppy, it helps you become familiar with what's normal for her. Any change in the status quo will alert you. That's the time to contact your veterinarian for an expert opinion and diagnosis. She'll be able to tell you what, if anything, needs to be done to address the change.

MEDICATING YOUR PUPPY

There will come times when you need to treat your puppy at home. Never fear, your veterinarian or the technician will be more than happy to demonstrate for you the best way to do this. Puppies who are ill may be sent home from the vets with medicine for you to administer. Well puppies often need preventative treatments—like flea medicine—that should be given at home.

Unfortunately, your pup just won't "open wide" and take her medicine on command. Treating your puppy could be compared to giving medicine to a reluctant four-year-old child. But with children, you can explain what's happening and cajole them into putting up with the process. Puppies won't understand or care why you're trying to give a pill. And the furred baby has needle-sharp teeth she'll use to express her displeasure. She's also tiny, squirmy, and difficult to safely hold.

Safe Puppy Restraints

Any time a puppy must be medicated or needs a dog medical treatment from being injured you may need to know how to restrain a puppy to keep him—or you—from being hurt. It's hard to tell him that you're "pilling" him for his own good, or that he must leave that sore alone or it won't heal. Struggling and getting upset won't help either his emotional or physical state.

Your veterinarian can demonstrate how to use an effective restraint for your individual puppy. Different techniques work best for small- to large-size breeds and the easiest methods employs an extra pair of hands makes medicating go much more smoothly. One of you restrains while the other medicates.

The puppy restraint technique you choose depends on which body part needs attention. For instance, a muzzle wouldn't be appropriate if you needed to treat a wound inside the mouth. Here are some of the most common types of restraints.

- **Hug restraint:** Used to immobilize the abdomen, legs, chest or back for treatment, the hug restraint works best on larger pups over 20 pounds. Bring one arm under and around the puppy's neck in a half-nelson posture, and hug. With the other arm, reach over and around his chest and pull him closer to your chest.
- **Stretch restraint:** Small pups may be restrained most easily against the tabletop or floor by grasping the loose skin at the back of the neck—scruff—with one hand. Capture both hind feet with the other hand. Then gently stretch him out flat. Warning: This restraint technique should not be used with puppies that have prominent eyes, like Pekingese.
- **Kneeling restraint:** This is the best technique for Pekingese and other prominent-eyed dogs, because pressure around their necks may cause prolapsed eyeballs—the eyes pop out of the socket. Kneeling restraint also works very well on any small puppy especially when you must medicate puppies by yourself. Place the pet on the floor between your knees, facing out. Then put one hand on top of the head, and the other beneath his jaw to hold him still.
- **Reclining restraint:** This technique works particularly well on medium to large pups. Place your pet on his side, with the treatment area facing up for easy access. Grasp the ankle of the foreleg that's nearest the ground while pressing your forearm across his shoulders to hold him gently down. Your other hand grasps the ankle of the hind leg that's against the ground while pressing that forearm across his hips.
- **Muzzle:** Frazzled doggy nerves or a painful touch may prompt the most loving puppy to snap in reflex. A muzzle gently holds the dog's mouth closed so he can't bite. A variety of commercial muzzles are available from pet supply stores that fit large to small, sharp- to snub-nosed dogs. You can also make your own muzzle with a length of soft

cloth, roll gauze, or even length of pantyhose. Tie a loop in the material and slip it around the pup's nose—you may need someone to help you steady his head. Snug the knot over the top of his nose, then bring the ends down underneath and tie a second knot below his chin. Finally, draw the ends back behind his neck and tie in a bow behind his ears.

- **Collar restraint:** Commercial cone-shaped collars that surround the pet's neck like the elaborate ruff of an Elizabethan noble are called Elizabethan collars. They come in a variety of sizes to fit any pet. However, some dogs strenuously object to wearing these collars because they have trouble eating or navigating with them on. Newer alternatives are softer versions, inflatable styles, or designed similar to the stiff cervical collars for people to wear after neck injuries. These collars are used to prevent dogs from pawing head wounds or from chewing body injuries. They are available at most pet supply stores or from your veterinarian.

- **Body restraints**: To protect shoulder and chest areas, fit the puppy with a tee shirt—his front legs go through the arms, his head through the neck, and the loose end is safety-pinned behind his rear legs beneath the tail. For body area protection, stand your pet on a towel or sheet, mark the positions of his feet on the material, and cut out holes in these places. Then put him back on the cloth with his feet through the openings. Pull it up over his legs, and secure over his back with safety pins.

In the best of all possible worlds, your puppy won't ever need to be restrained. If you know long enough in advance that medication is necessary, you can use clicker training to each your puppy to hold still, offer a paw for treatment, or open wide for a pill (followed by a treat!). But it's best to be prepared to know how to properly use restraint so that neither one of you will suffer any more angst than necessary.

Taking Puppy Temperature

Your puppy's temperature refers to the body's warmth as measured by a thermometer. An adult dog's normal body temperature ranges from 99 to 102.5 degrees. But a newborn puppy can't regulate body temperature. Without Mom-Dog's warmth, the pup's temperature may fall between 92 to 97 degrees. A body temperature either higher or lower than these normal ranges can indicate a health problem.

Temperatures higher than normal are referred to as a fever. Fever is the body's normal defense mechanism to fight infection, because a higher than normal body temperature helps fight viruses and bacteria. Fevers associated with infection may be caused by wide variety of illnesses, wounds or infections.

A higher than normal body temperature also can be due to overheating during exercise or to exposure to high temperatures that lead to heatstroke. Low body temperature, termed hypothermia, can develop from shock caused by a sudden injury or to prolonged exposure to cold.

Since normal body temperature varies between individual puppies, it's a good idea to know what constitutes your puppy's "normal." Taking your puppy's temperature at home also gets her used to being handled so that when the veterinarian does this, she won't be scared or object to this normal part of her puppy care routine.

1. Use a rectal thermometer, either digital or bulb, to take your pup's temperature. Most puppies don't mind the procedure, but if yours protests, be gentle and firm to get the job done.
2. For bulb thermometers, shake down the thermometer until it reads about 96 degrees. A digital thermometer won't need this but should be switched on.
3. Use baby oil, mineral oil or petroleum jelly to lubricate the tip.
4. Your pup will need to remain still for at least one minute, so allow her to choose a comfortable standing or reclining position.
5. Use one hand and firmly grasp and lift her tail to expose the anus. Your other hand gently inserts the greased end of the thermometer about one inch into the rectum.
6. Do not release the thermometer while taking the temperature, or it could fall out and in some cases actually be drawn too far into the pup's anus.
7. Speak calmly to your pup and offer a toy or gently stroke her so she won't wiggle away. After the thermometer remains in place for the specified time, remove and wipe clean, and read the temperature.
8. Clean and disinfect the thermometer after each use with alcohol or a comparable disinfectant.

Pilling Puppies

Routine heartworm or flea pills often are flavored so puppies take them like treats. Non-flavored medicines, pilling can be trickier and can risk your fingers. Pilling requires the pup to open his mouth so you can place the capsule or tablet on the back of the tongue and then encourage him to swallow. Bigger puppies are easier to pill because you have a good-size muzzle to grasp. Little pups and short-muzzled breeds can wiggle and require extra hands for them to cooperate.

An extra pair of hands can help with wiggly puppies. One person holds the baby dog while the other opens his mouth and pops in the pill. If you don't have help, wrap the youngster in a blanket with only his head exposed. For larger puppies, kneel on the floor and place the dog between your legs facing out. That way he can't squirm away and you've got two hands to manage his jaws.

Most dogs have incredible jaw strength that makes it difficult to lever the mouth open against their will. You might be able to force a puppy's mouth open but could easily hurt him. Instead, prompt the pup to open wide on his own.

1. Place the palm of one hand over the pup's face and muzzle so that the thumb on one side and middle finger on the other fit behind the upper canine (long) tooth on each side.
2. Tilt his head back so he's looking at the ceiling.
3. Gently press the pup's lips against his teeth to encourage him to open his mouth. Or, slip one finger inside his mouth and gently press the roof of his mouth and he'll open wide.
4. Then use your other hand to push the pill to the back of his tongue, quickly close his mouth, and stroke his throat until he swallows.
5. Have a squirt bottle of water handy to give him a quick drink afterwards so you're sure the pill goes down and doesn't stick in his throat.
6. A pill syringe available at most pet supply stores works well for some owners who don't want to risk putting their fingers in the pup's mouth. Your veterinarian can demonstrate its safe use so you won't hurt the back of your dog's throat.
7. Hiding medication in treats works very well with dogs, who tend to gulp food whole. Check with your veterinarian first, though, because some drugs should not be mixed with certain foods.
8. Use a hunk of cheese, a dab of peanut butter, or anything you're sure the dog will eat in one swallow.
9. Mixing medicine in the whole bowl of food isn't recommended, because the pup may not be properly medicated if he doesn't eat it all at once. Some smart canines learn to eat around the medicine.
10. Unless the medication is a time-release treatment that's supposed to dissolve slowly, the pill can be crushed and mixed into a strong-tasting treat or a dab of canned food. Use the bowl of a spoon to powder the pill and combine with a mouthful of canned food.
11. If you're hiding medication in treats, be sure to offer them before meals to ensure every bit is eaten. Your veterinarian or pharmacist may also be able to compound the medication into a tasty form the puppy takes like a treat.
12. Following any treatment, reward your puppy with positive attention. Give him lots of praise and play his favorite game so that he associates the activity with good things for him. That should help make the medication go down even more smoothly in the future.

Liquid Medicine

Puppies more readily accept oral medicines that are liquid. They also tend to be much easier to give to the baby, because you don't need to lever her mouth open. All you need is a medicine syringe or eyedropper, and the medicine.

Medicine syringes are available from your veterinarian. Often, liquid medicine comes with its own applicator, but the syringe—minus the needle, of course—should be a part of every pet owner's home medicine chest. They are easy to use, measure the dose accurately, and are well accepted by puppies and adult dogs alike.

Draw up the prescribed amount in the eyedropper or syringe. As with pilling, place the palm of one hand over your puppy's head to hold her still, and tip her head to the ceiling. Insert the end of the applicator into the corner of the puppy's mouth, between her lips. Then squirt the medicine into her cheek. Withdraw the syringe, and hold her mouth closed until you see her swallow.

After you treat your puppy and he's been a good boy and taken his medicine like a grown up dog, don't forget to praise him. When you associate the treatment with something he likes—such as a special treat, praise or a favorite game—your puppy better tolerates medication. And puppies who don't fight and get upset over treatment get well faster.

Ear Treatments

The key to ear treatments is hanging on to the puppy, and not allowing her to shake until you're finished. Otherwise, you'll end up with the medicine sprayed all over you, rather than inside her ear where it belongs. It's a good idea to wear an old shirt when you must treat puppy ears. Despite your best efforts, she's likely to nail you with at least some of the medicine when she shakes her head after you're finished.

There is a trick to safely cleaning a pet's ears. Care must be taken not to damage the fragile eardrum, and using Q-tips can be dangerous for that reason. Your veterinarian will demonstrate how to use these cotton swabs, if that's necessary to the treatment.

Most times, though, medicated drops or ointments are prescribed. Dripping two or three drops of the medicine or ointment into the ear may be all that's required. Tip the baby's head so the appropriate ear faces the ceiling, and let gravity do your work. Once the medicine is applied, gently massage the base of the puppy's ear. That spreads the ointment or drops deeper into the canal where it can do the most good. Often, the puppy will appreciate this massage, because it helps scratch a deep-seated itch she can't reach.

When the veterinarian has diagnosed ear mites, you'll need to clean the ears thoroughly, once a week for at least three to four weeks. That gets rid of any hatching mites that were missed during the first treatments. Commercial over-the-counter products are available, or your vet may prescribe a mite treatment.

Hold the puppy's head steady, apply several drops of the liquid mite medicine into the ear, and massage the base of the ear. Hang onto the tip of the ear with a firm grasp to keep her from shaking her head too early. Massaging the ear base helps flush mite debris out of the canal, so you can wipe it away with a cotton ball. It may take two or three sessions on each ear to get them clean.

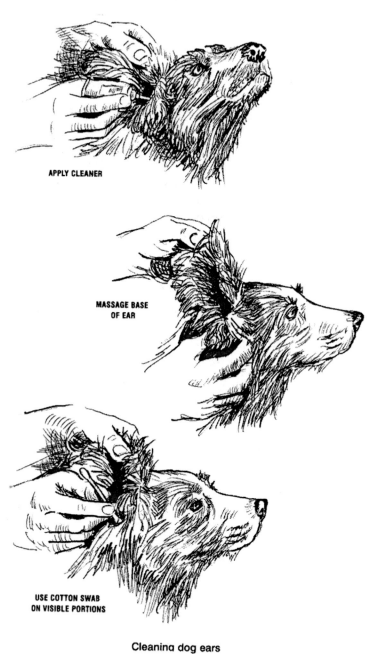

APPLY CLEANER

MASSAGE BASE OF EAR

USE COTTON SWAB ON VISIBLE PORTIONS

Cleaning dog ears

Holistic veterinarians advise that any type of oil—from mineral oil or baby oil, to vegetable oil—will work to cure ear mites. Oil suffocates the bugs. Of course, you must first be sure of the diagnosis. Then you can safely use something like olive oil to soothe the sore ear and kill the mites. Remember to treat the ears for at least three weeks to get all the bugs.

WARNING!

Ear infections or mite infestations can make the ears so sore and itchy the puppy may not allow you to touch her ears. Other times, she may damage herself with scratching until the ears bleed, or the ear flap swells like a tiny balloon. That's called an "aural hematoma." In these instances it's best to have the veterinarian provide the treatment she needs.

Eye Treatments

In most cases, you can gently tip the puppy's head toward the ceiling, and drip the liquid medicine into each eye. Sometimes, when it's an ointment, you'll need to apply it very carefully to keep from poking her.

A puppy face usually is small enough that you can hold her with one hand and gently open her eye at the same time. Carefully pull down her lower eyelid, squeeze the prescribed amount of ointment into the cupped tissue, and then close her eye. The natural motion of blinking will spread the ointment where it needs to go.

It's important to restrain your puppy while you medicate her, to ensure she's not hurt accidentally when she wiggles. If you don't have an extra person around to lend a hand, you can often restrain the baby with the Knee Restraint. Get down on the floor and place your puppy between your knees as you kneel above her. She should face out. You control the exit, and she can't back up anywhere to get away. This trick also leaves your hands free to medicate her ears or eyes, or give a pill.

And remember, whenever not contraindicated by her health, always follow a treatment with a tasty treat. That associates the unpleasantness with good things, so the puppy will be less likely to argue about subsequent treatments.

Skin Treatments

Putting medicine on the skin is probably the easiest treatment of all. The problem, though, is that puppies want to lick off the medicine as soon as it's applied. After you apply the ointment, salve or other medicine to the skin problem, distract the puppy with a game for ten to fifteen minutes, to allow the medicine to be absorbed.

An Elizabethan collar fits around the baby's neck, and extends several inches like the stand-up stiff decorative collars popularized by the English queen of the same name. This collar restraint keeps the dog from reaching her body with tongue or teeth, or from scratching her ears or face with a paw. Elizabethan collars are available from pet supply stores or the vet's office.

Elizabethan collars may not come in the right size for a tiny puppy, though. You can make a homemade "body suit" using a baby T-shirt that will protect skin sores from industrious licking. The puppy's head goes through the neck, her front feet fit through the armholes, and then safety-pin the excess under her tail.

PUPPY HEALTH CONCERNS

It's never a good idea to try to diagnose and treat a serious puppy health problem yourself. There's a reason that veterinarians go to school for 8 to 10 years to get a degree. They also have all kinds of tests to confirm their suspicions when a particular sign of illness points to a problem.

It is important, though, that you become familiar with some of the most common health problems your puppy might face. Most are easy to prevent. Many are treatable, particularly when you catch them early. And there are a few that have home treatment options, especially once your vet has suggested it's okay to do this.

BLOAT

Bloat in puppies goes beyond that cute pot-belly tummy common to youngsters after a full meal. A bloated stomach in puppies also may be a sign of intestinal worms. But the technical term for bloat--gastric dilation-volvulus (GDV)--is a leading cause of death among large and giant breed puppies.

Bloat develops from air that rapidly accumulates in the stomach until the puppy's tummy twists. That traps stomach contents that can't be expelled either by vomiting, burping, or traveling into the intestines.

Bloat also refers to stomach distention with or without the stomach rotation. The twist cuts off blood circulation to the stomach and spleen, and compresses a vein that returns blood to the heart, severely restricting normal blood circulation. That can cause death within hours.

Large and giant breeds have a threefold greater risk than mixed breeds. Nobody really knows for sure why the stomach ultimately rotates. Great Danes have the highest incidence with about a 40 percent chance they'll have an episode before they reach age seven. Dogs that are underweight also have an increased risk.

Dr. Larry Glickman of Purdue University conducted a five-year study of nearly 2,000 show dogs, funded by a grant from the AKC Canine Health Foundation, Morris Animal Foundation, and eleven dog breed clubs. His work suggested that deep narrow-chest conformation of certain breeds creates a more acute angle where the esophagus connects with the stomach. That may be what predisposes them to accumulate gas in their stomach.

But that alone isn't the cause of bloat. The puppy personality also influences risk. Anxious, irritable, nervous, and aggressive characteristics seem to make dogs predisposed. Some research indicates nervous dogs have a twelve times higher risk for bloat than calm, happy dogs. That means proper puppy socialization that reduces nerves and potential for fear can help prevent bloat as your puppy grows up. Dr. Glickman's study also confirmed that bloat risk increased with advancing age, larger breed size, greater chest depth/width ratio and having a sibling, offspring or parent with a history of bloat.

Symptoms Of Bloat

The pain of the swollen tummy makes affected pups act restless within just a few hours of eating. They'll whine and cry, get up and lie down again, and pace in an effort to get comfortable. The dog may strain to vomit or defecate but can't. You'll notice the stomach swells and becomes painful. Finally you'll see signs of shock—pale gums, irregular or shallow breathing, rapid heartbeat—followed by collapse and death.

Treatment sounds simple. The puppy's distended tummy is decompressed by the veterinarian passing a stomach tube down the throat. That allows the gas and stomach contents to empty. Early treatment is key to increase the chance for survival. A twisted stomach requires surgery to fix, though. And treatment for the shock also is important if your puppy is to survive.

Although bloat can't be completely prevented, predisposing factors can be reduced, particularly with large and giant dog breeds. Even when the stomach decompresses by stomach tube without surgery, experts recommend gastropexy surgery, which fixes the stomach to the body wall so it can't twist. That prevents a recurrence of the condition in more than 90 percent of cases.

Gastropexy surgery may be recommended as preventative, particularly in the Great Danes or other pups that have a family history of bloat. It can be done at the same time as spay or neuter surgery. Laproscopic surgery techniques can make the procedure much less invasive and reduce recovery time. Basically, gastropexy intentionally creates a scar that when it heals fixes the stomach to the body wall.

Dr. Glickman's study showed that limiting water and exercise before and after meals, commonly recommended in the past, in fact did not reduce the incidence of bloat. Another recommendation—-raising the food bowl—actually increased the risk of bloat by about 200 percent!

Multiple meal feedings of smaller quantities is a good idea, though. Don't give pups a bucket of water they can bury their head in and suck down five gallons at one go.

Eating too fast also increases risk, and to slow the rate of gulping, researchers recommend placing a heavy chain with large links in the bowl with the food.

That forces the dog to slow down to eat around the chain. Feeding your puppy with puzzle toys also forces them to slow down and not gulp food.

CORONAVIRUS

Canine coronavirus (CCV) is a highly contagious gastrointestinal disease that causes vomiting and diarrhea. It was first identified in 1971 in a group of military dogs in Germany. The virus has since been found in Europe, North America and Australia and occurs throughout the world.

Coronaviruses occur in all kinds of animals and often look similar or cause similar signs. For instance, the canine coronavirus is closely related to the feline forms that cause feline enteric disease and notably sometimes mutates into feline infectious peritonitis. However, CCV causes disease *only in wild and domestic dogs,* including coyotes, wolves and foxes.

All dogs are susceptible, but the signs are most severe in puppies, and may develop suddenly. Studies have shown that more than 25 percent of pet dogs have been exposed to CCV. The disease by itself is rarely fatal, and often is a mild disease with sporadic symptoms that you may not even notice.

But CCV can prove deadly when the puppy is already infected with intestinal parasites that compromise his health. In particular, dogs infected with both CCV and canine parvovirus at the same time have up to a 90 percent death rate.

Dogs usually are infected through contact with sick dogs or their droppings. A stressed pup may have reduced resistance to infection. The virus can remain in a recovered dog's body and continue to be shed for up to six months, so even well pups could continue to spread the infection.

Puppies explore their world by sniffing everything, and then tend to lick their nose, and that's a prime way for them to become infected. Once virus is swallowed, infection develops within one to three days. Signs vary with adult dogs perhaps showing only vomiting one time (if at all), or a sudden bout of explosive diarrhea--typically yellow-green to orange liquid. Many adult dogs will show no signs, while others become rapidly sick and die. Most cases are seen in kennel situations.

Early signs include loss of appetite, rarely fever, and more often vomiting and depression. This is followed by loose to liquid diarrhea which may contain blood or mucus, and has a characteristic foul odor. In puppies, life-threatening dehydration can develop quickly.

CCV infects a specific part of the lining of the small intestine. The small intestine is lined with hill-shaped structures called *villi* that are covered with tiny hair-like projections (microvilli) which absorb nutrients. CCV infects the "hilltops" of the villi, compromising the body's ability to process food.

The "valley" portion which contain microvilli-producing crypt cells can completely replace the tips about every three or four days. For that reason, the virus tends to produce only a mild to moderate, usually self-limiting disease. In most cases, dogs will recover within seven to ten days. Some dogs may relapse three or four weeks following apparent recovery.

Diagnosis is made on the basis of symptoms. However, since vomiting and diarrhea can also point to other diseases, a definitive test may require further tests such as serum (blood) tests or antibody tests. There is no specific treatment for CCV, but supportive care helps speed recovery.

Adult dogs may not need medication but puppies require extra attention. Diarrhea in severe cases may continue for nearly two weeks, and soft stool for even longer. Antibiotics may be indicated if secondary infection develops. But treatment is mostly aimed at counteracting dehydration from fluid loss, vomiting, and preventing secondary bacterial infection. Fluid therapy helps combat dehydration that often results from the vomiting and diarrhea, and antibiotics reduce the number of bacteria in the bowel so they do not infect the bloodstream through the compromised bowel lining. Medication is often prescribed to control the diarrhea and vomiting.

Prevention of the disease is best managed by avoiding contact with infected animals and their droppings. Sanitary procedures, such as picking up the yard and kennel area, help a great deal. Preventative vaccinations are available, and may be recommended for high-risk pups such as those exposed through kenneling or dog shows.

When you have more than one dog, be sure to quarantine the sick puppy during treatment and recovery, and take steps to keep him from infecting the other pets. Remember that even once he's gotten well, he may continue to shed infective virus for some time. So keep the other pets from making contact with his stool.

DIARRHEA

Puppies with diarrhea ranks near the top as a common puppy problem, and being familiar with dog diarrhea treatment is important. Mild cases may be treated at home and get better but diarrhea can be deadly for puppies. Diarrhea isn't a disease. It's a sign of illness, and may be caused by many different conditions.

Diarrhea can be associated with viruses such as parvovirus and distemper. It also can be caused by intestinal parasites like whipworms, hookworms; protozoan such as giardia, bacterium like salmonella and E. coli. Some types of intestinal parasites can be very difficult for veterinary tests to detect and it can take many tests over weeks to obtain a diagnosis.

Puppies also may develop diarrhea from a sudden change of diet. The stress of coming to a new home could prompt loose stools. Overfeeding or eating out of the garbage also causes tummy upsets. Without knowing the cause, the right treatment can't be suggested.

WARNING!

Diarrhea can point to conditions that could kill your puppy. Don't wait—the resulting dehydration can make puppies even sicker. See the veterinarian immediately if your puppy's diarrhea:

- Looks black with a tarlike consistency
- Smells extremely foul
- Contains large amounts of red blood
- Diarrhea is accompanied by vomiting, severe pain, fever, appetite loss or lethargy

How to Treat At Home

It's always best to get a vet check first. But your vet may recommend milder forms of diarrhea be treated at home. For instance, if it's been less than three days, the puppy still feels and acts well, and the diarrhea has a pudding like appearance, home care may help.

Until you see the vet, withhold food for 12 to 24 hours. That rests the gut and gives the irritation a chance to heal. Also, if there's nothing going into your pet, there won't be anything to come out. However, don't withhold food any longer than that without advice from your veterinarian.

Make sure that water remains always available. It's very easy for puppies to quickly become dehydrated. A sudden watery diarrhea can spill large amounts of fluid and important minerals out of the body. If your pet acts reluctant to drink, offer him ice cubes to lick. Pedialyte or Gatorade mixed 50/50 with water can counter the dehydration if he'll drink it.

Pepto-Bismol and Kaopectate may help your pup, if he likes the taste (some don't!). Use a needleless syringe or a turkey baster to squirt the medicine into his mouth. Your vet will let you know the proper dosage, if it's appropriate for your pup's situation.

It often takes a couple of days for your puppy's tummy to calm down, and a bland diet can help. Offer plain white rice or macaroni cooked until very soft in plain no-salt chicken broth. Stir in a tablespoon of low fat cottage cheese or plain yogurt for more flavor. Yogurt contains beneficial bacteria, which helps rebalance the disruption caused by the diarrhea. The high fiber of pumpkin can help with either constipation or diarrhea to help normalize the stool.

Although dealing with diarrhea stinks, knowing what to do can ensure that everything comes out all right. Literally.

DISTEMPER

Distemper in puppies, similar to the human measles virus, is the most common canine infectious disease of the nervous system. During their lifetime, most dogs will be exposed to distemper. Puppies have the highest risk. Distemper also infects the wolf, coyote, raccoon, ferret, mink, skunk, otter and weasel. Wild animals keep the virus alive so even effective vaccination for decades hasn't stamped out the disease. Vaccines are not 100 percent effective, either, but provide the best protection for your puppy.

Distemper is highly contagious and often fatal. Virus sheds in the saliva, respiratory secretions, urine and feces. Virus transmits by sneezing and coughing or and by your pup sniffing contaminated objects. Distemper spreads the same way a cold virus spreads in people.

Increased exposure to other dogs raises the risk so pups that are kenneled, regularly boarded, shown in competition or hunted are more susceptible. Pups adopted from stress-filled sources like animal shelters or pet stores most often get sick, especially during the nine-to-twelve-week age. They can look healthy while they incubate the disease—even after vaccination—and become sick once in their new home. Diagnosis typically can be made based on the signs of disease.

Incubation is the time it takes from exposure to the development of signs of disease. Within two days following infection, the virus spreads to lymph nodes and tonsils, and then throughout the body to bone marrow, spleen, and other lymph nodes.

Within five days, virus begins to destroy white blood cells and puppies develop a fever for a day or two. The virus attacks various body tissues, especially cells that line the surfaces of the body like the skin, the eyes, the respiratory and urinary tracts, and the mucus membranes lining the gastrointestinal tract. Virus also infects kidney, liver, spleen, and the brain and spinal cord. Whether or not the infected pup survives depends on the effectiveness of her individual immune system.

By nine to fourteen days following infection, 75 percent of dogs that have competent immune systems will kill the virus and won't become sick. But a young pup won't have a mature immune system. That's why about 85 percent of puppies exposed to the virus when they are less than a week old develop distemper within two to five weeks and die. Older puppies and adult dogs develop fatal disease only about 30 percent of the time.

Pups suffer loss of appetite, yellowish diarrhea, trouble breathing, and central nervous system signs such as seizures, behavior changes, weakness and incoordination. A characteristic thick white to yellow discharge from the eyes and nose often develops and looks like a runny nose from a cold. Puppies don't catch colds like humans do; this is a serious warning of illness.

Infection of the respiratory system prompts puppies to cough and develop pneumonia. Gastrointestinal infection can cause bloody or mucus-filled diarrhea. Infected eyes may ulcerate or even become blind, and the skin (particularly the footpads) may thicken, crack and bleed.

Pups with severe symptoms usually die within three weeks unless hospitalized and given supportive care. Owners can provide some nursing care at home.

Stricken dogs may be given antibiotics to combat infections that result from a suppressed immune system. Fluid therapy and medications help control diarrhea and vomiting to counteract dehydration. Anti-seizure medication may be necessary to control seizures. No single treatment is specific or always effective and it may take ongoing therapy for up to six weeks to conquer the disease.

Each pup responds differently to treatment. For some, symptoms get better and then worsen before recovery. Others show no improvement despite aggressive treatment. Consult with your veterinarian before making the heartbreaking decision to euthanize a sick puppy.

Recovered pups shed the virus for up to 90 days and can infection other healthy dogs. Sick dogs must be quarantined away from healthy animals. The virus can live in a frozen state for many years, thaw out, and still infect your dog. However, it is relatively unstable in hot or dry conditions, and can be killed by most disinfectants such as household bleach.

Dogs that survive infection during puppyhood may suffer enamel hypoplasia—poorly developed tooth enamel that's pitted and discolored. Even dogs that recover from infection may suffer permanent damage to the central nervous system that results in recurrent seizures or palsy for the rest of the dog's life. Protect your puppy with preventive vaccinations as recommended by your veterinarian, and prevent contact with other unvaccinated dogs.

HIP DYSPLASIA

Hip dysplasia in puppies is a progressive, degenerative disease of the hip joints, and is the most common cause of rear-end lameness in dogs. The pelvis cradles the head of the femur (thigh bone) in a cup-like socket of bone that forms the hip. Puppies typically are born normal, but as the puppy matures, the hip joint alignment becomes progressively worse.

Canine hip dysplasia is most often seen in large breeds like German Shepherd Dogs, Saint Bernards, and Greater Swiss Mountain Dogs, but any size dog may be affected and both male and female dogs are affected with equal frequency.

The cause of canine hip dysplasia isn't known. The condition is thought to have a genetic link, and dogs suffering from hip dysplasia should not be bred. Puppies from parents that have hip dysplasia will be two times more likely to develop the disease as puppies born to parents with normal hips. However, even dogs with normal parents can develop hip dysplasia.

As a young pet grows, if the alignment isn't just right due to bone abnormalities or laxity of the ligaments and muscles that hold the joint together, the misalignment causes wear and tear on the joint. Pups suffering from dysplasia typically have a very shallow socket and/or loose muscles and tendons. This allows the joint to work loose, which places abnormal stress and wear on the bones when they rub together, and causes further joint degeneration and pain. Bones respond to stress by growing thicker, which makes the fit even worse. As the dog matures, this damage predisposes to arthritic changes and painful joints.

Signs of Hip Dysplasia

Severe hip dysplasia may become noticeable as early as four months of age, but more typically is seen in the nine to twelve month old pup. The painful condition causes limping and favoring of limbs, difficulty rising, running or jumping. Dysplastic pups may exhibit an odd wavery gait when walking, and "bunny hop" when running which helps minimize joint stress. Stairs can prove a challenge to these dogs, and sore hips may prompt aggression causing the pup to snap or flinch when touched.

However, there are degrees of severity. Some pups may show few to no signs at all and mild cases may go undiagnosed until the dog reaches middle age or older. How quickly or to what extent degeneration occurs is in part determined by the pup's activity level. While healthy, normal hips probably won't be adversely affected by hard work or exuberant play, the dog with mild to moderate hip dysplasia develops more severe signs more quickly when excessive stress is placed on these joints.

Fortunately only a relatively small percentage of pets suffer the severest, crippling form of the disease. Genetics accounts for about 25 percent of a pup's chance for developing hip dysplasia, and even dogs with normal parents can develop the condition. Hip dysplasia is considered "poly-genetic" by veterinarians which means the genetic component of the disease can be influenced by lifestyle, nutrition, weight and activity level.

Outward signs may point to a problem, but for a conclusive diagnosis, X-rays are performed while the puppy is under anesthesia. The puppy is placed on his back and the veterinarian looks for the typical arthritic changes and subluxation (laxness) of the bone fit. Some changes may not be evident until the pup reaches two years old, and experts say there can be great changes from six to nine months to a year.

That's why OFA certification cannot be done prior to age two in dogs. The Orthopedic Foundation for Animals (OFA.org) provides a consulting service for purebred dog owners and breeders. OFA reviews hip X-rays provided by an owner to evaluate the dog's conformation and, when normal, certifies that fact.

PennHip testing method (http://info.antechimagingservices.com/pennhip) developed by Dr. Gail Smith, a veterinary orthopedic specialist at the University of Pennsylvania, also positions the pet on his back, but then fits a metal and acrylic form, called a "distracter," between the animal's hips. This brace positions the pup's rear legs sort of like a frog pose, to replicate what happens when standing. The resulting X-ray helps gauge the pet's laxity score or "distraction index" and allows veterinarians to determine the degree of joint looseness even before bone changes from damage occur. Whatever laxity or looseness they have at four months, they'll have for the rest of their life.

Reputable breeders have dog parents tested prior to breeding to make sure they do not have hip dysplasia and reduce the chance of the condition in puppies. Dogs can be certified free of hip dysplasia by sending appropriate X-rays to either the OFA registry or the PennHip registry. OFA costs less because there's only one X-ray taken. This is evaluated by three radiologists who score the hips fair, good or excellent. PennHip evaluation uses computer analysis to compare the X-rays to all the other dogs of that breed in the registry.

Management for Hip Dysplasia

There is no cure for hip dysplasia. Treatment is aimed at relieving pain and improving joint function. How well treatment works depends on the severity of the problem.

Often, mild to moderate cases of hip dysplasia can be managed with gentle exercise, a healthy diet, and oral pain relievers like buffered aspirin or Rimadyl as prescribed by the veterinarian. Moderate exercise helps maintain and improve the puppy's muscle tone, which alleviates painful wear and tear on the joint.

Studies have also shown that restricting the growth rate of pups during the first four months delays the development and severity of the condition. Therefore, it's important to feed your puppy appropriate foods that promote a moderate growth rate rather than accelerated growth, especially in the high-risk large breeds.

Encourage your dysplastic puppy to take short walks with you. Swimming is ideal exercise, but jumping and prolonged running should be discouraged. Keep him lean; obesity increases joint strain and can make the condition worse. Massage can also help him feel better.

Severe cases of hip dysplasia may benefit from surgery that rebuilds or removes bone, or alters the muscles and tendons to reduce pain. Such procedures may not fully restore joint function, but can give the dog improved movement and improve the pup's long term quality of life.

Triple Pelvic Osteotomy (TPO): When hip dysplasia can be diagnosed early before arthritis develops—ideally between seven to 12 months of age—the state-of-the-art surgical treatment is a triple pelvic osteotomy (TPO).

Osteotomy means cutting the bone, and a TPO procedure cuts the pelvis in three places with a surgical saw in order to rotate the socket to a better angle. Wire and a plate hold the reconfigured pelvis in position with the pelvis socket over the head of the femur, and the plate allows the pet to bear weight during the six weeks needed for the fractures to heal. The pup remains hospitalized for 24 to 48 hours and can then walk out the door.

Most surgeons perform TPO on one hip at a time, with a four to five week period between procedures to allow for healing and rehab. It requires intensive care from pet parents to manage these patients afterward, and the TPO is not cheap and may run about $2000 per hip.

Femoral Head Ostectomy (FHO): Once arthritis has developed, other surgical options offer better results. A femoral head ostectomy (FHO) removes the femoral head, or "ball" of the joint, and prompts the pup's body to create a new "false" joint from fibrous scar tissue. This procedure works best for pups that weigh less than 40 pounds.

Dog Hip Replacement: Hip replacement for dogs has been performed for 25 years, and today it mirrors the procedure done in people. The dog prosthetics are based on prototypes for human hip replacement. Companies like BioMedTrix.com make hip replacements and artificial joints for companion animals—for dogs weighing from three pounds to 170 pound. Human artificial hips, of course, are all nearly the same size.

The orthopedic surgeon removes the socket portion of the pelvis and replaces it with a plastic cup fixed in place with screws or cement. The ball portion of the femur is removed, and the end of the bone is hollowed to accept the titanium stem-and-ball inserted into the opening. The prosthetic is usually cemented in place. Other surgeons use press fits with no cements.

When finished, the dog has a new hip with no cartilage, no pain, and no chance of arthritis. They typically want to walk and bear weight on the new joint the same or next day, since the pain has gone away. Exercise is restricted for six to eight weeks, though, sometimes with rehab depending on the individual pup. Often only one hip replacement provides all they need, because the dog learns to transfer weight to the artificial hip and compensate. The cost varies across the country between $2,000 to $3,000 per hip.

Juvenile Pubic Symphysiodesis (JPS): Dr. Kyle Mathews, an assistant professor of small animal surgery at North Carolina State University's College of Veterinary Medicine, developed another prevention option called Juvenile Pubic Symphysiodesis (JPS) that is less invasive and expensive than standard TPO or hip replacement treatments. Dr. Mathews researched in collaboration with Dr. R. Tass Dueland at the University of Wisconsin.

During a 30-minute procedure, electrocautery via a groin incision heats and fuses the lower pelvic bone. That changes the growth of cells responsible for pelvic bone development. As a result, the pelvis grows at an angle that provides a better fit for the hip. When mature, the hip socket has rotated to a more horizontal angle, making it less likely for the ball on the end of the femur to slip out.

The procedure has the best result when performed on pups 12 to 18 weeks of age. After about 24 weeks of age that growth window has closed and the surgery won't help. That means early diagnosis is vital, either using PennHip or other factors to determine the pup's likelihood of developing hip dysplasia. JPS can be done at the same time as spay or neuter surgery and is much less expensive with very little recovery time compared to TPO or hip replacement procedures.

KENNEL COUGH

Canine infectious tracheobronchitis, generically referred to as kennel cough, is a highly contagious and common condition affecting puppies and adult dogs. The disease causes an inflammation of the dog's larynx, trachea, and bronchi--tubes leading to the lungs.

All dogs are susceptible, but the disease is most common in dogs exposed to crowded conditions found with bad breeders, or boarding kennels, dog shows, or other stressful conditions. Most cases cause only mild disease with signs that tend to be more aggravating to owners than dangerous to the dog. But kennel cough in puppies can cause stunted lung development, and/or develop into life-threatening pneumonia.

The disease can be caused by any one or combination of several different infectious agents. The most common culprits are bacteria called *Bordetella bronchiseptica*, the canine parainfluenza virus, and the canine adenovirus-2 (CAV-2). These agents attach themselves to the delicate hair-like cilia in the dog's trachea, or actually cause the removal of the cilia.

Cilia normally protect the tracheobronchial tract by clearing away irritants like bacteria and other microorganisms with wave-like motions similar to wind moving a grassy field. When they are destroyed—or the agent can't be dislodged from remaining cilia—the protective mechanism breaks down, resulting in further irritation to the puppy's respiratory tract.

Infection spreads through the saliva and nasal secretions. It can happen by direct nose-to-nose contact when your puppy sniffs another infected dog. However, coughing also transmits the agents through the air from one dog to another. Signs develop four to six days following exposure, which is another good reason to quarantine new puppies.

The typical sign of kennel cough is, in fact, a chronic high-pitched honking cough. It can easily be prompted by excitement, drinking, or gentle pressure applied to the base of the puppy's neck. Your puppy tugging at his leash may result in a paroxysm.

Rarely there is also a nasal or eye discharge, and some dogs may suffer a slight fever or loss of appetite. The signs can last from a few days to several weeks.

Your veterinarian diagnoses kennel cough based on the puppy's recent history and clinical signs. For instance, if coughs and also recently was adopted from a shelter or kennel, or spent time boarded at a similar facility, your puppy may in fact suffer from kennel cough.

Kennel cough can develop into a vicious cycle difficult to cure without help from your veterinarian. The infection causes irritation that prompts the cough. But the honking cough causes even more irritation. In most cases, a puppy that has kennel cough won't get better and needs medication to overcome the infection.

Cough suppressants to relieve persistent coughing are very important. Antibiotics may be required when bacterial infections are involved. Anti-inflammatory drugs and bronchodilators that open breathing passages to help the dog breathe may also be prescribed.

LEPTOSPIROSIS

This disease is caused by a *spirochete*, a type of spiral-shaped bacteria. Several varieties can cause leptospirosis in dogs: *canicola, icterohemorrhagiae, grippotyphosa,* and *pomona*. Dogs may be infected when livestock or wild animals pass the agents in their urine, contaminating food, soil or water. Most infections are mild and cause no problem. However, leptospirosis is extremely contagious and can be transmitted from infected dogs to people. Fortunately, canine leptospirosis is relatively uncommon.

The bacterium infects the dog by entering through a break in the skin, or when the dog swallows contaminated water or food. Drinking from standing water in cattle pens or from mud puddles are common routes of infection.

Owners probably won't notice signs of mild disease. But following recovery, untreated dogs can become carriers, and they'll shed bacteria in their urine for as much as a year.

Common symptoms include low-grade fever with mild to moderate listlessness, loss of appetite, and increased thirst and increased urination. Pain in the kidneys causes the dog to walk in a hunched posture. In severe disease, diarrhea and vomiting develop, and mouth ulcers can make eating painful. The dog may have blood-shot eyes or reddened gums, and a brownish coating on the tongue may be seen. Diagnosis can usually be made by the signs themselves, and the disease is confirmed by finding the bacteria in the dog's urine or blood. When diagnosed early and treated aggressively, most dogs recover.

To reduce the chance for human infection, dogs usually must be hospitalized. When the dog returns home, owners should wash their hands thoroughly with soapy warm water after handling the dog. Confine the dog away from where you prepare and eat your meals.

The bacteria are killed and further organ damage arrested using a combination of antibiotic therapies, such as penicillin and streptomycin. Antibiotics may be required for several weeks to ensure all the bacteria are eliminated. Diuretic drugs that promote urination help with the kidney failure. Supportive care such as fluid therapy to control dehydration, along with medication to help minimize vomiting and diarrhea, are often required. If hemorrhage is present, the dog may need blood transfusion.

Vaccinations are available, but they do not combine all agents and it can be difficult to recommend based on geographic region. Only dogs at risk for infection are recommended to receive this *noncore* vaccination. In addition, puppies less than 12 weeks of age may suffer mild-to-severe vaccination reactions, so vaccination is not recommended until after this age.

The best way to prevent leptospirosis in your dog is to prevent her opportunity for infection. Don't allow her to roam unsupervised, and provide fresh drinking water so she's less tempted to drink from contaminated puddles.

LYME DISEASE

Lyme disease is one of the most common tick-borne diseases in dogs and puppies. Youngsters appear to be more susceptible so it's important to protect your puppies from Lyme disease especially if you live in a region known to harbor the Lyme disease tick.

Lyme disease was first identified in 1975 when a cluster of childhood arthritis cases were reported in Lyme, Connecticut. It's caused by a spirochete, a type of bacteria named *Borrelia burgdorferi*, which occurs naturally in white-footed mice and deer. The organism is transmitted to people and dogs by deer ticks.

A number of tick species are able to carry B. Burgdorferi, but the deer tick, *Ixodes scapularis* is the most effective transmitter of the Lyme bacterium. It's found most commonly in the northeastern, north central, and Pacific Coast states.

Deer ticks mature in a two-year cycle, progressing from egg to larvae, nymph and then adult. Adult ticks prefer to feed on deer, but immature stages feed on white-footed mice and sometimes other warm-blooded animals.

The Lyme bacterium makes its home in deer and mice, which don't become sick, but spread the disease to ticks at any stage when they feed on infected blood. Both the nymph and adult tick are able to transmit the disease to people and dogs, and will make do with such victims when a preferred host isn't available.

Human symptoms include a red rash around the tick bite in a kind of "bullseye" pattern. Other early signs involve flu-like symptoms, including fever, headache, stiff joints and swollen lymph nodes. The disease can ultimately cause arthritis, lethargy, heart disorders and damage to the nervous system.

The most common sign of Lyme disease in dogs is a sudden (acute) lameness characterized by limping from painful swollen joints of one or more leg. Other times there may be "shifting leg lameness" where the pup limps on different legs as the discomfort comes and goes.

Affected pups may walk with a hunched back from pain, limp, be sensitive to touch, have difficulty breathing, run a fever, refused to eat, and act depressed. More serious problems happen with some dogs and include kidney damage, heart issues or even neurological problems. Labrador Retrievers, Golden

Retrievers and Bernese Mountain Dogs seem to be affected more often by kidney complications.

Diagnosis is based on the presence of these signs, a history of being in an endemic region, and blood tests as well as urinalysis to look for bacteria, parasites and/or fungi. The fluid in swollen joints may also be tested and X-rays may be indicated. Since arthritis most commonly affects older dogs, a puppy with lameness may be suspected to have Lyme disease. However, some blood tests simply indicate that exposure has taken place and are not a definitive diagnoses because in endemic regions, up to fifty percent of tested dogs will show they have been exposed to the bacterium, yet may show no signs of disease.

A positive reaction to antibiotic therapy is a better confirmation of diagnosis. Pups may refuse to walk, yet within 24 hours of antibiotic treatment appear to be fully recovered. Most dogs show signs of pain relief within three to five days of therapy, and antibiotics are most effective when given soon after onset of the symptoms. Typically the treatment is given for about four weeks. Sadly, some pups continue to show signs of joint pain even after the disease is eliminated, and my require ongoing treatment.

Preventing Lyme Disease

There is a preventative vaccine available for dogs; ask your veterinarian if it is appropriate for your situation. Deer ticks are found in high grass and weeds between the lawn and the woods, and pets and people that roam these areas are more likely to pick up ticks. Use veterinarian-approved tick repellents or insecticides which kills both fleas and ticks.

Prevention also includes removing ticks promptly. The tick must feed 18 to 24 hours before the organisms will be transmitted into the host. When your puppy comes inside, immediately inspect him for ticks, and remove them with tweezers to avoid exposing yourself. People don't become infected from their pets, but you can become sick by touching infected ticks, so wear gloves.

Application of insecticide directly to tick-infested environment is another method of control. However, since the tick's life cycle is two years, one application isn't enough.

People living in endemic areas should wear light-colored clothing, tape socks over pants cuffs, and use insect repellents on clothing and exposed skin when in tick-infested areas. For further information, call the Lyme Disease National Hotline at 1-800-886-LYME.

PARASITES

Puppies are the perfect target for parasites. They're low to the ground like furry dust mops and their fluffy fur is the perfect buggy habitat. Most times, skin parasites are more aggravating than dangerous, but with tiny puppies they can cause serious problems.

EAR MITES are tiny, spider-like critters related to spiders and ticks. *Otodectes cynotis* are a type of arthropod that resembles ticks. They colonize the puppy's ear where they feed on cellular debris and suck lymph from the skin. Only three or four adult mites in the ear can wreak considerable discomfort. Just imagine a tiny mosquito inside your own ear canal biting and making it itch and you'll understand how aggravating this can be to your puppy.

Ear mites are extremely contagious, and also affect cats, rabbits, ferrets and other pets. Puppies often catch ear mites from their mother. If one pet has ear mites, all animals in contact with that pet must be treated to prevent reinfestation. When left untreated, ear mites can lead to infections of the middle and inner ear which can damage hearing or affect balance.

The buggy life cycle takes three weeks. First, the eggs are laid and cemented in place within the ear canal. Eggs incubate only four days, then hatch into six-legged larvae which feed for another three to ten days.

The larvae develop into eight-legged protonymphs, which molt into the deutonymph stage. At this point, the immature deutonymph attaches itself to a mature male ear mite using suckers on the rear legs. If the deutonymph becomes a female adult, fertilization occurs and the female bears eggs.

Even the adult stage of ear mite is so tiny, it's difficult to see. But since all stages other than the eggs feed on your puppy's ears, he's miserable for all three weeks and then the life cycle starts over again. Ear mites are the most common cause of ear inflammation—called otitis. You'll see a brown crumbly debris in the ear canal, and/or crust formation. Mites biting and crawling about inside the ear cause intense itching, and puppies typically shake their heads, dig at their ears, or rub their heads against the floor or furniture and may cry.

Trauma to the ear often results when the pup's efforts to relieve the itch bruises the pinna, the external ear flap. Scratching and head shaking, especially in pendulous-eared breeds like Beagles and Basset Hounds, can cause a kind of blood blister called a hematoma where the pinna swells like a balloon.

Characteristic dark ear debris and behavior signs generally point to ear mites but it's important for the veterinarian to confirm the diagnosis by finding the mite in a sample of ear debris that's examined under the microscope. The parasite is tiny, white, and nearly impossible to see with the naked eye. Never treat your puppy for ear mites until the diagnosis has been confirmed, or you risk masking other ear problems, or complicating their proper diagnosis and treatment.

Your puppy's ears can be so sore that he won't want you or the vet to touch them. In those cases the veterinarian may need to sedate the pup before treating. Follow up treatment at home usually is recommended. Some pets are too difficult for owners to continue treating at home, and in certain instances, an injectable medication may be recommended. Some of the monthly heartworm and flea prevention treatments also prevent ear mites.

Many commercial products are available for treating ear mites. Ask your veterinarian for a recommendation. Once you get a diagnosis of ear mites from the vet, you may want to learn to treat ear mites at home. It involves cleaning the ears and/or treating with a liquid at least twice a week for three weeks or more. Otherwise the ear mite eggs left behind in the ear canal will hatch, and start the process all over again.

Ear mites sometimes travel outside of the ear to other parts of the puppy's body. Resulting sores may resemble an allergy to fleas; the condition is called otodectic mange. When your pup is diagnosed with ear mites, don't neglect the rest of his body. Flea products also kill ear mites, so choose an appropriate product and do whole-body treatments along with ear treatments.

Ear mites infest the environment for several months, and premise control is helpful particularly in homes with many pets. Follow the same procedures and use the same products for premise control of fleas to get rid of ear mites in the environment. Treat your house and yard for at least four weeks; experts suggest treating the environment two weeks beyond the pet's apparent cure.

FLEAS drive your pet nuts and with more than 2,200 species of fleas recognized worldwide, feel comforted that only a handful "bug" dogs in North America. The cat flea most often infests dogs and causes more than itching. Fleas can cause allergies, anemia, and transmit tapeworms as well as the agent that causes cat scratch disease. To pick the best bug weapons, you must first understand the enemy. The adult flea you find crawling through your puppy's fur represents only the tip of the buggy iceberg.

Puppies with fleas become quite itchy. Fleas seem to prefer the back end of dogs, so the pet may chew the flanks and above the tail region. Parting the fur also often reveals "flea dirt"—it looks like tiny black specks caught in fur. This digested blood is flea poop and turns red when placed on a damp cloth.

But with allergic pets, a single flea bite can cause all over itching. These pups become sensitive and react to flea saliva. Products that don't just kill but also repel fleas work best for allergic pups.

Adult fleas don't hop on and off your puppy. They stay there unless involuntarily dislodged, but they represent only five percent of the total flea population. The remaining 95 percent composed of flea eggs, larvae, and pupae lurk in the environment poised to belly up to the furry banquet.

Fleas can lay 20 to 40 eggs per day, and ten female fleas can create almost a quarter of a million different life stages in a month. Newly emerged flea larvae can survive two weeks without a blood meal, and pre-emerged (pupae/cocoon stage) can survive six months without feeding.

Flea products may address the egg, larvae and adult stages, but no insecticide can kill the cocoon stage. You must wait until it hatches to kill it. It takes fourteen to twenty-one days for the lifecycle to be complete.

Fleas hate direct sunlight and prefer outdoor shaded areas with sand, leaves or other debris. So the lifestyle of your puppy determines their exposure. Indoor couch potato pups won't need the same protection as hunting dogs that roam the field. But even pups that visit the yard on leash have enough exposure to warrant flea protection.

Age and health also influence the type of product you should choose. Look at the label to make sure the flea or tick protection says it's safe for your individual pets. Some are not safe for puppies.

While extremes of cold can kill parasites and they remain active only during warm months, owners have trouble predicting and anticipating a weather change that brings out the bugs. The Companion Animal Parasite Council (CAPCvet.org) recommends year-round protection against fleas and ticks.

Flea Treatment, Naturally

The safest and most "natural" flea control technique involves using a flea-comb. Frequent vacuuming of the carpet removes up to 90 percent of flea eggs and 50 percent of larvae. Don't neglect washing pet beds, carriers, blankets, and throw rugs as well as any sofa cushions or other favorite pet resting places.

For outdoor habitats, cut the grass short to allow sunlight to shoo away the bugs. Keeping your pets from problem areas and treating the bug habitats helps reduce the pest population. Nematodes—worms that eat immature fleas—are available from lawn and garden supply outlets.

Bathing puppies can get rid of existing fleas but won't necessarily keep them off. They often are safest for very young pups. Be cautious of so-called "natural" flea products as they may still be dangerous for youngsters. Spray products do a better job and have some residual effect.

But products that contain insect growth regulators (IGRs) are the best choice for premise control because they prevent immature fleas from maturing into biting adults. They typically last a long time with a single application, some as long as seven months.

Modern Pest Advances

IGRs attack insects but not the pet and are one of the safest of the flea ingredients around. For instance, methoprene fools flea larva into thinking it's a larva forever, so it never turns into a biting adult flea. Another early IGR called lufenuron (Program, once monthly pills) inhibits the development of the exoskeleton of the flea and sterilizes the bug so it can't reproduce. Pyriproxifen (Nylar) works like methoprene but with increased potency that also kills flea eggs and larva.

A better understanding of flea biology also helped develop active ingredients that attack the flea nervous system. These include fipronil (Frontline), imadacloprid (Advantage), nitenpyram (Capstar), and selectamin (Revolution) applied as spot-on treatments once a month. Each offers slightly different benefits.

Imidacloprid kills adult fleas and have a month-long effect. Fipronil also kills adult fleas for a month and in addition is labeled to kill ticks. Selamectin protects for a month against a host of pests including fleas, ear mites, heartworms and certain types of ticks. All four of these active ingredients take 24-48 hours to be effective. Nitenpyram, taken as a pill, kills adult fleas that feed on a treated pet within twenty minutes, but is only effective for 24 hours and isn't helpful for flea-allergic animals.

WARNING!

Electronic devises touted to use ultrasonic emissions to repel fleas don't work. Period. Save your money, and your puppy's peace of mind. In controlled studies, these products have been shown to bother the hearing of the pet more than that of the bugs.

Some of the most effective flea and tick products today combine an adulticide to kill adult fleas with an IGR to control the immature bug population. You'll find a fipronil and methoprene combination product that kills fleas and ticks (Frontline Plus), as well as etofenprox partnered with Nylar or methoprene in various over-the-counter spot-on products that help control fleas and ticks. Products that contain imidacloprid with permethrin (K-9 Advantix, dogs only) or spinosad (Comfortis for dogs) also are available. New products appear all the time.

Ask your veterinarian how best to protect your puppy in the bug wars. Some products only are available by prescription. If you choose an over-the-counter product, ensure that you look at the label and follow product instructions to ensure the health and safety of your pets.

MANGE is a generic term that describes a hair loss and skin condition caused by microscopic parasites, called mites that live on or in the skin. Mites are similar to insects, but are actually more closely related to spiders. Ear mites (discussed above) fall into this category.

DEMODICOSIS caused by the demodectic mange mite is not contagious. Puppies are infected the first two or three days after birth through close contact with an infected mother. In normal dogs, a few of these mites may be found in the hair follicles of the face. A normal immune system keeps the mite population in check, so that no disease results and the puppy's hair coat remains normal.

The life cycle of the mite is spent entirely in the host animal, and takes about 20 to 35 days to complete. Spindle-shaped eggs hatch into small, six-legged larvae, which molt into eight-legged nymphs, and then into eight-legged adults.

Demodicosis typically affects puppies three to twelve months old. Usually it is the immune-compromised individual unable to stop mite proliferation that develops disease. Two forms of demodectic mange occur: Localized and Generalized.

The condition always begins as the localized form, which is limited to a spot or two on the face and legs. **Localized demodicosis** is quite common in puppies, and typically is a mild disease that goes away by itself. It typically consists of one to five small, circular, red and scaly areas of hair loss around the eyes and lips, or on the forelegs. The lesions may or may not be itchy. In most cases, the localized form resolves as the dog's immune system matures and gets the bugs under control and rarely recurs.

When the localized form spreads, involving large areas of the body with severe disease, it is termed **generalized demodicosis** and is considered uncommon. Again, it is youngsters that are most commonly affected with generalized demodicosis, usually prior to the age 18 months. Such dogs may have a genetic defect in their immune system.

Any pup may develop the disease, but an inherited predisposition appears to increase the incidence of the disease in the Afghan Hound, American Staffordshire Terrier, Boston Terrier, Boxer, Chihuahua, Chinese Shar-pei, Collie, Dalmatian, Doberman Pinscher, English Bulldog, German Shepherd Dog, Great Dane, Old English Sheepdog, Pit Bull Terrier and Pug.

Generalized demodicosis is a severe disease characterized by massive patchy or generalized hair loss and skin inflammation, often complicated by bacterial infection that may cause the feet to swell. Mites (all stages) may also be found in lymph nodes, intestinal wall, blood, spleen, liver, kidney, bladder, lung, urine, and feces. The skin is red, crusty and warm, and has many pustules. It bleeds easily, becomes very tender, and has a strong "mousy" odor due to bacterial infection on skin. The condition can ultimately kill the puppy.

Diagnosis is based on signs of the disease, and finding the parasite in skin scrapings or biopsies. Occasionally treatment is not necessary for localized demodicosis, which may clears up by itself. Generalized demodicosis requires aggressive therapy, however. Typically, the pup is shaved to offer better access to the skin, and is given weekly or every-other-week whole-body dips with a miticidal preparation prescribed by the veterinarian. Some puppies and breeds are sensitive to these preparations, though, and may suffer side effects such as drowsiness, vomiting, lethargy, and drunken behavior. Use such products only with veterinary supervision.

Antibiotic therapy is required to fight secondary infections. Repeated baths with exfoliating shampoos such as those containing benzoyl peroxide are helpful. Unfortunately, dogs suffering from generalized demodicosis have a guarded prognosis and may never achieve a cure. Euthanasia is sometimes the kindest choice. Because of the potential heritable components involved in this disease, dogs that have suffered generalized demodicosis should not be bred.

SARCOPTIC MANGE, also known as canine scabies, is a parasite disease caused by a circular short-legged microscopic mite that burrows in the skin. Canine scabies can affect any dog regardless of age, breed, or coat type. It's rare for only one dog in a multi-pet home to exhibit clinical signs. It is like ear mites in that it is so contagious that usually if one is affected, all animals are infected.

The female mite burrows into the skin, forms a tunnel, and lays three to five eggs daily. Larvae emerge within another three to eight days, and after hatching, those that migrate across the surface of the skin often will die. But most larva stay in the tunnel or its extensions (called "molting pockets") where they develop into nymphs.

Some nymphs stay in the original tunnels and molting pockets, while others burrow and form new tunnels. A few wander on the skin surface, where the potential for transmission to yet another host becomes possible. The next molt produces adult male and female mites. The cycle from egg to adult takes 17 to 21 days. Adult females live about four to five weeks, while the males die shortly after mating.

The mite is usually transmitted by direct dog-to-dog contact. The mite lives out its entire life cycle on the dog, but mites can survive up to 48 hours off a host. This means your puppy could pick up the mites simply by sleeping on a blanket used by an infested dog, or by sharing grooming tools like brushes.

It takes as little as a week for signs of disease to develop following exposure. The mite prefers sparsely-furred areas of the body, like the hock, elbow, area surrounding the eyes and muzzle, stomach, ear flap and root of the tail. The puppy's back is rarely involved.

Burrowing mites produce intense itching which prompts the infested puppy to chew, scratch, and rub the affected areas. The scratch reflex in affected pups can be easily stimulated; by merely manipulating the pinnae (ear flap) the pup will often kick a hind leg in reaction.

Excessive scratching results in skin inflammation, and red papules and sores and secondary infections often develop. Crusts form on the surface of affected skin, and as the disease intensifies, the skin thickens. Untreated dogs will have dry, deeply wrinkled and thick skin. Damaged skin causes loosened hair to fall out, and the sparseness of hair in turn provides the mite with an even better environment in which to proliferate.

Left untreated, the disease may continue for months to years. Victims with advanced mite infestation become irritable and are restless, and subsequently begin to lose weight. Diagnosis is based on signs of disease, and on finding the mite in microscopic examination of skin scrapings.

Scabies can be difficult to diagnose because the mites can be hard to find; only about 30 percent of canine scabies cases actually locate a mite in skin scrapings. For this reason, the condition may be confused with seborrhea, flea allergy or other skin conditions.

Treatment is often the best diagnosis. Dogs that respond favorably to therapy are deemed to have scabies. Treatment consists of clipping the puppy's fur, bathing with an anti-seborrheic shampoo, and treating with a miticide solution from your veterinarian.

Because the condition is so contagious, all dogs and cats in contact with the affected animal should be treated. Some puppies may be carriers of the mite, without ever showing clinical signs themselves. Several effective scabicides are available from your veterinarian. Multiple treatments over several weeks are generally needed for satisfactory results. Ivermectin, which is the active ingredient in some heartworm preventatives, is also effective against sarcoptic mange.

Secondary infections generally respond to the medicated shampoos and miticidal therapy, so antibiotics are not usually necessary. However, in severe cases of sarcoptic infection, use of concurrent therapy may be warranted. A high quality, well balanced puppy diet for affected pups is important as well.

Canine scabies almost exclusively affects dogs, but can also cause skin disease in cats or in people. It most commonly affects owners who allow the pup to sleep in their bed or who hold the pup a great deal. In people, the mite causes itching and inflammation, and prolonged exposure may produce sores. However, the mite does not reproduce on people, and curing the puppy typically also cures the owner within seven to 28 days following treatment of the affected dog.

Once cured, dogs are not immune to reinfection. Part of the treatment should include disinfection of the dog's bedding, grooming tools, collar, and carriers, to prevent reinfestation. Reduced exposure to other dogs, and vigorous treatment at the earliest warning will keep your puppy free of this disease.

RINGWORM is a fungal parasite (dermatophyte) that causes skin disease in pets and people. The dermatophyte feeds on keratin, the outer dead surface of growing fur, skin and nails. There are many types of dermatophytes, but most cases of canine ringworm are caused by *Microsporum canis*. Another type of ringworm, carried by rodents, may infect pups that dig through rodent burrows. A third kind of ringworm lives in the soil.

Ringworm easily spreads to humans, too, and very young children, older folks, or those with a depressed immune system are most susceptible. In people, ringworm infections spread outward from a central spot. As the inside central sore heals, the "ring" of reddened inflammation surrounding the area gives it a characteristic look and name.

Puppies suffering from ringworm infection won't necessarily show this distinct pattern, though. Sores expand but not in rings, and can look like a variety of other pet skin diseases such as skin allergies.

Typically there is scaling and crusting at the margins of bald patches, with broken or stubbled hair in these areas along with variable itchiness. The dermatophyte lives only on hairs that actively grow. The infected hairs break off, and leave a stubby patchwork fur pattern, and mild to severe crusty sores also can develop.

Some pets become itchy, others do not. The inner hairless regions appear clear as they start to heal. The face, head and forelimbs are the first areas affected, but the fungus potentially can spread and affect the pup's whole body.

All dogs are at risk for ringworm, but the condition is most common in puppies less than a year old, and in older dogs with compromised immune systems. Healthy adult dogs often resist infection because their immune system squelches any exposure. Some healthy pets become "typhoid Mary" carriers, with no health problem themselves, but spread infection to other animals. Once a pet becomes infected, spores contaminate the environment and can remain infective for months.

The condition is transmitted by direct animal-to-animal contact usually from infected hair or skin debris. However, ringworm is also transmissible from contaminated grooming equipment, and can even be picked up from dermatophytes in the environment. If one pet in the house is diagnosed, all should be treated whether showing signs or not. Infected pets should be quarantined from those not showing signs.

Canine ringworm is diagnosed by identification of the fungus. The veterinarian may use a Wood's Lamp to screen suspect cases; about half of *M. canis* cases will "glow" when exposed to its ultraviolet light.

Other times, a skin scraping collects debris from the lesions, which is then examined microscopically. Many cases are identified using a culture test that grows the ringworm fungus. A sample from the lesion is placed in a special medium designed to grow ringworm. It may take up to three weeks before the test indicates a positive result.

In most cases, otherwise healthy dogs self-cure in 60 to 100 days without any treatment at all. However, in severe cases and when the infected pet may expose humans to infection, specific topical or oral antifungal treatment may be recommended. Be cautious about medicating sores with anything prior to veterinary examination. That may interfere with an accurate diagnosis. Treat only after your veterinarian diagnoses the condition, and follow his or her recommendation.

Ringworm fungus is difficult to eradicate. Human products like athlete's foot preparations aren't effective. Neither are captan, or ketoconazole shampoos. The only topical treatment proven to be effective in controlled studies is lime sulfur dip, but it smells like rotten eggs.

Longhaired puppies must be clipped first to reduce the amount of contaminated hair (remember to disinfect the clipper blades afterwards!). Avoid shampooing or scrubbing the pet when you bathe your puppy because that can make the infection worse by breaking off infected hairs and spreading the spores over the body.

A variety of drugs have been used. Ketoconazole (for dogs only!) and itraconazole (Sporanex) for cats probably are most common. The drug griseofulvin (Fulvacin) is also very effective in treating ringworm. Once swallowed, it is incorporated into the growing hair where it slows the growth of the fungus. Your veterinarian will recommend the best choice for your situation.

In addition to treating your puppy, you must clean the environment. That's easier said than done because the ringworm spores are nearly indestructible. Contaminated hairs and skin debris shed into the environment remain infective for over a year, and act as a reservoir for reinfection. Treating the environment helps reduce the numbers of fungal spores, and helps prevent reinfection.

Only concentrated bleach, cancer-causing chemicals, and enilconazole (toxic to cats) have been shown to effectively kill ringworm spores, and none of those options work well in your home. Currently, experts recommend environmental control by daily cleaning of all surfaces using a diluted bleach solution (one part bleach to ten parts water), along with thorough vacuuming.

Get rid of spore reservoirs such as carpet, drapes, pet bedding, and the like. Repeatedly bleach all surfaces with a 1:10 bleach and water solution. High temperature steam also may be effective. Vacuum repeatedly, but remember to toss out the bag every time, or you'll simply spread the spores. Disinfect the vacuum, too, with the bleach and water spray.

Sunlight also kills ringworm spores. Anything that can't be thrown away or bleached can be left outside in the bright sun for a couple of weeks.

You must treat the puppy and continue disinfecting the environment until follow up

TECHNICAL STUFF.
In an otherwise healthy pet, ringworm resolves in about 60 days, even without treatment. Treatment will speed up the recovery, though, and can help prevent reinfection. Ringworm fungus spores can live in the environment for over a year. Confine the ill puppy in one room that is easily cleaned with disinfectants like bleach solutions, to contain the household contamination.

cultures of the pet are negative. In a single pet home, treatment may be needed three to eight weeks and longer in multipet households. When an otherwise healthy pet develops ringworm and is not re-exposed, the lesions typically will self-heal in about three weeks even without medication.

TICKS not only cause skin irritation, they carry other diseases. There are more than 850 types of ticks recognized worldwide but only a few cause problems in pets in North America. The American dog tick and brown dog tick, the black-legged tick and lone-star tick are the most usual culprits. Ticks cause allergies and prompt hot spots, and carry a host of organisms able to transmit such disease as Lyme disease, ehrlichiosis, Rocky Mountain spotted fever, and babesiosis that make pets and people sick.

Ticks are amazingly adaptable, which makes them extremely difficult to control. These spider relatives also spend most of their life cycle in the environment. They can remain dormant for months, and a single female can lay four thousand eggs.

Three-host ticks prefer a different type of animal with each life stage. For instance, the tick that transmits Lyme prefers small rodents as a larvae, larger animals like raccoons, cats and humans as nymphs. And as adults they prefer deer but will settle for cattle, coyotes, dogs and other wildlife. The tick can be infected in either the larval or nymph stage when it bites an infected rodent, and then transmit Lyme to other victims it bites.

Eggs hatch into tiny six-legged larvae that suck blood, drop off the host to molt into eight-legged nymphs, and again seek a blood meal before dropping off the host and molting into the adult stage. Adult ticks usually must feed before mating. You'll see the tick body swell like a leathery balloon, with the head buried beneath the puppy's skin. Often the tick prefers the face and ear regions that are hard for the pet to scratch off, but ticks can be found all over your pet's body.

Ticks thrive in long grass or wooded habitats. So the lifestyle of your puppy determines exposure. Does your pet enjoy an indoor-outdoor lifestyle, or is Fluffy confined to the apartment? If the hunting dog roams the fields, or enjoys outings on leash in the yard, he's at risk for pests. Age and health also influence the type of product you should choose. Look at the label to make sure the tick protection says it's safe for your individual pets. Some are not safe for puppies.

Just handing ticks can spread disease to you, if you see a tick, use gloves or a tissue to remove it. It's even better to use blunt nose tweezers and grasp the tick body close to the puppy's skin and tick mouth parts and pull straight out-- gently and slowly. A tiny bit of flesh nearly always comes away with the tick head. If the head remains buried, don't worry, the skin will either absorb it or eject the foreign matter in a day or two. Flush the tick to get rid of it. Or if you live in a Lyme disease area and need to have the tick analyzed you can place it in a plastic bag with a moistened cotton swab and take to your vet for analysis.

For outdoor habitats, cut the grass short to allow sunlight to shoo away the bugs. Since the Lyme-carrying tick likes mice and deer hosts, clearing away vegetation that attracts these critters also helps eliminate the ticks. Keeping your pets from problem areas and treating the bug habitats helps reduce the pest population. Vacuum inside and wash puppy bedding regularly.

A better understanding of parasite biology also helped develop active ingredients that attack bug nervous system. Many of the current flea products also protect puppies against ticks. Ask your veterinarian how best to protect your puppy in the bug wars.

HEARTWORMS can kill your puppy. Dogs are the natural host for heartworms, which have been a problem at least since 1922 when they were first discovered. Today heartworms are found all over the world. The heartworm *Dirofilaria immitis* belongs to a group of parasites called filarids, and is a type of roundworm. They live in the right heart chambers and pulmonary arteries—the lungs—of infected dogs. As you can imagine, lungs and heart filled with worms can damage and interfere with normal organ function.

An intermediate host, the mosquito, is necessary to transmit the disease. Mosquitoes ingest baby heartworms called *microfilariae* when taking a blood meal from an already infected dog.

The immature parasites spend about three weeks developing inside the mosquito and migrate to the mouthparts of the insect. When the mosquito again takes a blood meal, larvae are deposited upon the skin and gain entrance to the new host's body through the bite wound left by the mosquito.

Once inside the dog's body, the immature heartworm undergoes many more molts and development stages. Finally it migrates to the heart and pulmonary arteries where it matures.

Adult worms can reach four to twelve inches in length. It's not uncommon for infected dogs to carry dozens of worms; more than 250 have been found in a single dog. Adult worms mate and females shed as many as 5000 microfilariae each day into the dog's bloodstream. These microfilariae must be ingested by a mosquito to continue their development, but can remain alive and infective in the dog's bloodstream for up to three years.

The life cycle takes about six to seven months. Puppies can be infected with microfilariae and not show signs of disease even when tested for many months. They might not show symptoms for years, but damage continues as long as they're infected.

All dogs can get the disease, but those exposed more often to mosquitoes. That means outdoor puppies that live near prime mosquito breeding grounds like swamps or standing water are at highest risk.

Heartworms can live in the dog for up to five years. Initially, the dog may not show any ill effects, but symptoms develop and grow worse over time. Common signs are coughing, shortness of breath, and reluctance to exercise. Infected pups may faint after exuberant play or games.

Eventually the dog becomes weak, listless, loses weight, and may cough up blood. Severe signs of late-stage disease are congestive heart failure that may result in sudden collapse and death.

Traditional tests look for microfilariae in the bloodstream. The veterinarian draws a sample of the dog's blood, and looks at it under the microscope to find the baby worms. But modern diagnosis is based on a combination of factors. Rather than visually searching for the microfilaria, blood screening antigen tests can detect the presence of adult female worms even before they've had babies. X-rays and echocardiography examine heart and lung changes, and urinalysis looks for telltale signs of protein.

Dogs fall into four categories once diagnosed. The lowest risk category, Class 1, tend to be young dogs or those with early infections and few symptoms, with no heart damage visible. Moderately affected Class II dogs have mild or intermittent symptoms though still relatively health, but have evidence of heart damage. Class III dogs are severely affected. Class IV Caval Syndrome dogs collapse and will die from their worm-load unless the worms are surgically removed.

Treatment

Heartworm treatment addresses the different life stages of the parasite. The newborn microfilariae swimming in the bloodstream, and the "adolescent" stages migrating through the dog's skin, must be eliminated first. That serves two purposes.

If only the adult worms in the heart are treated these immature parasites would replace them as they mature. Killing these immature parasites first also reduces the numbers of adults that later need to be treated. Some of the monthly preventive medications can be given by the owner at home for two or three months to safely eliminate these immature heartworms before treating the adults.

Once the immature parasites have been treated, the adult worms are killed with a series of two or three treatments of a worm-killing poison called melarsomine dihydrochloride. This substance is related to arsenic and injected in the muscles of the dog's back. This treatment can be hard on even a healthy dog's body. The injection hurts and may require pain medication and follow up care to prevent potential abscess.

The treated dog can go home, but must be confined for at least a month. That allows the dead worms to be absorbed by the body. Exercise could cause dead worm debris to move into the blood stream and cause a blockage—embolism—that damages the lungs or prompt heart failure.

It is much easier and less expensive to prevent heartworm disease in your puppy. According to Dr. Wallace Graham, president of the American Heartworm Society, puppies should begin preventatives at six to eight weeks of age. For pups six months old or older that haven't been on preventative, a heartworm test should be given before starting medication and the dog tested six months later to be sure there are no parasites. Annual tests thereafter ensure your puppy stays healthy. Although some geographic regions like the southern states and Mississippi Delta region have a higher incidence of heartworms, the disease has been found in all fifty states.

There are several heartworm preventive medications available, some in chewable tablets and others combined with flea or other parasite preventive products as a spot-on treatment. Ask your veterinarian to recommend the best option for your puppy.

INTESTINAL PARASITES

INTESTINAL PARASITES can set up colonies in the baby's digestive track and make her very sick. They tend to interfere with the body's ability to properly process food. Consequently, diarrhea is a common sign associated with these parasites.

Many kinds of intestinal parasites affect pets, but the most common complaints for puppies include coccidia and giardia (protozoan), hookworms, roundworms, whipworms and tapeworms. There's no home treatment for these problems, but it's a good idea to be able to recognize the signs so you can get your puppy prompt veterinary care.

COCCIDIA and GIARDIA are primitive single-cell organisms. Coccidia colonize and attack the lining of the puppy's intestines. Infected puppies can develop a fatal diarrhea that's mixed with blood-tinged mucus. Giardia gets in the way of nutrient absorption, so the puppy suffers intermittent soft, smelly diarrhea, poor hair coat from malnutrition, and problems gaining or maintaining weight.

Puppies contract these bugs by swallowing the infective stage of the parasite which is often found in contaminated soil. Drinking from mud puddles may be all it takes to pick up giardia, and puppies can spread it between themselves, too. Diagnosis is made by examining a stool sample under the microscope. Drugs are available to get rid of these parasites. There is also a preventative vaccine for giardia.

HOOKWORMS are a common intestinal parasite of puppies, and grow to less than half an inch long. Depending on the species, they suck blood and/or take bites out of the wall of the dog's small intestine, which can result in severe bleeding. All dogs are susceptible, but puppies are at highest risk.

That's because puppies may not have the immunity to the worms that adult dogs usually develop. Dogs typically become immune to the worms after several bouts of infection; however, immunity doesn't necessarily clear all the parasites, but does help diminish their effects.

Several kinds of hookworms affect dogs. *Ancylostoma caninum* is the most important, and along with *Ancylostoma braziliense* it is found in warm climates. *Uncinaria stenocephala* also occasionally affects dogs, and is found in cool climates. The highest incidence of disease is found in southern states where higher humidity and temperature conditions provide an ideal environment for the parasite.

The adult hookworms mate inside the pup's intestine, and females lay eggs which are passed with the stool. The eggs hatch in about a week, then develop further in the environment into infective larvae. In warm and wet conditions, larvae may live for two months. They prefer sandy soil, but may crawl onto grass seeking a host.

Dogs can be infected in several ways. Swallowing the parasite after sniffing or licking is a common route of infection. Puppies can picks up larvae from soil or feces. Larvae are also able to penetrate the skin directly, most usually the dog's footpads. Infective hookworm larvae are capable of penetrating human skin, causing Cutaneous Larval Migrans in which migrating larvae in the skin cause small, red itchy trails.

Puppies often contract hookworms through trans-mammary infection—by drinking infested mother's milk—or less often, before birth while in the uterus. Dogs also may be infected by eating an infected mouse or cockroach.

After being swallowed or penetrating the skin, it takes about two weeks for the immature worms to migrate into the bloodstream, through the lungs, and into the intestine where they mature. When the dog is older and has an established immunity to the parasite, the larvae may never reach the lungs, and instead remain in arrested development in various tissues throughout the body.

When a dog becomes pregnant, the worms migrate to the mammary glands or, less commonly, the uterus, and subsequently infect puppies before or shortly after birth. In males and non-pregnant females, tissue-infesting larvae may "leak" back into circulation, mature, and become reproducing adults.

The most common clinical sign of infection is blood loss resulting in anemia. When young puppies are exposed to hookworms for the first time, they have no natural defense and can quickly become overwhelmed by a massive infestation. Acute hookworm disease arises suddenly, and in addition to signs of profound anemia, these pups may have a bloody to black tar-like diarrhea. A severe infestation can cause sudden collapse and death.

Adult dogs more typically develop chronic, or ongoing, disease. Dogs that are stressed, malnourished, or in an endemic region are at highest risk, and chronic infection typically is characterized by mild diarrhea or vomiting. But if the dog's immunity fully breaks down, chronic hookworm disease can turn deadly even in adults; signs are similar to the acute infection. This is an emergency situation, which may require hospitalization, a blood transfusion, and supportive care.

Hookworms are diagnosed by finding eggs during microscopic examination of the stool. However, young puppies may suffer acute disease without any eggs being present if the worms are too young to reproduce. Medications are given in doses timed to kill adult worms and maturing larva, but may not clear larvae in arrested development in other tissues. It's important to follow your veterinarian's instructions in treating your puppy to be sure all the worms are eliminated.

Sometimes older dogs with ongoing exposure to the parasite develop a hookworm dermatitis at the site of skin penetration. This most commonly affects the footpads, and is referred to as pododermatitis. The dog's feet become painful, swell, feel hot, and become soft and spongy. Without treatment, the footpads may separate, nails become deformed, and the pads turn dry, thick and cracked. Treatment is the same as for intestinal infestation, but in addition, a medicated paste is applied to affected skin to kill the larvae.

Preventing hookworm infection can be easily done simply by giving a heartworm preventative that also prevents hookworms. Otherwise, female dogs that are to be bred should receive worm medication given prior to the birth will help kill the larvae that may infect her puppies.

The best prevention is to practice good hygiene. Clean up stools promptly from the yard, because it takes six days for larvae to leave the stool. Outdoor exposure has the greatest risk in damp, shaded areas so keep kennel areas dry and clean.

Direct sunlight will help curb the worm population in the environment. Gravel or sandy runs may benefit from applications of rock salt or borax, which will kill the larvae; however, these substances also kill grass. Concrete runs should be washed down with a one percent solution of bleach.

ROUNDWORMS are one the most common intestinal parasites of puppies. Even puppies that come from pristine kennels and environments often develop roundworms because it is found in almost all puppies at birth. There are several types of roundworms, technically called nematodes, but the species *Toxocara canis* most commonly affects dogs. Roundworms are passed in the stool or vomited, and look like masses of spaghetti.

Dogs can become infected in four different ways. Puppies may be infected before they are born when immature worms the mom-dog harbors migrate to the uterus. Puppies may also contract roundworms from nursing the mother's infected milk. The parasite can also be contracted when a puppy or adult dog swallows infective larvae found in the environment, or by eating an infected host like a mouse or bird.

When a puppy swallows infective eggs, the larvae that hatch in the intestines later migrate to the liver and lungs. They are coughed up, and swallowed again, and then mature once they return to the intestines.

The parasites grow into one to seven inch long adult worms. Mature females can lay 200,000 hard-shelled eggs in a single day, which pass with the stool and can live in the environment for months to years. Eggs hatch into infective larvae, completing the cycle.

Older dogs that swallow infective larvae are more resistant to the worms, and their immune system tends to arrest the worm's development. Such larvae simply stop developing, and remain wherever they happen to alight. In other words, they can lodge in the pet's muscles, kidneys, brain, or even the eyes. In male dogs, and females that are spayed or never bred, the larvae remain permanently frozen in time.

But when a female dog becomes pregnant, the same hormones that promote the unborn puppies' development also stimulate the worms to grow. Immature roundworms begin again to migrate and typically cross into the placenta or the mammary glands to infect the puppies before or shortly after birth.

Roundworms are rarely life-threatening, but massive infestations may cause intestinal damage, or rarely bowel obstruction or even rupture. More commonly, roundworms interfere with absorption of puppy food.

Puppies with roundworms often have a potbellied appearance. They may also develop a dull coat since the worms take away nutrients that keep the coat looking healthy. Heavy worm loads can cause diarrhea, or mucus in the stool. Puppy owners typically diagnose the worms themselves when they see the spaghetti-like masses passed in the stool or vomited. Your veterinarian also can diagnose roundworms by examining a sample of the puppy's stool under the microscope and finding the immature eggs, which confirms adult worms are present in the intestines.

Veterinarians usually prescribe medication for roundworms as a matter of course. These treatments are considered safe even in quite young puppies. Many heartworm preventatives also protect against roundworms, since heartworm is a kind of nematode as well. This is important because roundworms can also affect children.

Children may be at risk for infection with *Toxocara canis*, primarily from accidentally ingesting infective stages of the worm. Ewww! But actually, this most commonly occurs when the kids taste or eat contaminated dirt.

The parasite causes a disease in humans called *visceral larva migrans* in which immature worms never reach maturity, but simply migrate throughout the body. Symptoms include fever, anemia, liver enlargement, pneumonia, and other problems. Because of this human risk, the Centers for Disease Control (CDC) recommend that all puppies and their mothers undergo deworming treatments, whether diagnosed with the parasite or not.

These precautions, along with simple sanitation procedures, will protect both puppies and human family members from roundworms. Clean up feces from the puppy's yard at least once a week, and prevent young children from playing in the dog's "toilet area."

TAPEWORMS are ribbon-like flat worms that live in the intestines of puppies. There are several varieties, but *Dipylidium caninum* is seen most often in cats and dogs. While tapeworms are rarely a serious health risk, they can pose nutritional problems interfering with the puppy food your baby dog eats, or other serious health risks. It's important to understand how your puppy contracts tapeworms to know how to get rid of the parasite and prevent its return.

Immature worms must spend developmental time inside an intermediary host before being able to infest your puppy. The flea serves this purpose. If your puppy is infested with fleas, she is also highly likely to have tapeworms. That's why incidence of tapeworms closely parallels the summer months of flea season.

Tapeworm eggs are eaten by the flea larvae, which then develops as the flea itself matures. When a pet nibbles to relieve that itch, she often swallows the flea and infects herself with tapeworm.

The head of the tapeworm, called the scolex or holdfast, is equipped with hooks and suckers that are used to anchor itself to the wall of the small intestine. There is no mouth as such; in fact tapeworms don't even have a digestive system. Instead, nutrients are absorbed through their segmented body.

Called proglottids, these segments are linked together like a chain. The parasite continuously grows new segments that are added from the neck down. Adult worms continue to add segments as long as they live, sometimes attaining lengths of two feet or more composed of hundreds of segments. Can you imagine several two-foot-long tapeworms inside your little puppy? That gives you an idea about the potential for problems.

Each proglottid contains both male and female reproductive organs. When mature, the segment produces up to 200 eggs. Segments furthest from the scolex are most mature, and once "ripe" they are shed from the worm's body, and pass in the puppy's feces.

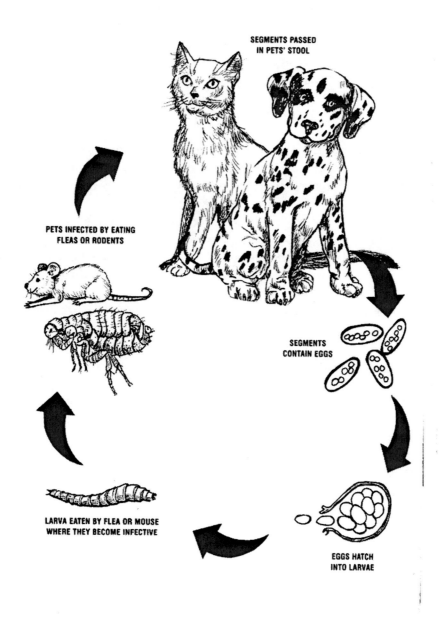

SEGMENTS PASSED IN PETS' STOOL

PETS INFECTED BY EATING FLEAS OR RODENTS

SEGMENTS CONTAIN EGGS

LARVA EATEN BY FLEA OR MOUSE WHERE THEY BECOME INFECTIVE

EGGS HATCH INTO LARVAE

Tapeworm life cycle

Once outside the body, each segment can move independently like tiny inchworms, but when dry they look like grains of rice. Infested pups typically have segments stuck to the hair surrounding the anal area, or in their bedding. Eventually, the segments dry and rupture, releasing the eggs they contain into the environment. The life cycle is complete in two to four weeks.

Tapeworm eggs are passed and shed so sporadically, that your veterinarian examining the pup's stool for telltale evidence may often be inconclusive. It's considered diagnostic to find the segments on the pet.

Tapeworms are rarely a medical problem, and are usually considered an unpleasant annoyance. The moving proglottids may cause irritation to the anal region, which may prompt puppies to excessively lick themselves or "scoot" their rear against the floor or ground.

Without treatment, however, massive tapeworm infestations potentially interfere with digesting food and/or elimination. Puppies may suffer intestinal blockage should too many worms become suspended the length of the intestinal tract.

Also, the hooks of the holdfast can damage the intestinal wall. Diarrhea with mucus and occasionally blood may be signs of tapeworm infestation. Long-term infestation can result in an unkempt, dry-looking coat and generally unhealthy appearance, and reduced energy.

Flea tapeworms are the most common kind of cestodes affecting dogs. However, other species may be contracted if the dog eats wild animals like mice or rabbits. When I was a child, our first Sheltie came from a backyard breeder (yes, we didn't know any better) and was diagnosed with rabbit tapeworms that took forever to eliminate!

There are several safe and highly effective treatments for tapeworms, which may be administered either as a pill or injection. Unless constantly exposed to reinfestation by fleas, a one-dose treatment will eliminate the tapeworms. Controlling fleas is the best way to prevent tapeworm infestation.

WHIPWORMS (*Trichuris vulpis*) are thin, two to three inch long thread-like intestinal parasite worms that narrow at one end like a whip. All dogs are at risk, but puppies may be more profoundly affected.

Dogs contract the parasite by ingesting eggs found in the soil. Eggs can live for five years in the soil of cold climates. Consequently, whipworms may cause more problems in northern states than in southern climes where the eggs are more readily killed.

The eggs hatch and mature in the dog's large intestine in about 70 to 90 days. The parasite feeds on blood by burrowing into the wall of the intestine. In small numbers, whipworms cause few problems. The female worm produces fewer offspring than many other kinds of intestinal parasites, like roundworms so typically the infestation is light.

Puppies infected with whipworms often are also infected with other parasites, such as hookworms, and the combination can be devastating. A heavy worm load of whipworms may cause diarrhea, vomiting, anemia and weight loss, and such dogs typically have a rough coat or "unthrifty" appearance.

Diagnosis is made by finding eggs during microscopic examination of the stool. But dogs may show clinical signs for several weeks before worm eggs will be shed in the stool. Later, eggs may only be shed intermittently, continuing to make diagnosis difficult.

Effective medications are available, but once whipworms are in the environment, infestations can be hard to contain since dogs are often re-infected from egg-contaminated soil. Treatment for three months or longer may be necessary to totally eliminate the infestation.

Good hygiene is the only way to reduce the chance of your dog contracting whipworms. Pick up the yard after your puppy at least weekly, and oftener is much better. Heartworm preventatives can prevent whipworms as well as some other parasites such as fleas.

PARVOVIRUS

Parvovirus, a highly contagious and often lethal virus was first identified in 1978, and is found throughout the world. It is believed that parvo arose as a mutation from wildlife or from the feline parvovirus (feline distemper virus). Parvo also affects coyotes and some other wild canids.

Parvo affects dogs of any age but puppies are the most susceptible with up to a twenty percent mortality rate even in pups that receive treatment. Puppies stressed from fleas or ticks or from tail docking or ear cropping are at highest risk for severe disease. Rottweilers and Doberman Pinschers seem to be more severely affected by parvovirus than other breeds. The highest incidence of parvo occurs in kennels, pet stores, shelters, and poor-quality breeding facilities.

The virus is shed in the droppings of infected dogs for about two weeks, and the disease is spread by direct contact with this infected material. Dogs are usually infected when they swallow the virus after licking contaminated material. Following exposure, symptoms usually occur in five to eleven days.

Symptoms include depression, usually a fever of 104 to 106 degrees, refusal to eat or drink, and severe vomiting along with diarrhea. Vomiting is often the first sign, with diarrhea usually appearing within 24 to 48 hours. Vomit may be clear, yellow or blood-tinged; diarrhea is often bloody, smells rotten, and may have mucus present. Because these signs are not restricted to parvo, diagnosis is only confirmed by finding the virus in the feces.

The acute form of the disease, however, may result in sudden severe stomach pain and depression, followed by shock and sudden death before any other symptom becomes apparent. A long illness is rare; dogs typically either recover quickly, or they die.

Parvovirus causes two forms of disease. Myocarditis affects the heart muscles in young puppies four to eight weeks old, and was more common when the disease first appeared. Affected puppies are infected before birth or shortly thereafter and typically stop nursing, gasp for breath and may cry in distress.

Retching, convulsions and foaming at the nostrils or mouth may occur. Other times, the disease causes a sudden death syndrome that may occur within hours or a few days of onset.

Those pups that survive initial infection may develop congestive heart failure and die weeks to months later. Today, this form is rare because puppies are usually protected by maternal antibodies.

The more common enteric form of parvo affects the intestines. The tonsils are infected first, and from there the virus travels to the lymphatic system which routes it to the bloodstream. Then virus travels throughout the body, ultimately infecting the crypt cells of the intestinal lining.

The small intestine is lined with hill-shaped villi containing tiny hair-like projections called microvilli. It's here the majority of digestive absorption takes place. Crypt cells down in the 'valleys' replace the microvilli every three to four days, and these new microvilli migrate toward the 'hilltops' of the villi. Parvovirus kills the crypt cells that make the nutrient-absorbing microvilli. It takes three to four days for crypt cells to heal, and begin to re-populate the villi. During that time, the puppy's body can't process food and water.

Sick pups die from dehydration, electrolyte imbalance, shock, or secondary infections. Puppies often collapse and die in as little as twelve hours following the onset of symptoms. Immediate veterinary help is critical.

There is no cure or specific treatment for parvovirus, but early detection and treatment increase chance for survival. Therapy is centered upon good nursing and supportive care. Essentially, a sick dog must be kept alive long enough for his own immune system to suppress and clear the virus from his body. Dogs that survive for three to four days following the onset of vomiting and diarrhea generally recover rapidly, and will become immune to the enteric form of the disease.

Food and water are usually withheld for two to four days to give the digestive system a chance to rest. Fluid therapy helps counter the devastating dehydration and returns electrolyte balance to normal. Antibiotics may be administered to fight secondary infection, along with medications to control vomiting and diarrhea. Once vomiting and diarrhea have subsided, water and a bland food like cottage cheese and rice or veterinary prescribed diet are offered in small amounts several times daily. The normal diet is then reintroduced gradually as the dog recovers over the next several days.

Strict isolation and quarantine helps control the spread of disease. Sick dogs should remain isolated for thirty days after recovery and bathed thoroughly before being brought into contact with other dogs.

Parvo can live in the environment for at least five months and sometimes for years. Direct dog-to-dog contact spreads distemper, for example, isn't necessary to spread parvo. Virus can be picked up simply by walking through a yard contaminated with infected feces, or by contact with kennels or other objects that have been contaminated by an infected pet. You could carry the virus to your puppy on your shoes after you've walked through an infective area.

The virus is resistant to most common disinfectants and household detergents. But thorough cleaning with household bleach will kill the virus. A dilution of one part bleach to thirty parts water is recommended.

Protecting puppies with vaccination reduce the risk of your puppy catching the disease. Be sure your puppy stays away from exposure to other dogs until fully protected.

RABIES

Rabies is caused by a bullet-shaped virus that belongs to the family *Rhabdoviridae*. It causes a devastating neurological disease that affects the brain, causing symptoms that are similar to meningitis. Once symptoms develop, the disease is always fatal.

Rabies is an ancient scourge that has been around for centuries, and continues to appear throughout the world. The disease affects all mammals, most commonly wild animal populations, but also afflicts dogs, cats, and people. However, since 1884 when Louis Pasteur developed the first vaccine, rabies has been preventable. Some areas such as Hawaii and Great Britain eliminated the disease using strict quarantine protocols.

Rabies still appears today in pets or people as a result of disease "spillover" from wild animals, and parallels the incidence of rabies in these feral reservoirs. Animals most often associated with the disease include raccoons in the north eastern United States (New York, Connecticut, New Jersey, Maryland and spreading), coyotes and gray foxes in Texas and the southwest, foxes in Alaska and skunks in Kansas. Bats are also often associated with rabies. Pets allowed to roam in these regions are at highest risk for encountering a rabid animal, and getting sick. Consequently, such high-risk pets place owners in danger as well.

Infection requires direct contact with an infected animal. The usual transmission is through a bite that introduces infective saliva into the wound. There, the virus proliferates until it reaches the nerves, which carry the infection to the spinal cord. Ultimately the virus reaches the brain, whereupon symptoms develop.

Puppies allowed outside risk wildlife encounters. It's not just the aggravation of having to remove skunk smell, but could prove deadly. Even puppies confined to yards or the house could be exposed to "high risk" wildlife, which includes the skunk, coyote, fox, raccoon and bat. When sick, animals lose all fear and may wander into fenced yards, through pet doors, down chimneys, or attack litters of puppies or kittens.

Finding the dead animal where pets have access qualifies as exposure. Even when the skunk can't be tested for the disease (too badly decomposed, or too damaged for brain analysis), the law requires it be treated as though rabid. That's because pets can also be exposed by playing with the dead body, or coming in contact with infective material.

Signs of Rabies

Rabies has three recognized states of clinical disease: 1) incubation, 2) clinical signs, and 3) paralysis terminating in death. The incubation period -- the time from exposure (bite) to development of symptoms -- takes 14 days to 24 months to incubate, with an average of three to eight weeks for most species. From the brain, the virus spreads to other tissues, like the salivary glands.

Clinical signs are mild to severe behavior changes. The first symptoms are refusal to eat or drink, and the stricken dog typically seeks solitude. The disease then progresses to one of two forms; paralytic or dumb rabies, and furious rabies.

In the dumb form, dogs act depressed, become insensitive to pain, and develop paralysis of the throat and jaw muscles. It may look like they are choking or have something stuck in their throat as they salivate and drool. Pets with dumb rabies usually fall into a coma and die within three to ten days of initial signs.

Furious rabies is the classic presentation of "mad dog" symptoms. Dogs become extremely vicious and violent, and any noise prompts attack. Such dogs snap and bite at real or imaginary objects, and may roam for miles attacking anything in their path. They lose all fear of natural enemies, and commonly chew or swallow inedible objects like stones or wood. Death occurs four to seven days after onset of clinical signs as a result of progressive paralysis.

The signs and course of rabies in people are similar to animals, and incubation ranges from two weeks to twelve months. There is no cure for rabies. Once signs appear, the mortality rate for the animal or person is virtually 100 percent.

Diagnosis of rabies can only be accomplished by microscopic examination of brain tissue from the suspect animal; this cannot be done while the animal is alive. Wild animals that act suspiciously, or attack humans or pets should be euthanized immediately, and the brain examined for evidence of rabies. Any pet that is bitten by an animal that cannot be tested for the disease should be considered exposed to rabies.

The Law and Rabies

Pets must be protected with rabies vaccination by state law, because they come in such close contact with people and may transmit the virus to humans after being infected by a rabid animal. But each state has established its own rules regarding rabies exposure in pets.

Animals are thought to be infectious only shortly before and during the time they show symptoms. Therefore, a biting animal capable of transmitting disease at the time of the bite will typically develop signs within a ten-day period. For that reason, ten days is the recommended period of quarantine in such cases.

The human risk is so high when handling suspect animals that it's safest that unvaccinated pets exposed to rabies be euthanized, and then tested for the disease. However, some local or state laws may allow an exposed pet to live under stringent quarantine for six months and, if no signs develop, be vaccinated prior to release. Recommendations for pets' current on rabies vaccination that are exposed to the disease include immediate revaccination and strict owner control/observation for not less than 45 days.

Preventing Rabies

Prevent exposure and protect your dog and yourself by restricting roaming. Keeping his rabies vaccination current also protects your puppy from the risk of being euthanized for testing, if he's ever exposed. Any contact with wild animals acting in an abnormal behavior, including stray or feral cats or dogs, increases the risk.

The rabies virus is sensitive to many household detergents and soaps. Should you or your puppy suffer a bite, thoroughly wash the wounds with soap and hot water to kill as much virus as possible, and then consult a doctor and/or veterinarian immediately. The post-exposure vaccine available for people is virtually 100 percent effective when administered in the right period of time.

VOMITING

Vomiting is not a disease but rather a sign of potential problems. Vomiting is the forcible expulsion of the stomach's contents up the dog's throat and out of the mouth. Dogs tend to vomit more readily than almost all other animals.

Vomiting is different than regurgitation, which is a passive process without strong muscle contractions. Regurgitation can occur minutes to hours after your puppy eats his food, and the expelled material is undigested and may even be tube-shaped like the throat. Occasional regurgitation isn't a cause for concern unless it interferes with nutrition and what you feed your puppy. Chronic regurgitation typically is seen in a young puppy that as a result grows very slowly.

In cases of poisoning or swallowing dangerous objects, you may need to induce vomiting. Learning how to make puppies vomit can save his life.

When the "vomit center" of the brain is stimulated, the puppy begins to salivate and swallow repeatedly. Your puppy may seek attention or look anxious. Then, the stomach and abdominal muscles forcibly and repeatedly contract, while at the same time the esophagus relaxes. The puppy extends her neck, opens her mouth and makes a strained gagging sound as the stomach empties.

Vomiting should never be considered normal. Most cases of adult dog vomiting result from gastric irritation due to swallowed grass, eating inedible objects, spoiled or rich food (raiding the garbage, table scraps) or simply eating too much too fast. You can prevent puppies from eating the wrong thing with these puppy-proofing tips. Dogs and puppies also may vomit from motion sickness during car rides.

The most common cause of vomiting in dogs is gluttony. Dogs that gorge their food tend to lose it just as quickly, particularly if they exercise shortly after finishing a meal. This type of vomiting isn't particularly dangerous, but is annoying.

Repeated vomiting, vomiting along with diarrhea, unproductive vomiting, vomiting not associated with eating, and/or the puppy acts like she feels bad before or after the event is a cause for alarm.

Vomiting can be a sign of canine distemper virus or canine parvovirus, which can be prevented by proper vaccinations. In deep chested breeds, unproductive vomiting may be a sign of bloat. If the vomit contains blood or fecal material, if it lasts longer than 24 hours, or if other signs such as diarrhea accompany the vomiting, contact your veterinarian immediately.

Slowing down how fast your puppy eats relieves mealtime vomiting. Feed puppies in separate bowls to cut down on "competition" eating, or place a large non-swallowable ball in the dish so the puppy is forced to eat around it. Meal-feeding several times a day rather than once will also alleviate overeating. A few dogs vomit when they're excited or fearful.

Vomiting that happens only once or twice isn't a cause for concern as long as the puppy acts normal before and after. Rest the digestive tract for 12 to 24 hours or so usually resolves the gastric irritation in older pups and adult dogs. But very young puppies and especially Toy-size breeds shouldn't go without a meal for longer than about six to eight hours, though, so you'll need vet help with tiny pups.

Pick up the food bowl and give only small amounts of water. Vomiting makes pups feel thirsty but drinking can upset the tummy even further. So offer water in a syringe every 15 or 20 minutes, or offer an ice cube for her to lick.

You can safely give Pepto-Bismol to manage doggy vomiting. It coats the stomach wall, soothes the upset and the bismuth absorbs bacterial toxins that prompt vomiting. The dose is about ½ to 1 teaspoon per 5 pounds of body weight up to three times a day.

Vomiting may be a sign of serious illness, though. Even if it's not due to a virus, vomiting for any reason can result in dehydration that can kill puppies very quickly. Anytime your pup vomits three or more times in a single day, or two or more days in a row, you should take her to the vet.

11: First Aid & Common Emergencies

Puppies are not only accident-prone, they are fragile and more likely to become injured. The Christopher Columbus kitties, those with boundless energy and curiosity, are the most likely to get into trouble because of their desire to explore. Also, puppies learn by example and experience. They are innocents when it comes to many dangerous situations and simply don't know any better than to approach a strange animal, dart in front of a car, or fall into the hot tub.

Of course, preventing accidents is the best choice. But if the unthinkable happens, you can save your puppy's life by knowing emergency first aid. You should always follow up with professional veterinary treatment as well. Here are some of the most common emergencies, and what you can do.

Animal Bites

Puppy teeth are like needles, and just playing with the other furry babies can expose your youngster to bites. In nearly all cases, playful bites are inhibited so they don't break the skin.

Worse bites come from adult dogs and cats, particularly those not willing to put up with the puppy's pestering antics. Adult cat teeth are also sharp and make puncture wounds that plant bacteria deep beneath the skin and that can cause infection even when the bite looks minor. Without prompt treatment, a cat bite typically swells and gets hot when it becomes infected and can turn into an abscess.

The most dangerous bites are from dogs. They may not look bad, because the entry wound can be small from the long fang-like canine teeth. But dogs tend to grab and then shake—so the muscle is torn beneath the skin. Even worse, the puppy's internal organs could be bruised or punctured. If your puppy is bitten, here's what to do.

1. Separate the animals by spraying water at them from the hose, or tossing a blanket on top of them. That way you don't risk being bitten.
2. If the wound bleeds, put a soft, absorbent cloth like a towel or washcloth against the bite, and apply firm pressure.
3. When the puppy's abdomen gapes open from a bite, which can happen with dog teeth tears, cover the area with a wet cloth, and hold in place by wrapping Saran wrap all the way around the body.
4. Severe bites may cause the baby to stop breathing. Administer artificial respiration until you can get help, as described below.
5. Finally, bundle the puppy in a soft blanket or towel to keep her warm, and place her in an open box or carrier for the ride to the veterinarian's office.

Artificial Resuscitation

All kinds of puppy accidents may cause her to stop breathing. In these instances, you must immediately breathe for her and try to resuscitate your puppy, or she will die within three to five minutes. Rescue breathing can be performed on the way to the veterinary emergency room—puppies can, and do, survive life-threatening accidents when their people are able to provide rescue breathing. Here's what to do.

1. First, make sure the baby has stopped breathing, by feeling for warm air coming from her mouth and nose, and watching for the rise and fall of her chest. Pets that have stopped breathing will be unconscious, and insensitive to your voice.
2. Cradle your puppy in your lap while another person drives the car to the emergency room. Straighten her neck by lifting the chin so her throat offers a straight shot into her lungs.
3. Mouth-to-mouth breathing won't work. Too much air escapes because you can't seal pet lips with your mouth. Use one hand to close your puppy's mouth.
4. Put your mouth completely over her nose and gently blow—imagine you're puffing breath to inflate a paper bag. Use your other hand to feel her lungs expand. Air will go directly through the nose and into her

lungs when the mouth seals correctly. Don't blow too hard or you could hurt the baby—it doesn't take much breath to do the job.

5. Between breaths, let the air naturally escape out of her lungs before giving the next breath. Give 10 to 15 breaths a minute until she begins breathing on her own or you reach the veterinarian.

Car Accidents

When I worked in veterinary offices as a technician, we abbreviated this as HBC—or "hit-by-car." This kind of trauma can be deadly, and if the puppy is to survive, immediate veterinary emergency care is vital.

Being struck by a car can cause a wide range of damage, from broken bones and bleeding to internal injuries and stopped breathing. Even if the puppy seems okay and walks away, problems can develop from shock or hidden damage within minutes to hours later.

Puppies may be so small that it's nearly impossible to do anything for broken legs—and a fractured leg usually is the least life-threatening of possible injuries. But spinal injury can be devastating, and it's hard to tell how extensive the injuries are without an exam. Here's what to do if your puppy loses a contest with a car:

1. When the puppy has stopped breathing, perform artificial resuscitation, as described previously.
2. Control bleeding by applying direct pressure, as described in Animal Bites.
3. It's important to transport the puppy to the emergency room as soon as possible—but you must move her very carefully to prevent more injuries. To do that, you should slide her—don't lift!—onto a solid, rigid surface. A rigid cookie sheet, breadboard, or even a coffee-table book will work. Place a towel across the puppy's body, and tape over the cloth behind her front legs and in front of the rear ones to hold her secure, so she won't move during transport. If you have nothing else, use a towel or other length of material (perhaps a jacket?), spread on the ground beside the puppy, and slide her onto the fabric. Grasp the four corners, and use as a stretcher.
4. Have somebody call your veterinarian to warn her a HBC case will shortly arrive. Then drive to the emergency room.

Drowning

Puppies and dogs instinctively know how to swim. But they run into trouble if they fall into water and can't get out, and become exhausted. Hot tubs, swimming pools, toilets or—for very small puppies, a water bowl—could cause drowning. You may find your pet floating, or nearby a body of water where she collapsed after dragging herself out.

Drowning causes suffocation—the puppy can't breathe—and she'll quickly fall unconscious. You have a very short time period to give first aid, if she is to be saved. When the water is very cold, you may have an extra few minutes to spare because the low temperature can slow down body function and help protect the puppy brain from damage. Here's what to do if you suspect your puppy has drowned:

1. Grasp her by the hind legs, and hang her upside down. Have a second person pat or thump her briskly on both sides of the chest for ten or fifteen seconds, and shake her a bit. That helps drain away water still in the mouth, windpipe or lungs, and it may be enough to jump-start her breathing again. If it doesn't, begin rescue breathing, as described above.

2. After two or three breaths, make sure her heart is beating by listening to her chest. If there's no heartbeat, start heart compressions (CPR or cardiopulmonary resuscitation). Cradle her chest in your right hand with your thumb over the left side behind her "elbow" (above the heart), and your fingers on the other side. Squeeze rhythmically to compress up to 50 percent. Alternate one to two chest compressions with ten to fifteen breaths a minute.

3. As soon as she starts breathing, dry her off and warm her up. Most pets drown in water colder than their body temperature. Wrap her in a dry towel, and get her to the emergency room.

Electrocution

Puppies love nothing so much as to chew anything that doesn't move faster than they do. Prime targets include lamp and computer cords, spiral telephone lines, and even the lights from holiday decorations. And when a bite penetrates the electrical cord, the puppy risks electrocution.

You'll know your puppy is in trouble if you find her unconscious near an electrical cord. Even if she remains alert, electrocution damages the internal organs. That causes the lungs to fill up with fluid and makes it hard to breathe. Often, the breathing and heartbeat stop. Here's what you should do:

1. Before anything else, shut off the power to that particular outlet. Often the electricity causes the pet to bite down even harder on the electrical cord and not let go. And you can get shocked if you touch a pet that's still in contact with the electricity. If you can't turn off the power, then try to knock the puppy out of contact with the power using a yardstick or the handle of a broom.

2. Once it's safe to handle the baby, check her for breathing. If you hear gurgling sounds, turn her upside down by her hind legs (as in drowning) for ten to fifteen seconds to help clear the lungs.

3. If the puppy has stopped breathing, begin immediate artificial mouth-to-nose respiration, as described previously. Check for a heartbeat, and begin CPR if necessary.
4. Wrap the baby in a warm towel, and get to medical help as soon as possible.

Low Blood Sugar (Hypoglycemia)

Low blood sugar can affect puppies much more often than adult dogs, even when your puppy is healthy, so it's important to learn about low blood sugar symptoms and what to do. The technical term is hypoglycemia. Sugar moves into the cells with the help of insulin, and too much insulin can cause hypoglycemia.

Puppies can develop low blood sugar due to intestinal parasites that compromise digestion. Very small puppies, especially Toy breeds like the Chihuahua or Pomeranian, are so tiny, they have very few fat stores. Fat is body fuel, and when there's not enough, the blood sugar levels fall. Adult pets can make up this difference when their liver churns out the necessary sugar. But immature livers can't manufacture enough necessary sugar and as a result, these tiny pups develop hypoglycemia.

The signs of low blood sugar can be vague. It's important to watch out for them especially if your puppy is a tiny breed that's most susceptible. Without enough sugar, the puppy's heartbeat rate and breathing slows down and that triggers a cascade effect of other symptoms. Be alert for any one or combination of the following signs.

- The puppy acts weak.
- The puppy becomes sleepy.
- The puppy seems disoriented.
- He develops a wobbly "drunk" gait.
- His eyes look 'glassy' and unfocussed.
- The puppy starts to twitch, shake or tremble/shiver.
- His head tilts to one side.
- He develops seizures.
- The puppy falls unconscious and can't be wakened.

Without prompt help and first aid, your puppy could die. But fortunately, when you recognize the signs early in the process, low blood sugar is easy to treat and reverse at home.

In almost all cases, the puppy will respond very quickly to treatment, within five or ten minutes. However, it treatment doesn't reverse the symptoms within this time frame take your puppy to the veterinarian immediately as something else could have caused the signs. Even when your baby dog responds quickly it's a good idea to have the vet check your puppy sometime that day to be sure everything is as it should be.

When you catch the symptoms early and treat with first aid immediately, most puppies are fine. But without prompt help puppies can fall into a coma, and their breathing and/or heartbeat may stop. Refer to the articles on rescue breathing and puppy CPR to save your pet's life.

For All Symptoms. When the blood sugar drops, puppies can't regulate their body temperature. It's important to keep him warm until the glucose level rises enough to burn for energy. Wrap your puppy in a blanket, and snuggle him with a hot water bottle or heating pad. This can also slow down the effects of shock.

For Sleepy/Woozy Behavior. Getting sugar into the puppy will counteract all these symptoms. Often, you'll notice the wooziness when it's been a while since the puppy's last meal. So as soon as you notice puppy woozy behavior, offer him something to eat. Make it something smelly and yummy that you know he'll eagerly snarf up, like a tablespoon or two of canned food.

For Drunk/Shivery Behavior. A highly concentrated sugar source like Karo syrup, pancake syrup or honey can work even more quickly. Just be sure your puppy is still able to swallow before giving him about a teaspoonful of the sugar source. If he's very groggy, offer a bit of water first and if he won't lap it up, give some with a syringe. Check to be sure he swallows, and then offer the syrup. He should be able to lap it up from the spoon.

For Seizures/Unconscious. Refer to the tips outlined in the article about seizures in puppies. Once the seizure has finished, or when the puppy has fallen unconscious, you can still administer a sugar source. He doesn't need to swallow. It will be absorbed directly through the mucus membranes in the puppy's mouth and transferred into the bloodstream. Honey works best for this. Rub the honey on the inside of his lips and gums, and watch for recovery in five to 15 minutes. You can drive your puppy to the vet clinic during this period.

Preventing Low Blood Sugar

When your puppy has suffered from a bout of hypoglycemia, you'll know to be alert for the signs of low blood sugar in the future. You can also take steps to prevent the problem, especially if your puppy is a high-risk pet.

Add two tablespoons Karo syrup to your puppy's water for all day sipping. Be sure to dump out and add fresh each day or the sugar water could grow bacteria.

Schedule several meals every day. Toy breed adults and any young puppy have trouble eating enough food at one setting. So a small meal several times a day helps keep the blood sugar levels normal.

Provide dry food out all the time, in a puzzle toy ball, for intermittent snacking. You can measure this amount, too, and regulate how much the pup gets to help keep him slim, prevent puppy obesity, but provide health blood sugar levels.

Most adult dogs won't have problems with hypoglycemia. However, playing and running too hard without rest can cause low blood sugar even in adults that are not Toy breed dogs. It's up to pet parents to stay watchful and make sure the puppy and maturing dog eat right and maintain healthy food habits.

POISONS

Puppies, like all babies, tend to put things in their mouths—even dangerous substances that can poison them. And puppies are so sensitive, many otherwise safe substances for people or adult dogs are toxic to your baby dog. Often the best way to deal with poisoning is to make your puppy vomit. Here's how.

- First, feed the pup a small meal. This helps dilute the toxin and delay its absorption. Having something of "substance" in the stomach also makes it much easier to induce vomiting.
- Give your pet 3% hydrogen peroxide, one to two teaspoons for every 10 pounds the pup weighs. Squirt to the back of the pet's tongue with an eyedropper, needleless syringe, or turkey baster. The taste and foaming prompts vomiting within five minutes. If it doesn't work the first time, you can repeat two or three times, with five minutes between doses.
- Syrup of Ipecac is effective for dogs. Ipecac takes longer to work than hydrogen peroxide, though, and the dose should only be given once. Give one teaspoon for dogs less than 35 pounds, and up to a tablespoon for larger dogs.
- If you have nothing else available, table salt prompts vomiting after the first or second dose. Give it dry, onto the back of the pet's tongue— one teaspoonful at a time for little pups or a tablespoonful for adult-size pups. Repeat in three minutes if the first dose doesn't work.
- Call the veterinarian for further instructions after the pet has emptied his stomach. If you can't induce vomiting after a couple of tries, prompt veterinary care is even more important.

Swallowed Medicine

The most common puppy poisonings happen when human medicine is swallowed. That can happen accidentally when the baby plays with pill bottles by batting them around and mouthing them. Other times, the wrong dose is given by mistake. And all too often, human medicine like aspirin or Tylenol is given by the owner with the best of intentions, but both are very toxic to puppies.

- If you see your puppy swallow pills she shouldn't, or realize you've given the wrong dose, the best thing to do is to make her vomit, as described.

- When you only suspect your puppy has eaten the wrong medicine, call your veterinarian before anything else. Describe the type of medicine, so she can advise you what best to do. If the puppy vomits, take a sample along with the medicine to the doctor's office so they can analyze the poison and know what antidote is best.

Chocolate and Xylitol Poisoning

Chocolate poisoning usually happens around the holidays—Halloween, Thanksgiving, Christmas, Valentine's Day, Easter—when lots of candy is available. Chocolate is made from the roasted seeds of cocoa plants and contains theobromine, a stimulant related to caffeine, and both are toxic to pets. Eating too much chocolate shifts your puppy's heart into overdrive and can kill him.

Xylitol, an artificial sweetener in chewing gum and many other products, is also toxic to pets. It can cause devastating hypoglycemia (low blood sugar) in as little as 30 minutes after ingestion.

All pets are at risk for sweet poisoning. But puppies get into chocolate most often because of their curious nature and their canine sweet tooth. And their smaller size increases the risk for chocolate and xylitol poisoning even if they munch a small amount.

Milk chocolate usually doesn't cause life-threatening problems because it takes nearly two pounds of milk chocolate to poison a seven-pound puppy. Milk chocolate found in candy bars contains about 42 milligrams of theobromine per ounce. Typically, a toxic dose of milk chocolate is five ounces per pound of body weight. While a bite of chocolate generally isn't a concern, a 10-pound puppy can still get very sick from eating as little as eight ounces of milk chocolate.

Unsweetened baking chocolate is much more dangerous. It contains nearly ten times as much theobromine as milk chocolate, about 450 milligrams of theobromine per ounce. Baking chocolate is used to make truffles, brownies, chocolate cake, and other deserts. A lethal dose of theobromine is .67 to 1.3 ounces of baking chocolate per 2.2 pounds of dog. That means your ten pound puppy can become sick or even die simply by licking off the chocolate frosting on a large cake, swiping a truffle or lapping up your hot cocoa.

The theobromine and caffeine are stimulants that affect the puppy's nervous system, causing hyperactive behavior along with other signs. Poisoned pups may pass large amounts of urine due to the diuretic effect of the drug which also relaxes bladder control. Pups poisoned with chocolate drool, act thirsty, and suffer vomiting and/or have bouts of diarrhea. Even if not life-threatening, the diarrhea and vomiting can leave you with potty accidents to clean up.

If your puppy stops breathing you may need to perform rescue breathing. The drug may either increase the pet's heart rate or cause irregular heartbeat. The signs of poisoning may eventually include muscle spasms or tremors, seizures, coma, and ultimately death.

There is no antidote for chocolate poisoning. Affected dogs are offered supportive treatment from the veterinarian to prevent further absorption of the poison and hasten elimination, along with symptomatic treatment.

Activated charcoal may be administered to help prevent additional absorption of the theobromine into the puppy's system. Signs of shock are addressed with fluid therapy, and seizures, heart irregularities, vomiting and diarrhea are each specifically treated with appropriate medications. The treatment is often prolonged, because the half-life of theobromine—the time it takes the body to eliminate it—is 72 hours in dogs.

If you catch your puppy snacking on such things, induce vomiting as soon as you can to get rid of the poison. Even if you don't see the dirty deed but find suspicious evidence such as chewed up candy wrappers, it's a good idea to get him to purge. Chocolate isn't absorbed very quickly, so making him vomit may be helpful even a couple of hours after ingestion.

But for xylitol toxicity, call your vet if you don't see him eat it but only find evidence. Xylitol poisoning may prompt vomiting, weakness, seizures and coma. It can be dangerous to induce vomiting if the pup acts woozy.

The best way to deal with sweet poison is to prevent the problem from ever happening. Most puppies have a sweet tooth, so keep chocolate out of reach and be especially vigilant around the holidays.

Poisonous Plants

Puppies indulge in recreational chewing a lot and plants often are the target of their teeth. The ASPCA lists poisonous plants, so you know what to avoid. Depending on the plant, you should either offer the puppy water or milk to soothe mouth or stomach irritation, or induce vomiting (as described above). It's a good idea to contact your veterinarian or poison control center for specific instructions. You should also keep handy the telephone numbers of both your local and the ASPCA National Animal Poison Control Center (1-888-426-4435).

Induce Vomiting: Crown of Thorns, English Ivy, Chinaberry, Foxglove, Holly, Larkspur, Lily, Lily of the Valley, Mistletoe, Monkshood, Morning Glory, Oleander, Periwinkle

DO NOT Induce Vomiting: Caladium, Dieffenbachia, Philodendron, Jerusalem Cherry, Potato (green parts and eyes), Mother-In-Law Plant, Nightshade. Keep airway open, CPR if necessary, offer milk or water to wash mouth.

DO NOT Induce Vomiting: Azalea, Daffodil, Tulip, Wisteria Bulbs. Give water and/or milk to wash stomach, dilute poison and coat stomach.

Heatstroke

Normal puppy body temperature ranges from about 100 to 102.5 degrees. Dogs pant to cool off when it's hot but that's not very effective. And when the outside temperature is the same or warmer than their body temperature, they can overheat with devastating results. Usually, heatstroke happens when the puppy has no access to shade to get out of the sun, is trapped in a closed car in the sun, and/or has no cool water to drink. Puppies can also suffer heatstroke, as well as body trauma and head injuries, if they get shut in the hot clothes dryer.

Body temperature between 104 to 106 degrees, with bright red gums and tongue, sticky saliva, and panting indicate mild heatstroke. Body temperatures over 106 are a symptom of severe heatstroke that can kill—the gums turn pale, the puppy acts weak or dizzy, and can develop a bloody nose, and bloody vomiting or diarrhea. You must give immediate first aid to save the baby's life.

- For mild heatstroke, offer the puppy cool water to drink, and put the baby in front of the air conditioning or a fan. Usually, mild heatstroke victims recover pretty quickly when the outside temperature becomes lower than their body.
- Severe heatstroke requires an immediate cool (not cold!) water bath. Continue to monitor the puppy's body temperature, until it falls to 106 or below. Then get the puppy to the veterinarian for further treatment.

Hypothermia

Cold temperature can be as dangerous as hot weather. Adult dogs that have full coats of fur are better able to protect themselves from cold, but very young puppies have trouble regulating their body temperature and keeping warm. As the body temperature falls, her breathing and heartbeat slows down, she shivers, and acts sleepy. And with severe hypothermia, she can lose consciousness, and die. Here's what to do to save your puppy's life.

- As long as the puppy still shivers, her body will try to warm itself up. Simply wrap the baby up in a warm blanket and set her in front of the heat vent. You can offer her some warm chicken broth to help warm her up from the inside. If you're outside without access to warmth, put the puppy inside your clothes so your own body temperature warms her up.
- The shiver reflex stops when the body temperature drops too far. You'll need veterinary help to warm up the baby when this happens. But for the trip to the vet, keep her as warm as possible with a warm blanket, and a hot water bottle wrapped in a towel cuddled to her tummy.

Swallowed Objects

Puppies explore their world by mouthing, tasting, and chewing and as a result, swallowed objects get them into trouble. Puppies may gulp some things accidentally when a piece of a toy breaks off. Other dangerous objects prove too tempting--used tampons, and even grease-smeared foil proves irresistible to puppies who troll the waste baskets for scraps. Foreign body obstruction in puppies can be a medical emergency that costs you money and could cost your puppy his life.

Whole toys or parts of toys, jewelry, coins, pins, erasers, and paper clips are often swallowed. String, thread (with or without the needle), fishing hooks and lines, Christmas tree tinsel, and yarn are extremely dangerous. String from turkey roasts is particularly appealing so watch out for those holiday food hazards. And for puppies able to crunch up the object, pieces of wood or bone prove hazardous. Even too much of a rawhide chew can stop up his innards. Puppies may even eat rocks.

If the item was swallowed within two hours it's probably still in the stomach. If the object isn't sharp, feed your pet a small meal first, and then induce vomiting. The food helps cushion the object and protect the tummy, and also pets vomit more easily if the stomach is full. If he won't vomit, you'll need to see a veterinarian.

For sharp objects go to the vet immediately. It could cause as much damage coming back up if the puppy vomits.

WARNING!
Never pull on the visible end of string--either out the mouth or hanging out the puppy's rectum. String and thread is often attached to a needle or fishhook that's embedded in tissue further down the digestive tract. Pulling the string at your end could further injure the intestines, and kill the dog.

After two hours, the object will have passed into the intestines and vomiting won't help. Most objects small enough to pass through the digestive system may be eliminated with the feces and cause no problems. Feed a bulky meal of dry food to cushion stones or other heavy objects, and help them move on out. Food also turns on the digestive juices, which can help soften wads of rawhide treats, so they pass more readily. In most cases as long as it is small enough, objects pass harmlessly through the body and end up on the lawn. Monitor your puppy's productivity. Use a disposable popsicle stick or plastic knife to chop up and search through the puppy droppings for the object.

The exception to allowing small objects pass are swallowed metal objects like coins or batteries. DON'T WAIT, get your puppy seen immediately. Stomach acids interact with these metal objects and cause zinc or lead poisoning. String is another dangerous object when swallowed and requires you to seek professional help.

If you've seen the pet swallow something he shouldn't but it doesn't pass, or the puppy begins vomiting, retching without result, won't eat, looks or behaves distressed, or coughs repeatedly, seek help immediately. Any object, even tiny ones, potentially may lodge in and block the intestinal tract.

Diagnosis can be based seeing the puppy swallow something or based on symptoms. It's generally confirmed by X-rays or other diagnostics like an endoscope to determine the exact location and size of the blockage, and sometimes to identify the object itself. Specific signs depend on where the blockage is located and the type of object.

An object caught in the stomach or intestines causes vomiting which may come and go for days or weeks if the blockage is not complete and food can pass around it.

Complete blockage is a medical emergency that results in a bloated, painful stomach with sudden, constant vomiting. The dog refuses food, and immediately throws up anything she drinks.

Signs of zinc toxicity (from coins) include pale gums, bloody urine, jaundice—a yellow tinge to the whites of the eyes or inside the ears—along with vomiting, diarrhea, and refusal to eat. Lead poisoning from batteries can also cause teeth grinding, seizures and hyperactivity, loss of appetite and vomiting. Copper poisoning has similar signs plus a swollen tummy. String-type articles may be caught between the teeth in the mouth, with the rest swallowed.

Intestines propel food using muscle contractions called peristalsis that move through the entire length of the intestine (kind of like an earthworm) to help push the contents through. But when a foreign object like string is caught at one end, the intestine literally "gathers" itself like fabric on a thread, resulting in a kind of accordion formation. The result is sudden severe vomiting and diarrhea, and rapid dehydration. Your veterinarian should evaluate any blockage situation to determine the best course of treatment. Surgery is often necessary to remove the obstruction.

If blockage is not promptly addressed, the resulting damage may become irreparable. Sharp objects may slice or puncture the bowel, and obstruction may interfere with blood flow to the organs and cause bowel tissue to die. Peritonitis is the end result in either case, and usually kills the victim.

Once located, the object is removed. The veterinarian can sometimes do this with an endoscope down the puppy's throat or the other direction up through his rectum, or with surgery. Any internal damage is repaired. If surgery can correct the problem before peritonitis sets in, most puppies fully recover. Should tissue die, the damaged sections of the intestine may be removed and the living portions of bowel reattached; these puppies typically have a good prognosis.

Most puppies outgrow indiscriminate munching. The best course is preventing your dog from swallowing dangerous items. Choose dog-safe toys that can't be chewed into tiny pieces, and supervise object play. Anything a child would put in his mouth is fair game for puppies. Puppy-proof your home by thinking like your dog, so that you won't be caught off guard when your dog eats the rubber bumpers off the door stops.

PART FOUR:

PUPPY SOCIABILITY

AND TRAINING

12: Making Sense of Puppy Talk

Dogs are social creatures that live together, and so they need a dog language in order to get along. How dogs communicate—what I like to call "dogma"— is based on a system of common signals.

Your cute puppy's ancestors survived by forming packs that hunted together, communally protected young, and defended territory from outsiders. And while two individuals can get along, the more individuals added to a group increase the chance of arguments. Constant fights and injuries weaken the group. Survival depends on every dog—and puppy—in the group staying healthy and productive.

Dog language not only allows dogs to communicate and understand each other. It also is a system used for conflict resolution, including calming signals that head off fights. In fact, once you understand how dogs communicate and the way they interpret your verbal and silent body language, you can learn how to talk to your puppy.

HOW DOGS COMMUNICATE

Canine communication is a complex system of sign language, vocalization, and even scent cues. These signals reinforce the dog's social position within the group. Dogs are pretty flexible with members of their family group. That's why it's so important to socialize your puppy early and continue throughout his or her life. Your dog considers you—and other people and pets in the household—to be a part of his family group, and acts accordingly.

Why Understanding Dog Language Matters

Most behavior problems arise from normal dog behaviors. For instance, eating poop and targeting things that smell like you for puppy chewing are normal dog behaviors. From your puppy's perspective, he's done nothing wrong. And when you get upset with him, he communicates the only way he know show—with puppy language.

If your relationship is to reach its full potential, it is important that you understand what he's saying so that you can teach him what you want. Don't expect puppies (or adult dogs for that matter) to automatically understand and read your mind. Puppies make behavior mistakes because they don't know any better.

Kinds of Canine Communication

Compared to your puppy, humans are hearing-deaf and scent-blind. That makes it impossible for us to understand some of these subtle signals of canine language. But by paying attention to the vocal cues we can hear and watching body language, we can learn to interpret the more obvious canine signals.

Dogs evolved with an ability and fascination of paying close attention to the humans they love. So your puppy will meet you halfway, given a chance, and learn a large human vocabulary, particularly when words are used with consistency.

Dogs use vocalizations, scent, and body language alone or in combination. Each type of communication has advantages and disadvantages.

Sound carries over long distances. Howls, barks, yips, snarls, growls and more are included in the "dogma" repertoire. However, a bark may alert adversaries as well as pack members, so it's not effective for stealth communication.

While a vocalization can only be sustained one breath at a time, a body posture can be held nearly forever. Dogs "talk" with their ears, eyes, body posture, fur elevation, tail semaphore and more.

Scent signals don't require the dog's presence to get a message across. "Pee-mail" can be left behind for others to read the way people leave messages on the answering machine.

Dogs use combinations of each technique to communicate meaning. Very basically, canine communication is used to either decrease the distance between individuals with signals that ask for attention—a wagging puppy tail, for example—or to increase distance between individuals with warning signals such as growls.

Scent Communication

Dog marking behaviors use smell communication and leg lifting to spray urine and mark territory. Although they primarily use urine, some pups also scratch the ground after eliminating to leave visual signs while the paw pads leave scent cues.

The scent of urine tends to fade as soon as it contacts the air. That's why dogs constantly freshened with new markings on top or nearby the original. Some pups become so enthusiastic, they seem intent on throwing their hip out of joint to "baptize" everything they can reach!

Both male and female dogs urine mark, but typically it is the male that is most enthusiastic. And, it is the intact dog able to produce puppies that exhibit the most prominent behavior. Females may leg-cock to announce their breeding availability to male dogs.

Dog Marking Vs. Puppy Potty Training

Marking is different than elimination behavior. When the purpose is to simply void a full bladder, female dogs usually urinate downward in a crouched position over a flat surface like the ground. Male dogs also often squat to urinate. All puppies squat to urinate and the urge to actually mark develops with maturity from about five months on, depending on the individual pup.

In contrast, marking is done from a standing position by cocking a rear leg and aiming the urine stream at a (usually) vertical object. This places the scent at a convenient nose sniffing level, just as people would place a Post-It Note at eye level to attract the most attention.

It takes very little urine to send the intended Pee-Mail message. During walks with your pup, he may stop you every five yards or so to leg-cock against a tuft of grass, telephone pole, or other obvious landmark. By the end of the walk, he may run out of urine but continue to leg-cock, in effect simply going through the motions. Just the pose can be a visual signal to any watching dogs.

However, they sometimes get carried away and mark inappropriate targets. Extremely dominant dogs may even urinate against a person's leg, and intact indoor dogs often feel compelled to scent their household top to bottom. Neutering and spaying greatly reduces leg-cocking behavior, curtailing the baptism of bedroom walls, tires, and furniture.

Sounding Off—Vocalizations

When your crying puppy drives you crazy with whimpers, yelps, barks and howls, how can you understand all those puppy sounds? Canine communication helps reinforce your puppy's social position within his family. Puppy talk may invite you to come closer or warn to keep away. It can be confusing because puppies use barks and growls during play as well as when they mean business.

Most often, vocalizations punctuate what the body movements are saying in the same way people use inflection to impart emotion and meaning. And because dogs realize people rely on verbal communication our pets have become much more vocal than their ancestors.

Barking

For instance, barking is rare in wolves, but is the most common vocal signal in dogs. It's used during play, defense, and as a greeting. Barks are categorized as a dominance signal. But that does not mean barking necessarily equals aggression.

Barking is a canine fire alarm, a call to action that alerts the family group to the unusual. This may be anything from the arrival of friend or foe, to an unexpected sound like thunder, or the strange sight of you wearing a hat. Some dogs bark to relieve boredom, particularly when left alone for hours at a time, and dogs can be taught to stop barking.

But dogs won't stop barking any more than people would cease talking to express themselves. Dogs also bark together as a joyful expression of happiness; that's why yelling at a dog to stop barking rarely works—he thinks you're joining in a communal bark-fest, and barks even louder.

Howls

Dogs use howls to express emotion, and to announce their location to missing pack members. Usually, a howl is a canine cry of loneliness that implores others to come join him. Puppies left home alone, or sequestered by themselves in a room may howl.

Some puppy breeds howl more than others. These include Northern type dog breeds such as Alaskan Malamutes and Siberian Huskies that may be closer to wolfy forebears than others. Hound breeds also tend to howl more often since they were bred to "bay" as a way to announce their tracking or hunting progress in the field.

Howls seem to be contagious, with a single lone call often answered by any other dog within hearing. Dogs may interpret a siren as a howl, and respond with an enthusiastic reply. My German shepherd, Magic, howls along whenever I sing—maybe he's a critic, or perhaps he simply wants to join in the happy chorus.

Whines, Whimpers and Yelps

Whines, whimpers and yelps communicate submission, pain or fear. The actual meaning depends on what the rest of the body "says." When your puppy vocalizes with whines, whimpers or yelps while trying to keep her distance from you or some other situation, the sounds indicate fear. Puppy injury often gets announced with repeated yelps, and holding up or favoring the hurt paw. But whines, whimpers and yelps also are used as solicitations to a dominant individual (usually the owner). In other words, your baby uses these techniques to beg for attention, food, or to go in or out.

Growls and Snarls

Growls and snarls are warnings. Dogs use these as distance-increasing signals to tell others to back off and stay away. Snarls display the teeth and aren't always accompanied by sound; they signify slight fear. Growls indicate deeper concern, and can be made with the mouth open or closed. A dog's growl is used in defense, and as a threat. They often are used during play when your puppy attacks a toy or wrestles with other pups.

While a threatening growl and snarl can be scary, these sounds can be very important communication tools for your pup and to you. Puppies taught to never growl are more likely to bite without warning. That makes it especially important for all pups to learn proper bite inhibition. It's important for your puppy to snarl and growl in appropriate circumstances—during play, when frightened or in pain—so you have fair warning and can adjust your own behavior accordingly.

Laughing

Yes, dogs laugh! It doesn't sound exactly how you'd expect, either. And while puppies and dogs use the other whines, growls and barks in other contexts, the dog laugh appears to happen only during play.

A dog laugh sounds similar to a human saying, "Ha-ha-ha-ha!" but without sounding the "a" vowel. It's simply a breathy exhalation, according to researcher P.R. Simonet. There's also research that points to a dog sneeze in certain circumstances to being similar to a "canine giggle" of delight.

Recordings of the panting-laugh sound played at shelters has helped calm dogs' stress. Sneezing can prompt a reciprocal sneeze in your puppy, too-- because after all, laughter is catching and good medicine. Try it!

Mixed Signals

Puppies aren't always sure how they feel. They can mix up vocal signals and make it difficult for owners to understand what they mean. Puppies that aren't sure how they feel may bark, whimper, snarl and yelp all at the same time. That usually means they're more scared than aggressive. By learning to understand what your puppy says, you can help prevent dog bites and ensure you maintain a great relationship.

FEARFUL AGGRESSION

DOMINANT AGGRESSION

ALERT-INQUISITIVE

INVITING PLAY

Canine body positions

Puppy Body Language

Even puppies use dog body language to "talk" to each other and their owners. Dogs are most highly attuned to puppy body language, and this silent communication is given the greatest weight. Your pup's dedicated observation can make him appear psychic—he always hides when a bath is imminent—when in fact he's simply reacting to non-verbal cues you may be unaware you're broadcasting. That's why when you smile as you reprimand Junior for stealing your socks, the puppy reads amusement rather than reproach, and acts accordingly.

Canine language serves to smooth relationships, offering a way for dogs to get along with each other and the people who make up their families. Silent canine communication makes use of the dog's body from nose to tail. The position and movement of his tail, his facial expression, even his posture is telling.

Eye Talk

Eyes communicate volumes. Droopy eyelids indicate pleasure, and your pup may squint and moan with delight when his ears are rubbed. Alert pups keep their eyes open wide. An unblinking stare is a challenge and shows dominance, while averting the eyes shows canine submission.

The pupils of a dog's eyes indicate aggression and imminent attack when they suddenly dilate wide. Avoid locking eyes with a strange dog. That's a challenge and may prompt him to challenge you back with aggression.

Mouth Talk

The dog's mouth is also quite expressive. Your pup uses his lips, teeth and even his tongue to communicate.

In general, when the lips lift vertically to show the long dagger-shaped canines, the dog is showing aggression or fear. Lips pull back horizontally to show more teeth in a canine grin of submission, which is often used as an appeasement gesture toward a dominant individual. But grabbing the other dog's muzzle or neck with his mouth--with inhibited bite--shows dominance.

A flicking tongue signals intent to lick, which when aimed at the face or hands is also an appeasement gesture. The relaxed, happy pup may sit with his mouth half-open and tongue lolling out as he pants.

Ear Talk

The ears are barometers of puppy mood. The shape of the dog's ears—whether erect and termed "prick ears" or floppy and pendulous—also influence how easy ear language is to understand. For the sake of this discussion, the ear conformation of the German Shepherd Dog will be used.

When erect and facing forward, the dog is interested and possibly aggressive. The ears flatten against the head by degrees depending on how fearful or submissive the dog feels.

Tail Talk

Tail talk is perhaps the dog's most obvious signal to people. Again, the conformation of the dog's tail -- from long to docked, corkscrew or curled -- will determine the extent of your dog's tail semaphore.

In most cases, a wagging tail is a distance-reducing signal that declares the dog to be friendly.

However, what the tail says depends to a great degree on what the rest of the body is doing. Learn more about your puppy's tail talk in this article.

Puppy tail wagging is part of dog language and is a complex system of (mostly) sign language, some vocalization, and even scent cues people can't detect. Many of these signals define and reinforce your puppy's social position within the family group. That includes other dogs, humans, or other animals.

Why should you care what your puppy's tail talk means? Misreading a dog's clear signal can get you bit. Even if the bite isn't serious, it can result in the pup losing his home—or even his life.

Signals that ask for attention seek to decrease the distance between individuals while warning signs are designed to increase distance between individuals. For instance, a warning growl means, "stay away!" while most folks interpret a wagging tail as invitation to approach.

But puppies don't just "talk" from one end of their body. They use the same signal—a wagging tail—to mean very different things depending on the context. For instance, they may "pretend" to be aggressive with lots of growls, but use a wagging tail to tell you it's only play.

TECHNICAL STUFF. A research article published in Current Biology by a neuroscientist and veterinarians at Italy universities suggests tail wag directions also have meaning. When puppies feel positive about you, the tail wags more to the right. Negative feelings prompt more tail wags to the left.

The whole repertoire of signals that must be read together, from nose tip to tail, to understand what your puppy really intends. What the tail says depends to a great degree on what the rest of the body is doing.

- A relaxed pup's tail curves down and back up in a gentle U. The more interest he feels, the higher the tail.
- Dominant and confident pups hold their tails high, and wag rapidly in tight sharp arcs.
- But aggressive dogs also hold their tails high, often tightly arched over their back with just the end jerking very quickly back and forth.
- A high-held stiff tail signals imminent attack. The dog may or may not include aggressive facial or vocal expressions such as snarls and growls. Many dominant or aggressive dogs use very subtle warnings—or none at all—before they bite, especially if the puppy has been taught NOT to growl a warning.
- Holding the tail in a low position indicates submission or fear. A dog shows his low standing relative to you (or another animal) with loose, wide low arcing wags that often include hip wags as well.
- Tucking the tail between the legs signals submission and fear. A tucked tail is the canine equivalent of hiding his face because it covers the genitals, and interferes with the sniffing behavior that identifies him to other dogs.
- Fearful pups also bite, though, if they can't escape the frightening situation. Watch for fluffed fur along the back (hackles), and a show of teeth with or without growls.
- Some dogs can't decide how they feel and wag at one end while snarling from the other.

Remember that tail shape and display (conformation) also influences how and what dogs say. Northern breeds such as Alaskan Malamutes with curled tails automatically "signal" dominance to other canines, whether they truly feel that way or not. Tailless dogs literally have one avenue of communication cut off and other dogs may not understand them as well.

Educate yourself—and especially your children—to the many "faces" of your puppy's wags. In almost every instance, King very clearly tells us that he wants petting, or fears you, or warns strangers to keep their distance. Problems arise when humans either don't understand—or don't listen.

Body Position

Your puppy's carriage shows how he feels. Dogs bump, push or lean against people or other animals as a sign of dominance. Extremely bossy dogs may even indulge in body slamming and bowling over the other dog--or person.

Erect posture is a sign of confidence typical of dominant dogs, who seem to nearly stand on tiptoe when in the presence of another dog they want to impress. The aggressive dog leans forward toward whoever they want to cow, while the fearful dog leans backward.

Dogs also stand or "loom" over top of the dominated individual to show their social position. The more dominant dog will rest his head, chin, and/or paws over the neck or body of the more subordinate dog. Older dogs putting a puppy in his place may grab the muzzle or neck of the other pup to drive home his point, and engage in mounting or clasping behavior.

The opposite is true when a dog shows submission. Puppies that feel insecure or recognize others as being in charge try to look small. Dogs cry uncle by flattening their ears, tucking their tail, crouching as low as possible and perhaps offering a paw. Holding up a paw is a placating gesture in prelude to rolling over to expose the tummy. Exposing the tummy, perhaps even urinating in this position or when crouched before the aggressor, is the dog's ultimate sign of deference.

Fur Talk

Piloerection—fur standing upright along the ridge of his back, called the hackles—makes the dog look bigger and more impressive. It's not a conscious thing and may happen simply when the dog becomes aroused. Raised hackles can mean serious business or can be a bluff. Both fearful and aggressive dogs raise their hackles.

Meta Signals

Puppies also "pretend" to be aggressive to invite play, and indicate it's a game by using exaggerated behaviors, called meta signals. Dogs also can "pretend" to be submissive to entice more subordinate playmates to engage in games.

All these signals must be read together to place your dog's meaning in proper context. Often, mixed signals may be sent, with the snarling front half of the dog indicating aggression while the back half wags submissively. In general, any sort of fearful or aggressive sign can prompt a bite and should be taken seriously.

Communicating submission to a dominant individual reinforces each's position within the family group. For the most part, place is determined simply by posturing alone, and fights are rarely necessary.

MAKING SENSE OF SENSES

Puppies and dogs sensory ability goes far beyond that of humans. Their hearing and scent ability far outshines our own, and feeds into your puppy's two-way communication. You may "say" one thing while he "hears" (or smells) something else entirely. Further, while a puppy's vision isn't the same as ours, it's helpful to compare the two so that you better understand what he perceives—or misses.

What Puppy Sees

Puppy eyes work quite similarly to our own. Light passes through the clear window-like cornea on the front surface of the eye, through the dark round opening called the pupil, and enters the lens which focuses the light images onto the retina at the back of the eye. Unlike human eyes, all dogs have a "third eyelid" called the haw or nictitating membrane which is located in the inner corner of the eye that acts as a windshield wiper that sweeps horizontally across the eye.

Most dogs are emmetropic—normal sighted or slightly near sighted. Dogs tend to rely more on motion than focus, though. They have trouble seeing objects closer than about 10 inches and must use their noses to find the kibble that spills out of the bowl. The visual acuity of dogs is about 20/75, although the German Shepherd, Rottweiler and Schnauzer appear to be even more near sighted

Depth Perception

Prey animal like rabbits and deer can watch in two directions at once with eyes on each side of the head. But predators—dogs and cats—have eyes toward the front of the face that gives them depth perception and binocular vision so they can correctly time pursuit and pounce.

Eyes placed closer together have a greater degree of visual overlap—improved binocular vision—compared to those placed further apart. The binocular vision and field of vision varies somewhat between dog breeds depending on conformation of the face.

The eye placement of brachycephalic dogs like Pugs are situated more toward the front of the face, while the narrow-headed sighthound breeds like the Collie tend to have eyes more on the sides of the face. Most dogs have only about 30-60 degrees of binocular overlap versus approximately 140 degrees of humans. Therefore dog's depth perception is not as acute as people's. He may see the movement of hand signals from a long distance but not recognize a hat-wearing owner until scent or voice further identifies you.

Peripheral Vision

But dogs are champions when it comes to visual field of view—seeing all around in peripheral vision. That means when your puppy looks straight ahead he can still see 240 degrees, compared to 180 degrees in humans.

Dogs are potentially even better at peripheral vision because they have a high density line of vision cells across the retina, called a visual streak. That lets them see sharp focused object at a distance even in the extremes of peripheral vision—out of the corners of their eyes. It is believed this extension of cones improves the animal's ability to see particularly along the horizon and serves as an adaptation based on the evolutionary requirement of the dog.

Motion Detection

A reliance on motion makes sense from an evolutionary standpoint. The dog breeds developed to hunt by sight like Greyhounds and Afghan Hounds scan the distance for prey. Most dogs can detect strong hand signals from as far away as a mile.

While dogs tend to ignore stationary objects, this visual streak triggers their instinctive urge to chase whenever something moves in their peripheral vision. That makes dogs great guard dogs because they alert to even small movements humans probably would never see. The visual streak is most pronounced in long-nosed dogs—the sight hound dogs developed to hunt and chase. That's why herding breeds, for instance, may trigger on a bicycle or car and turn into chase maniacs.

How Puppy Hears

Your puppy's ears are sensory organs of hearing, and also provide a sense of equilibrium, or balance. Canine hearing is remarkably acute; it's used in hunting, protection, and play, and is an important tool that keeps dogs in touch with their world.

Puppies are born virtually deaf. Their ears and eyes are sealed at birth so they rely on vibration and scent for this period of life. Even though the ears and sound detection are not yet fully functional, the balance function of the ears allows the babies to move about, recognize when they tip over and struggle to right themselves. Once the ears become unsealed at about two weeks of age during this early puppy development, and the baby dog learning to recognize and react to different sounds.

Canine Ear Structure

The structure and function are categorized as the external, middle, and inner ear. The visible portion, called the pinna, is a triangular cartilage flap covered on both sides by skin and fur. The size and shape varies among breeds. Some are erect (prick ears) like the German Shepherd Dog, folded to some degree (drop ear) as in the Collie, or pendulous as in Cocker Spaniels. The pinna of some dogs is surgically altered by cropping to conform to a breed standard.

The pinna is extremely mobile, with more than twenty separate muscles that provide 180 degrees of movement. This mobility helps collect, capture and direct sound further into the organ. It also aids in canine communication by offering a host of expressive ear positions.

The pinna funnels sound down the L-shaped auditory canal. This configuration, a vertical passageway ending in a right-angle turn inward (the foot of the L), helps protect interior structures. However, it also makes dogs prone to ear infections when debris collects in the foot of the L. Hair that grows in the ears of a number of dog breeds may compound the problem.

Sound waves pass through the auditory canal, and strike the tympanic membrane, or eardrum. The resulting vibration is passed to a chain of three tiny ossicles (bones called the hammer, anvil and stirrup) of the middle ear. The eustachian tube which helps equalize pressure within the ear is also located in the middle ear, and connects this area to the back of the throat.

Vibrations are transmitted by ossicles to the inner ear, a bony chamber containing four fluid-filled organs responsible for hearing and balance. Chalk-like particles float in the fluid inside the semicircular canals, utricle and saccule, and as the dog moves his head they brush against tiny hairs that line these organs. That signals directional information to the brain, and gives the dog his sense of equilibrium.

Sound vibration is read by the fluid-filled cochlea, a snailshell-like coil of tubing lined with a membrane called the cochlear duct that spirals its length. The "organ of Corti," a specialized area of this lining, is where hearing actually takes place. Vibration-sensitive hairs that cover the organ of Corti pass information through the auditory nerve to the brain, where the vibration is interpreted as sound.

These intricate organs enable your dog to hear sounds you cannot detect, particularly at high frequencies and at soft volumes. People are able to hear low-pitch tones about as well as dogs, but while we typically hear sound waves up to 20,000 cycles per second, dogs may hear frequencies as high as 100,000 cycles per second. The size of the dog doesn't matter, with Chihuahuas able to hear just as well as Great Danes. However, age tends to temper the dog's hearing, and young dogs hear better than old dogs.

How Puppy Smells

A puppy nose structure and scent ability rules his life. The canine nose contains the scent-detecting organs that provide the puppy with olfaction, or dog sense of smell. More than looks or a name, it is scent that identifies each puppy as an individual among other dogs. Smell distinguishes friend from foe, provides sexual information, and is important to communication and social interaction.

The shape and size of the external nose, which is part of the muzzle, varies greatly between dog breeds. The profile of flat-faced (brachiocephalic) dogs like the Pekingese, which have a "break" or indentation at the eyes, may be many inches shorter than that of Roman-nosed and long-muzzled breeds like the Collie, and there are many breeds that fall in between the two extremes.

In fact, the short skulls of certain snub-nosed breed dogs can distort and narrow the nasal passages and airways. Dogs like Bulldogs and Boston Terriers may have abnormally small nasal openings and excessively long soft palates, which makes them work harder to breathe. When the condition results in breathing problems, it's referred to as brachycephalic upper-airway syndrome. Physical activity, excessive heat, or stress make breathing more difficult, and can prompt wheezing and noisy breathing; affected dogs often snore. Surgery to increase the size of air passages may be necessary.

Canine Nose Structure

The hairless end of the nose is called the leather, and is usually dark, but may be brown, pink or spotted to match the coat color. The leather contains the nostrils (nares) through which air-borne scent enters. The leather is typically cool and moist from mucus glands that lubricate the area.

Nostrils open into the nasal cavity that is enclosed in bone and cartilage and runs the length of the muzzle. This cavity empties into the throat behind the soft palate. Open spaces in the bone (sinuses) connecting to the nasal cavity help shape your puppy's vocalizations.

The nasal septum is a midline partition made of bone and cartilage and lined by mucus membrane. It divides the nasal cavity into two halves, one for each nostril. Within the nasal cavity are a series of scrolled bony plates, called turbinates. Those situated nearest the nostrils clean, warm and humidify air as it's inhaled. This protects the puppy's delicate internal nasal structures by screening the air before passing it on to the sensitive scent-detecting portions.

Further inside, additional turbinates are covered by thick, spongy membrane, called the olfactory mucosa. It is this structure which contains the scent-detecting nerves and cells. Depending on the breed and size of the muzzle, dogs have from seven to 60 square inches of olfactory mucosa, compared to the human's one square inch.

A long muzzle accommodates more scent-detecting equipment, which is why longer-nosed breeds tend to be better sniffers and hunters than the flat-faced dogs. Humans have between five to 20 million scent analyzing cells, but canine scent sense varies between breeds. For instance, the Dachshund has about 125 million such cells, compared to the German Shepherd's 200 million. The best sniffer of them all—the Bloodhound—is said to have 300 million olfactory cells. The flat-faced breeds have far less, but no matter their conformation, all dogs have an extraordinary ability to detect scent.

Odor particles that are inhaled must first be dissolved in the moist layer of mucus that coats the inside of the nose. Millions of microscopic hair-like cilia sprout from the olfactory cells up into this thin layer of mucus. Odor-detecting receptors are found on the cilia. When the dissolved odor particle makes contact, it somehow excites the receptor which in turn feeds the impulse down to the olfactory cell.

Every odor is thought to have a distinctive molecular "shape" which defines the amount of excitement stimulated in a given nerve cell. In turn, these nerves signal the olfactory bulbs, which send the information directly to the brain where the smell is interpreted as a rabbit, or whatever. A second scenting mechanism, called the Jacobson's Organ, may play a role in interpreting pheromones and especially sexually-related chemical signals.

The internal structures of the canine nose are also protected by a layer of moisture produced by serous glands and mucus glands throughout the nasal cavity. The muco-ciliary blanket is composed of microscopic cells covered with hair-like filaments called cilia that move the moisture toward the nostrils and throat. This mucus coating protects the body against infection by trapping foreign material.

13: Games Puppies Play

Play is a normal function of puppy life. Babies begin playing as early as two to three weeks of age, and dog play continues for the rest of her life. It not only is fun for the puppy and entertaining for people. It's healthy both physically and emotionally.

Historically, puppy play has been considered an instinctual method to "practice" for adult life issues, such as hunting. Adult pet dogs that played were thought to act out these behaviors as a substitute for frustrated hunting activities. That seems simplistic, though, and falls short of the whole answer when you consider that many adult animals in the wild continue to play.

Play does, in fact, help hone the puppy's various skills by practicing use of bite and grab, stalk and chase. More than that, it teaches them how to react to the world around them. The puppy learns that patting a leaf makes it move, that biting her brother prompts a squeal and retaliation, or that she can shake and "kill" a toy into submission. Play activity teaches puppies limits on what they can do, and how their actions and reactions impact the world around them. Puppies use their mouths to grab objects, and paws to reach out and "test" objects in play behavior to see how it feels and moves. They can learn inhibit their bite when playing with siblings—or humans.

Play also serves as a natural body-building exercise. A puppy's brain is almost fully mature at five weeks, but physical and motor development takes longer. Practice hones dexterity, builds physical prowess and skill, and keeps muscles toned and the mind engaged. Play is a great stress-buster for puppies and adults alike. It builds trust and reinforces social ties between individuals, and encourages loving relationships. Play can boost confidence in shy puppies, and reduce obnoxious aggression in bullies. Most importantly of all, play is fun.

To puppies, everything is a potential toy, even hiding a toy in the leaves.

Why Puppies Play

Puppy play makes us smile but often makes us wonder why puppies play. There are broad categories of play and how puppies play varies between individuals. Experts call these activities "play" because they don't seem to have any clear purpose other than fun.

In the past, we assumed puppy play was instinctive behavior designed to develop survival skills necessary for life in the wild. Preferred play styles often are specific to a puppy's breed, too. But that didn't answer the question why adult dogs continue to play, if they've already honed these skills. So we assumed that adult dogs were frustrated by modern domestication and continued to play as a replacement for hunting or defense urges. Today we know a bit more.

Studies have specifically examined the role of canine play and how it influences the dog's behavior. Even wild animals continue to play as adults. Dogs that get to hunt or herd and so practice the so-called survival or instinctive skills also continue to play. Today, many researchers agree that puppy play (and adult dog play) has many purposes and benefits.

- Play helps puppies develop, and adult dogs continue to practice, communication skills. During play, puppies learn the doggy rules of the road, how to inhibit bites, and practice all the must-know doggy athletic skills. Play practices running, jumping, biting, wrestling, sniffing and more.
- Play teaches puppies about their world. They learn cause-and-effect through play—for instance, that pouncing on a ball sends it bouncing away. And that chasing a cat makes it go fast—or hiss and swat.
- Playing together reinforces social bonds between group members.
- Play builds muscle, burns fat, and keeps puppies active and healthy.
- Puppy play relieves stress and tension. It allows aggressive dogs to release energy in a legal, productive way by attacking that stuffed toy and shaking it into submission. Play boosts the confidence of shy dogs when they grab the tug-toy and win the game. Play distracts fearful dogs during thunderstorms.
- Because a puppy considers you her best friend, playing with your puppy strengthens the bond you share.

Dogs are such social creatures and appear to have an innate need to play. Play behavior is also an expression of emotion and seems to characterize an individual dog's personality. The joy expressed by the puppy in full-on play-mode can't be denied. Play is great fun for dogs--and for humans who get to watch. Play for the fun of it should be enough.

This adult dog "play bows" to incite the puppy to play—and show "no threat."

How Puppies Play

How puppies play depends a great deal on the breed. Socialization and age also influences what games puppies play. It makes sense that sighthound breeds react more to seeing toys move while "gripping" breeds relish tug-of-war, and terriers like chase, grab and shake games.

Canine play is composed of exaggerated and highly ritualized gestures used in doggy communication. That allows dogs to "play fight" for instance, yet avoid misunderstandings which might result in real fights.

Play behavior begins as early as puppies can toddle around—about three weeks of age. Puppies of both sexes may exhibit sexual behavior as early as four weeks of age, mounting each other during play games.

Prey killing behavior like pouncing and object shaking is also seen, and the language of dominance and submission is learned. Puppies at these early ages practice being both the top dog and the bottom-of-the-heap, so they learn how to communicate with each other. Temperament extremes—a bully puppy or shrinking violet pooch—expressed in play by young puppies is not necessarily a good predictor of future status. Temperament tests are more accurate when conducted on older puppies.

Social Play

Social play is interactive. In other words, social play involves playing with another puppy, the owner or even the cat. Examples of social play include wrestling, biting, play-fighting, and chase games.

Puppies begin social play as early as three weeks of age, with play-biting and pawing, and barking.

The intensity escalates and becomes more complex as the dog matures. The first play-eliciting gesture seen in puppies is the raised paw. The play bow -- butt end up, front down -- is the classic invitation for a canine romp and is used by older pups and adults, along with barking, leaping forward to nose-poke and then withdrawing, face pawing or licking.

Self-Directed Play

Self-directed play, such as tail chasing or pouncing on imaginary objects, is thought to be a replacement for social play when a play-partner isn't available. Puppies that indulge in extremes of tail chasing or habitually target "invisible" objects—snapping at nonexistent bugs—should be checked by the vet. These may be indications of obsessive-compulsive or seizure conditions.

Locomotory Play

Locomotory play simply means the puppy is in motion. That can involve solo play or include interaction with others. Locomotory play in adult dogs usually involves a pair or group of dogs. But puppies may indulge in games of "ghost-tag" running, jumping and rolling about when they're by themselves.

Object Play

Object play is interaction with stuff. Chasing or pawing/grabbing a ball, rag or stick are examples. Some puppies target water and love chasing the hose or sprinkler. My German Shepherd, Magic, loves to play "hose tag."

"Just Kidding" During Play

Dogs use exaggerated behaviors, called meta signals, to tell other dogs all action that comes after is not serious but a game. For instance, the play-bow is a butt-in-the-air with front-end down position where the pup's forelegs dance back and forth to invite play. When your puppy first play-bows, he's telling you that any growls or wrestling that comes after are meant as fun and games.

Adult dogs often "pretend" to be subordinate to a puppy—with play-bows or rolling on the back—to build up the pup's confidence and invite him to play. This "just kidding" game allows lower-ranking pups to practice being in charge with play bites, mounting behavior, and wrestling games. Once the play is over, the higher-ranking dog again assumes his more "mature" behavior that tells the pup to respect his leadership.

Bad vs Good Play—Knowing The Difference

Dogs of all ages enjoy playing. Behaviors for fighting and fun are similar, but you must know how to tell the difference between aggression and play-acting. Watch for "meta signals" which tells participants that whatever comes after is meant in a "play" context.

Dogs commonly drop toys on your feet or lap to solicit a game, and offer toys to other dogs in the same way. A play bow—the dog sticks his butt and tail into the air, and bows forward on lowered forelegs that dance side to side— is the classic signal and invitation for the games to begin. Often, the "fighting" behaviors seen during such games will be exaggerated to indicate play, or the "fight" behavior sequences may be jumbled.

Play includes inhibited mouth-open bites often aimed at the legs and paws of other dogs. Dogs also paw and bat each other without force to hurt. In appropriate play, all the dogs willingly participate. If you suspect one of the dogs doesn't like the activity (one dog repeatedly tries to escape or hide), gently separate the pair to see if they go back for more. If the play session was too rough, one will sneak away.

Inappropriate play results in one or more dog frightened, hurt, or overwhelmed. Bully dogs always end up on top, while in appropriate play you'll see dogs take turns chasing and pinning each other during wrestling. Mouthing aimed primarily at the head or neck, or uninhibited bites means play has gotten out of hand. You'll hear yelps from the bitten dog.

Consistent play up on hind legs may indicate problems. Ongoing mounting, clasping and thrusting also can lead to problems, as can resting of paws, heads or whole bodies across other dog's shoulders to intimidate or achieve social status.

Growls don't usually indicate problems, but play can be so exciting that the action escalates into aggression. Listen for louder, lower pitched growls, and be prepared to break up the session before they get too aroused.

A variety of toys appeal to different puppies. This rope toy offers legal bite options as well as a fun shake-and-kill-it game, both very popular with dogs of all ages.

Play as a Bonding and Training Tool

Puppies look on humans as surrogate parents. To your puppy, you are the Mom-dog figure because all the food, attention, and fun stuff come directly from you. It's up to you to provide guidance, promote good behaviors, and improve or correct negative habits before they become problems. Playing with your puppy can be a powerful bonding and training tool.

Make a point to play with your puppy for at least twenty minutes, twice a day. Longer and more frequent play periods are even better. This helps exercise her body so she wears out and is less likely to find trouble. It also engages her puppy brain—create puzzles for her to solve, to keep her interested. For instance, show her a treat, and hide it beneath a scarf, then encourage her to find it.

Playing such games increases the bond your puppy feels with you. When a puppy is shy, it can build her confidence and help her become a more even-tempered pet. A stuffed toy she can bite and shake, or a toy she can play fetch, chase and capture—what a brave puppy!—offer positive results.

These games are self-rewarding. She wins and has fun at the same time.

For rambunctious puppies and those who have developed poor bite habits, play can teach them to temper these behaviors. It also gives them a "legal" outlet to go crazy and be wild canines. Play is a particularly effective training tool that can be used as a reward for good behavior, or a lure to prompt your puppy to do the right thing.

Remember, the best way to alter an unacceptable behavior is to offer your puppy a better alternative. Taking away the poor target—your fingers, for example—leaves a void that your puppy will fill with something else that's potentially just as objectionable—like your ankles. Puppies love to bite, so give her a toy that allows her to indulge in this normal puppy behavior.

14: Training Your Puppy

How Dogs Learn

All dogs can be trained, but frankly, the younger they are the faster they learn. Puppyhood is the ideal time to begin your baby's education.

Puppies learn from the moment they're born. Mom teaches them by example how to be dogs, how to eat solid food and pick up and carry toys. They may learn to fear children, for instance, if Mom-dog reacts unfavorably to them.

Learning can be categorized a couple of different ways. **Classical conditioning** forms an association between an outside event, like running the water in the sink, and a reaction, such as a bath. Depending on the reaction, the puppy associates the event with a pleasant or unpleasant experience and behaves accordingly.

Operant conditioning deals with relationships between stimuli, responses, and consequences. The puppy learns that what he does is critical to what happens next. For instance, he receives a treat for a good behavior like pooping outside in the right place.

Puppies behave in certain ways because the action is self-rewarding. It feels good to scratch an itch or go to the bathroom as soon as the urge strikes. Trial and error lessons are the most powerful because it self-trains them when the action (sniffing the cricket) rewards the behavior (the cricket jumps—what fun!).

WARNING!

Puppies use some of these same training techniques on you. For instance, when your puppy wants to be fed he creates a stimulus (whining and pawing your leg) to motivate you to feed him. When you give in and feed him, he stops crying— that rewards you and reinforces the training. Of course, when you give in and offer food, you've also rewarded him for pestering you.

In the same way, Puppies learn that biting Mom-dog's tail prompts a scary GRRRRR! and an end to the game. That's no fun at all. When they play nice, though, they are rewarded with Mom's fun interaction.

The key to successful puppy training is to figure out what motivates your puppy do what he does, and use that to train the response you want. In effect, puppy training fools the puppy into believing it was all his idea. You'll need a good understanding of puppy language, social structure, and behavior to create effective puppy motivations. Puppies are insatiable when it comes to learning. In most instances, they need to be instructed only once or twice to understand what you want.

Socialization and Bonding Benefits

Socialization refers to how baby dogs learn to interact with the world around them—you, other dogs and animals, and other people. Canine learning involves both nature (genetics) and nurture (environment). Puppies that inherit the potential for aggression and shyness, for example, may never exhibit these problems if properly socialized.

Dogs can be trained at any age, and continue to learn throughout their lives. But the prime socialization period falls in a narrow window during babyhood when learning the "wrong" lessons can emotionally cripple the pet. During the prime socialization period from age three to 12-14 weeks of age, puppies develop canine social and communication skills, learning to identify acceptable and unacceptable members of the canine clan. Mother dogs teach many lessons by example. If Mom-Dog becomes hysterical around men, her pups will pay attention and copy her behavior.

People raising litters must begin positive lessons before the babies go to new homes. Socialization continues through age 16 weeks, and through the juvenile period (18 months) in some cases. It's vital that the babies be exposed to positive experiences with other pets and people if they are to accept them as part of their "family" and become loving, well-adjusted pets.

It's important for puppies to be socialized to children—and for kids to learn about dogs!

Some animals experience a "fearful" period anywhere from age six to 12 months. Strive for a positive outcome for the dog in all new situations, and continue to provide exposure to a variety of people (wearing hats, uniforms, and of different ages), places (home, grandma's, the mall), and novel situations and objects to explore.

Many training schools or veterinary hospitals provide "puppy classes" that can help your new baby learn the ropes, particularly around other dogs. Don't neglect encouraging the pup to walk and eliminate on novel surfaces. Dogs only used to kennels or cement floor may refuse to potty on grass.

For a good puppy class, look for puppies who are off-leash all the time and have interruptions of their play at 15 second intervals. This allows them to learn bite inhibition from each other, while socializing them to other dogs.

Create a puppy kindergarten for your new dog. While human kids are taught the three R's in school, puppies can be socialized based on the three T's— Touching, Talking, and Timing.

Touching the youngster not only feels good to you both, it teaches him that contact with people is pleasant, not scary, and self-rewarding. Petting also places your scent on him, so he associates your smell with feelings of wellbeing. Petting is one of the first sensations newborns feel when Mom licks and grooms them, and petting harkens back to this wonderful safe experience.

Pleasant touch also prompts a reduction in blood pressure and heart rate, and can change brain wave activity. Studies have shown that handling furry babies for five minutes a day during their first three weeks increases the pet's ability to learn later in life.

Talking is equally important, and teaches the youngster to listen and pay attention to your voice. They may not understand all the words, but will recognize if you're happy with them, aggravated, amused, or affectionate. The more you speak to your dogs, the better they will learn to understand and react to what you want. That enhances and improves your relationship.

Teach the phrase, 'say hi,' so dogs learn that means they get to meet somebody. That's especially helpful for fearful dogs, who then know that person is safe and nothing to fear. You can also teach "look" or "check it out" while pointing to various objects, to tell the pup it's safe to investigate. Increase healthy curiosity and confidence by hiding tasty treats underneath a towel or cushion, toy or other object so when the dog investigates, there's a reward waiting.

Timing is the third "T" in the equation. Puppies won't know what's right and what's wrong unless you tell them at the right time to point out exactly what you like—or dislike. If he leaves a deposit under the piano, for example, and you find it 20 minutes later, he won't have a clue why you're angry. Only by catching him in the act (or within 30 seconds) will the youngster be able to connect your displeasure with the incident. It's more powerful to use timing to catch him doing something RIGHT. Offer a treat when he greets the mailman with a wag. Celebrate with a favorite game when the puppy and adult pets play together nicely—they've graduated pet kindergarten with flying colors.

PUPPY WAGS.
A "time out" works wonders for soothing upset feelings. I'm talking about you as well as your puppy. Training requires a calm temper. Anger won't get you anywhere, and losing control of yourself can actually backfire. To be effective, training must be positive and fun for the puppy. Scaring him by getting aggravated or angry may even cause some backsliding. So when you feel tempers flare, give yourselves a break. Give the baby a time out in his own room. Meanwhile, you take a nice walk, or count to ten.

Patience Is Key

Don't expect to wave a magic wand and have your puppy trained. After all, you are dealing with a baby. Babies make mistakes. Mistakes are part of the learning process—puppies learn through trial and error. Frankly, so do people. So have patience with your new puppy and patience with yourself. Give yourself permission to experiment, and figure out what works best in your situation.

Remember, there is a communication gap between you and your puppy. Both of you are learning about each other's language. Misunderstandings are inevitable, but you can reduce these setbacks by paying attention to how he reacts to you. Every puppy is different. What works for one puppy may be the wrong approach for another.

5 Common Misunderstandings

Your puppy is not a mind reader and what's "normal" behavior for people may be a totally foreign language and offensive to dogs. Humans are primates. We touch and hug, gesture with our hands, and when we get upset our tone of voice often gets louder and higher pitched. All of these things can be confusing or even threatening to puppies especially, but also to adult dogs.

Leaning over your puppy. We're taller than pups, and it's natural to lean down to talk or pet them. But "looming" over top of a dog intimidates him because in dog talk, this means "I'm the boss, I'm in control." That can be upsetting or even frightening to pups that already accept your status as the boss. They may use appeasement gestures such as submissive wetting to show they're no threat.

Strange dogs that don't know you may become aggressive or defensive when you lean over them. They simply fight back what they think of as a challenge. Instead of leaning over top of the puppy, give him space so he can approach you. Turn sideways and crouch or kneel on the floor so your height and stance doesn't seem a challenge.

Staring with hard eye contact. Sure, she's a little doll-baby pup but direct eye contact also can be intimidating. Use the pup's own calming signals to tell him you mean no harm. Turn your head away and avert your eyes, and move slowly to give the pup time to build up courage to stand her ground or even approach.

Pats on the head. Imagine you are puppy-size and a hand half the size of your whole body swoops down toward the top of your head—YIKES! Wouldn't you dodge and yelp, and run for cover, too?

Instead, think how puppies and dogs meet each other—smell communication with sniffs first, contact later. So offer your hand, palm down, for the baby dog to sniff the back of your fingers without risk of being grabbed. Then offer a scratch on the front of his chest or side of his neck. Avoid patting tops of puppy and dog heads until you know the pet very well and they've shown a good understanding of "human talk."

Hugging. For puppies and dogs, hugs are not a sign of affection. Our pets use clasping to grab and wrestle during play or fights, during mating behavior, or simply to show dominance.

Forgo the hugging and teach your children alternate ways to show affection to dogs. Otherwise, the puppy may lash out in retaliation of what she perceives to be an attack.

Kissing. Yes, I know the new puppy seems to lick-lick-lick you all the time, sort of like a kissing maniac-dawg. We often think of kissing as exclusively an expression of love and affection. But even among people, a kiss also can signify respect rather than adoration.

Dogs and puppies show their love in other ways. Licking is instead used to show deference, respect, and a declaration that, "I am no threat." Subordinate dogs lick a more dominant dog—or person's—face or side of the mouth as an appeasement gesture.

If you or your child try to mimic this doggy signal and "kiss" the dog on or near the mouth or eyes, in dog language this tells him that you're submissive to him. That could get you both into trouble. A large majority of dog bites target kid faces because the child hugged or tried to kiss the dog.

HOW TO TALK TO PUPPIES

Now that you understand what your own body language means, use it to talk dog to your puppy. When you want your juvenile delinquent pup to straighten up and mind, or you want to encourage the shy pup to be more confident, just communicate with him like a canine. And nope, you don't have to wag your tail!

Assertive Signals

- Use a calm, low-pitched tone of voice, and short clipped words. High-pitched upset voices can sound whiny and send the wrong signals that you are not in charge.

- Use the same words for the same thing each time so your pup learns your language with repetition. He won't know that "wait" and "stay here" and "I'll be right back" or "don't move" mean the same thing to you. Choose one. Puppies thrive on routine. A clicker training technique works particularly well to communicate what these words mean.

- Stand tall. Dogs in charge don't have to make a production out of it, they simply carry themselves like the boss. And everyone believes them so they don't have to prove it.

- Dogs don't use hands to control other's movements—they use body blocks, shove and lean, and control space. Think of the way a shepherd dog herds livestock and prompts sheep to move without ever touching. You can do the same thing, by using your body to control puppy movements. If he's leaping at you, simply tuck your hands close to your body and LEAN toward him before he leaps. You invade and control the space first and he'll back off.

Calming Signals

- For shy pups, think of ways to relieve the angst the same way dogs do. A higher pitched, slow and soothing voice can tell the baby you're no threat.
- Don't loom and lean over top of him. Crouch or kneel. Let the pup approach you rather than chasing after her. If you really want to pique puppy curiosity and show you're no threat, lie motionless on the ground.
- If you must approach, curve in at an oblique angle instead of walking or running toward the puppy directly. Lick your lips or yawn, while looking away.
- Try a dog laugh. Sneeze and see of the pup sneezes back. Or mimic the unvoiced breathy "ha-ha-ha-ha" dog laugh sound that dogs use exclusively in play to say you mean no harm.

PUPPY WAGS.

Finish each training session on a positive note. You want the puppy to have fun, not be stressed or worn out from failure. A great technique is to begin and end each training session with a favorite game, particularly if what you're teaching is new or challenging to the baby. Or end on a drill that your baby dog knows how to "win" so if he already knows how to "sit" on command, make that the last drill of the day.

Timing Is Everything

Puppies learn using the three T's. We've already covered touching and talking. Timing is equally important, for several reasons. First, puppies have the attention span of about a four-year-old child. They are oh-so-bright, and absorb information very quickly. They are also easily distracted.

Create a routine that your puppy can anticipate, and look forward to. Routine is comforting to puppies and dogs. Even if the exercise is new, your pup will feel most comfortable when trained in the same place and same time each day.

Keep training sessions brief, no more than five to ten minutes for puppies younger than 12 weeks old, and up to 15 minute periods for older puppies. Several short sessions throughout the day are much more effective than one marathon session.

Timing is even more important when correcting misbehavior. That's because puppies have a memory for infractions that lasts about 60 seconds. In other words, if your pup has a potty accident, he'll only remember what he's done for a brief time. Corrections too long after the infraction *do not work*. Pups won't be able to associate your upset with the mess he made unless he is literally caught in the act. If you come home and find teeth marks on your new shoes, there is no way to effectively tell the dog he made a mistake.

It is vital that any correction be timed to coincide with the inappropriate behavior. A simultaneous correction is best. Catch him in the act, or within ten seconds of the infraction, so he associates the "wrong" behavior with the correction. That's the only way he'll learn the misdeed results in an unpleasant consequence, and so know to avoid it.

Modern Dog Training

The theory of operant conditioning and reward training deals with relationships between stimuli, responses, and consequences—the puppy learns that what he does is critical to what happens next. Instead of simply reacting to avoid punishment the puppy learns to think—associate your "come" command with receiving positive attention. Puppies are encouraged to want to perform the task on their own. This dog-centric training method puts you in your puppy's paw-steps to look at training from the dog's point of view. Training should be efficient, effective, easy, and enjoyable, so that both pet owners and the dogs are eager to do it.

Training Equipment

Some of the newest training tools reflect this evolution in training philosophy. Tools like the Easy Walk Harness communicate with dogs in a natural fashion with gentle pressure, preventing them from jumping up or lunging forward. The Halti and the Gentle Leader head halters fits over the dog's face, and with gentle guidance, gets even giant-size dogs to go where guided—no jerking necessary.

The more traditional slip, Martingale or "choke" collars must be fitted appropriately and used correctly. A quick jerk-release directs the dog's actions. But if fitted wrong, the collar won't release the pressure, so a pet owner can easily hurt the dog by accident. Puppies and Toy dog breeds are particularly prone to injuries like collapsed trachea and can be permanently damaged by a jerk to the neck.

Electronic collars—those that deliver a remote-controlled low-impulse shock to correct poor behavior--are even more controversial. Many ethicists object to their use altogether. Even proponents agree that only professional trainers are qualified to use electronic training tools. E-collars train based on punishing bad actions rather than rewarding good behavior, and dogs often revert to old habits and run away unless they wear the collar all of the time.

No puppy should EVER be fitted with a shock collar. Period!

Reward training teaches puppies THEY are in control of getting good stuff—and the reward varies depending on what your puppy loves. It could be a special treat, toy, or even a "sniff" reward.

Reward Training

Reward training teaches pets to recognize a desired behavior by linking the action to appropriately timed verbal praise, sound signals such as a clicker training tool, or "cookie" (food) rewards. Whether you use a head halter, a clicker or verbal command, or cookie power, the major part of training involves teaching the puppy or adult dog *to want to comply.*

'If you sit, Fido, I'll open the door.' Or 'If you sit, I'll put your leash on.' 'If you sit, I'll throw the tennis ball.' Once your puppy has the light bulb go off, he learns to LOVE sitting because the pup can control whether he gets the reward or not. Teaching your pup the meaning of the word "sit" is only five percent of the training; 95 percent of training teaches the dog, "Why do it?"

For dogs, one of the most effective rewards is verbal praise. Puppies appreciate praise, too. Be sure to fill your voice with emotion that says how pleased you are. "What a *smart* puppy you are!" Verbal praise works best when partnered with a more tangible reward, like petting. Or treats. My Magical-Dawg will do just about anything for the promise of a treat.

Use petting and scratches in all your puppy's most favorite places as a reward, too. Pay attention to his sweet spots such as under his chin and above his tail.

Toys and games are a favorite, and really get the tail a-wagging when used in

WARNING!

Effective correction interrupts the behavior or takes place immediately after (within ten seconds) the behavior. By contrast, punishment is a way to get back at the puppy, to revenge the behavior. Please, get rid of the punish idea altogether! Granted, it may help vent anger in the short term, but causes long-term damage to any relationship with the puppy. And it won't cure the behavior. Revenge has no place in puppy training, or training any pet, for that matter. Puppies associate punishment with your presence—and learn to fear you. For more about effective and humane puppy corrections, turn to Chapter 15.

training. Again, it depends on the puppy which toy or game should be used. Perhaps he loves a game of fetch with a ball, or a game of tug with a dental rope toy. Once you've figured out his favorite, reserve it for use only as a reward. Make him earn it before the games begin!

Food rewards are legal, and bar none, treats are the most universally effective training tool for dogs and puppies. The treat should be something completely different than his usual diet and reserved only for those training sessions, or rewarding particularly good behavior. If he usually eats dry food, for example, then treat him with canned food. Commercial treats are designed to not upset the nutritional balance of his diet, and that's an important consideration with puppies. You don't need much—just a taste is all it takes.

Anything your puppy really likes to eat could be a potential bribe to use for training. For instance, my dog Magic loves cat food so much, that just a tiny smear on the end of my index finger does the trick. Strong-smelling treats work best, though. Tiny amounts are enough to prompt the right behavior, and won't unbalance his diet. If you use commercial treats, break them into pieces so one treat provides two or more rewards. Liverwurst often is a doggy favorite for training.

When To Start Puppy Training

Puppies are little sponges and they absorb lessons quickly. Your baby dog starts to learn the moment he sets paw in your home, and one of the most important lessons is to teach him that learning is FUN.

By six to eight weeks of age, your puppy can easily learn basic commands simply by teaching him how to learn. Puppies that enjoy training eagerly lap up more challenging tricks and commands as they mature.

Please avoid using the word "no!" when your puppy does something wrong. It's so overused that some puppies begin to believe that "no" is their name. Remember that training is learning, and puppies learn by making mistakes so they know what WON'T work, and choose better options.

A more powerful training word is "yes." Find opportunities to say "yes!" by catching your puppy in the act of doing something you like. If he does something unacceptable, instead of shouting "no!" try to find a method that encourages him into a legal alternate behavior. Look for opportunities to reward good behavior and replace bad choices with acceptable ones.

Puppies have short attention spans. Several short training sessions of about five to ten minutes each will be more successful than a single marathon training time. Set up a schedule in your routine so that you know your puppy has the energy and eagerness to learn. A good time is before meals because you can use a portion of his meals as treat rewards during training, without upsetting his nutrition.

How To Clicker Train

A great way to teach puppies to learn, think, and please you is a dog training technique called clicker training--clicker training puppies is easy, too. Puppies—and people—will repeat behaviors that reward them and naturally avoid behaviors that offer no benefit. Owners don't have to be master dog trainers to use this technique and puppies learn very quickly how to behave.

An added benefit is the puppy figures how that HE controls the outcome. That's empowering for the baby, and encourages him to think of ways to get you to do what he wants by guessing the good behavior you'll reward. It also teaches your dog to enjoy and eagerly look forward to dog training lessons because they become a game and way for you to communicate with each other.

My dog Magic learned using clicker training very quickly. By ten weeks of age, he performed "puppy push-ups" (sit-down-sit-down) on the local TV station. Your puppy can learn just as easily, and in fact, puppies are sponges eager for new things to learn. Give them a constructive · energy.

Clicker training lets your puppy stumble upon the b⟨ do. He will perform many "wrong" behaviors befor⟨ gets a reward. The puppy figures out that he'll get ⟨ and perform—the behavior you want. The more wro⟨ better he learns what won't work. You don't use com⟨ direction with clicker training, it's all puppy motivated, so the pup⟨ punished—but he's only rewarded for the right choice.

Here's how it works. Instead of waiting for your puppy to do something wrong, catch him doing something right. Mark that behavior with a distinctive signal so the puppy understands THAT action (the sit, for example) is what you like. You can use a special word like YES!, or a signal like the click from a clicker. The clicker simply explains to the puppy he was right. Then reward him with praise, treats, or a toy. Choose whatever floats your puppy's boat, and reserve the most prized reward for these training sessions.

Explaining the "Click"

To speed up the process, trainers recommend you load" the clicker so that the pup quickly identifies the sound with a forthcoming reward. Here's how to do that.

- Fill a shallow dish with smelly treats. Liver bits, cheese, slices of hotdog or other strong scented morsels work best. This isn't about filling his tummy and spoiling his proper nutrition, so the tidbits shouldn't be bigger than the tip of your little finger. You want the pup to appreciate the smell and taste and want more.
- Get comfortable on the floor with the dish within reach but so the pup can't access. Get a treat ready in one hand with the clicker in the other.
- CLICK the clicker, and when the pup's ears twitch or he otherwise comes to investigate, immediately give the treat. He won't know why or care at first—it'll be all about getting that next taste.
- Repeat the sequence over and over. Always click first, then treat. Click-treat. Click-treat. Click-treat. Be sure he has a chance to swallow before proceeding to the next click-treat.
- Very quickly, the pup should look at your treat hand as soon as the click sounds. Eureka! That means his puppy brain has connected the dots and he understands that CLICK signals a treat coming for him.
- Once the pup understands what the click-treat sequence is about, you can use the signal to point out the behavior you like, and reward with the treat. You simply wait for the puppy to plant his tail in a sit, for example, and immediately click-treat.

The pup may look confused. He'll come to you, perhaps paw your leg, run around, trying to figure out what made the "click" sound. When he again sits, click/treat . . . and watch the wheels turn. After only two-to-four repeats, many puppies figure out they control if they get a treat by their behavior.

Puppies understand cause-and-effect (their action makes you click-treat) very quickly. Before long, your baby will volunteer all sorts of behaviors in an attempt to make you click and give a treat. He figures out that he can turn you into a treat-dispenser once he figures out what you want. Puppies trained using clicker training spend time doing just that—trying to please you. Don't you perform better when you anticipate being paid for a good effort?

PUPPY POTTY TRAINING

A new puppy brings great joy, but potty training puppies can lead to frustration. Puppy potty accidents start your relationship off on the wrong paw. Without the right training he won't know how to please you.

Dogs can be potty trained at any age, but puppies learn much more quickly than adults. Puppies are so cute that owners forgive puppy-size accidents, but adult-size deposits aren't cute and often lose the grown-up pet his home. Use these 8 puppy potty training tips to housebreak puppies and ensure he grows up to be the best friend he's meant to be.

Think of potty training from your puppy's point of view. When he has to go he won't wait-he simply squats in place. He won't understand why you're always mad when you come home. If he's punished but not shown what you want, he'll think you don't want him to potty at all. Rubbing his nose in it makes him wonder, "She want me to eat that stuff?" Punishing teaches puppies to potty when you're not watching, or to hide deposits more carefully.

Catch Him In The Act

Timing is key when teaching cause-and-effect. He won't understand your anger has anything to do with the deposit he created five minutes ago. Unless caught in the act or pointed out within 30-90 seconds, correcting the baby won't work.

Instead, catch the pup in the act…of doing something right. Then throw a happy-dance praise party to tell him how smart he is! People work more eagerly for a bonus than a reprimand and dogs are no different. Once he learns he gets paid to go in the right spot—positive reinforcement—he'll virtually cross his legs to please you.

How Long Can He "Hold It?"

Pups need a bathroom break after every meal, nap, and playtime. Depending on his age and breed, he'll be fed two to four or more times a day. Prevent potty accidents by anticipating when the puppy needs a break. Your pup has a baby-size bladder and limited capacity to "hold it" no matter his best intentions. It can vary a bit between breeds with large and giant breeds having a bit more "storage" capacity and Toy breeds a bit less. And yes, that means potty breaks in the middle of the night, too.

But in general, here's what to expect:

- Two-month-old pups need a break about every two hours
- Three-month-old pups can hold it for four hours.
- Four-month-old pups can wait five hours
- Five-month-olds can wait about six hours
- Seven-month-old pups should be able to wait about eight hours.

8 Puppy Potty Training Steps

- **Create a schedule.** Base potty breaks on the pup's age, activity level, and mealtimes.
- **Choose a location.** Dogs rely on scent cues to remind them what's expected. Whether you create an indoor toilet spot with newspaper, pee-pads or a doggy litter box, or select an outdoor potty, take him to the same place each time.
- **Concentrate on business.** Keep him on leash until he's productive, or he'll only play and then have an accident inside. Take off the leash for a playtime as part of his reward for eliminating.
- **Name the deed.** When he squats, say a cue word that identifies the action. My dog knows "take a break" means to get down to business, while some folks use "hurry up" or "potty." Make sure your entire family uses the selected cue consistently. Once the puppy has been productive, reward with lots of praise, play or a tiny treat that doesn't upset his regular nutrition.
- **Confine and supervise.** Puppies don't want to live up close and personal to their own waste, so confinement can be a great tool to teach a quick lesson. A small room won't work-he can poop in one corner and sleep in the other. If the pup isn't productive after fifteen minutes during potty break, confine in a crate for fifteen minutes and then try again. If he potties in the crate, that confines the mess to an easily cleaned area. He'll have to live with his mistake for a short time. The next time he'll be more likely to empty when offered the opportunity. Alternatively, hook his leash to your belt so he can't sneak away and do the dirty deed.
- **Watch for warnings.** Puppies sniff the ground and walk in circles before they pose. If he squats inside, pick him up so he stops the process, and move him to the designated legal toilet area. Give your cue word, and praise when he's successful in the right spot.

- **Clean accidents.** Use an odor neutralizer to eliminate the smells that lure your puppy back to the scene of the crime.
- **Roll up newspaper.** When you find an accident, it means you've not paid attention to his needs. If you're feeling really aggravated, don't hold back. Roll up that newspaper—and hit yourself over the head with it, and resolve to do better next time. Just like puppies, owners take time and patience to learn important lessons.

Submissive Urination

Puppies wetting isn't always about house training because they use a wide range of communication signals to show deference behavior, including submissive urination. Squatting and peeing is normal behavior used by puppies (and sometimes adult dogs) to "cry uncle" and proclaim the owner—or another dog—to be the boss. Since puppies naturally will be at the bottom of the doggy hierarchy as babies, they use these signals to diffuse situations in which they feel threatened.

Puppies usually outgrow the wetting behavior, but some very submissive dogs continue as adults. In puppies, the scent of the urine also tells the other dog about the baby's sexual status and maturity level, and that also serves to tell other dogs that the puppy is no threat. However, adolescent boy puppy urine has a much higher content of testosterone, which signals mature dogs they should "teach him well" before he gets too big for his furry britches. These adults can put on quite a show, even if no injury is intended, and the pup's submissive urination helps stop the adult dog's schooling.

In this ultimate display of submission, puppies typically throw themselves at the owner's feet. He'll wiggle with lots of loose, low-held tail wags, and avert his eyes in the opposite of a steady hard eye stare, which is a challenge in dog language. He places his body position as low a position as possible. Finally the pup squats close the floor, and wets. Sometimes he turns onto his back before wetting. Submissive wetting behavior most commonly happens during greetings when you return home after an absence.

What NOT To Do

Owners of new puppies understandably object to the dog wetting on the floor. Even youngsters that have been properly potty trained can display submissive urination during greeting displays or when they feel stressed around older dogs or strangers. Some of the same behaviors that look like a guilty puppy may include submissive wetting designed to appease your upset feelings. But remember that because the behavior is instinctive and used to diffuse the angry actions of the scary other dog (or human), your anger can actually make it worse.

Think of it from your puppy's viewpoint. He pees. You yell, and he thinks, "Oh no, now he's REALLY upset so I must not be submissive enough!" So he pees some more.

Any actions on your part that communicate you being in charge--yelling, shaming, touching, or even making eye contact—communicates to your puppy that he's not yet submissive enough. In dog body language, the top dog put a paw across the puppy's shoulders, or leans his chin across the baby dog's neck to show they're in charge. When you pat your puppy on the head, that's sending a similar message.

So how do you stop puppy submissive urination? Teach him better control and more confidence so he doesn't feel the urge to wet. Much of this confidence and control come with maturity, but you can help with these tips.

- Ignore the behavior. I know, that's hard to do, but refrain from making a big deal out of this. Stay silent and simply mop up the mess as you avoid eye contact.

- If your puppy wets for another dog, this is an opportunity for the baby to learn from the older pet. Allow the adult canine make his point, nosing the pup for example, before calling him away. Then again, clean up the spot without saying a word.

- We love those exuberant puppy greetings when we return home. But if Puppy wets during homecomings, you need to IGNORE the little guy—at least at first. Walk through the door and ignore puppy for ten minutes to give him time to calm down. Turn your back and walk away without speaking to him. Paying attention to ANY of the other dogs nearby also could prompt the puppy to wet, so delay your greetings.

- A big hand coming down toward a small puppy's head looks intimidating. That's what pushy dogs do using chin rest and body leanings to prove their status to other canines. So instead of head pats, learn how to pet your puppy so it doesn't intimidate him. Scratch his chest or beneath his chin but only after he's calmed down.

- Try a softer, gentler voice. Avoid baby talk, and be matter of act. Sometimes confident people and especially men with low voices sound gruff without meaning to and that can turn on the puppy pee-works.

- Avoid "looming" over top of a puppy. Instead, give your puppy space and some busy work for his brain to think so he's distracted from feeling submissive.

- Rather than standing still, back away from the puppy while you ask him to COME and then SIT. As soon as he does, back away and repeat the COME and SIT practice. Have the other dogs practice obedience and reward them, too, to give the puppy a good role model to copy.

- Keep backing up, ignore the "wet" sits, and gently praise and offer food rewards for dry sits so your pup learns that NOT wetting prompts the payday.

Be patient and understanding. In time, almost all puppies outgrow this behavior. And then you can greet each other with the happy expressions you've saved up along the way.

CRATE TRAINING

Is crate training puppies cruel? Why would you want to "cage" that new puppy? The way Junior-Dawg howls and yelps, you'd think she's been beaten. Isn't locking up the pup cruel?

Actually, it's not. Most puppies and adult dogs feel more secure in a small, enclosed den-like area. That's not to say your new puppy should be in the crate for outrageous lengths of time. A youngster should be introduced slowly to the crate when possible and not left unattended longer than he's able to "hold it" for potty training. But crate training is a useful tool for your new puppy.

A crate works well as a bed. Because it's enclosed, the puppy crate also serves as a safe retreat to get away from other pets or pestering children. Don't you want a private place of your own where you won't be bothered? Puppies are no different.

A crate also can be safe place to confine that rambunctious puppy. That keeps him out of trouble when you aren't able to watch him. Besides, most dogs must be confined from time to time, when they travel by car or stay at the veterinarian, for example. So already knowing about and accepting a crate should be part of your puppy's training. It is one of the best tools available for helping to potty train your puppy.

The perfect crate should be just large enough for a puppy to go inside, turn around, and lie down to sleep. It can be a solid hard plastic container or a wire mesh cage.

Of course, puppies grow. So take into account your pup's future adult size before investing in a pricy dog crate. Large crates are available with partitions for you to "shrink" to puppy size, and then enlarge the area as your puppy grows. You can also purchase an adult-size crate, and insert a barrier like a plastic storage box that shrinks the space to puppy proportions until your pet grows into the size. While soft-sided pet carriers work great for transport, they may be too small and prove too tempting for chew-aholic pups to work well for safe confinement.

5 Tips to Crate Train Puppies

Introduce correctly, your puppy will welcome and even enjoy spending time in his crate. The puppy's crate should never be a place of punishment if you want him to consider it a pleasant experience. So use these tips to help your puppy claim the space as his own home-sweet-home.

1. **Make It Familiar.** While well-adjusted puppies tend to be curious, some tend toward shyness. Anything new prompts suspicion. So make the crate "part of the furniture" and set it out in the family room for your new puppy to explore. Leave the door open and let him sniff it inside and out.

2. **Make It A Happy Place.** Place a snuggly blanket or dog bed inside. Or you can toss a toy inside, and encourage him to go get it. You want him to have positive experiences with the crate.

3. **Offer A Treat.** Find a puzzle toy that can be stuffed with a smelly, tasty treat. This should be a treat your puppy loves, but he ONLY gets the treat when inside the crate. Show it to him, let him smell and taste the treat, and then toss it inside the crate and shut the door—with the puppy outside the crate and the treat on the inside. That shows him that an absolutely scrumptious puppy treat is inside, out of paw-reach. And after he's begged and scratched and whined to get inside, open the door and let him get the toy. Allow him to chew and enjoy it for five minutes with the door shut.

4. **Teach Him Tolerance.** Some pups settle down and enjoy their treat with no fanfare. Others throw a fit and want out. So if your puppy fusses let him out—but lock the treat back inside. You're teaching him that wonderful things can be found inside the crate. Most pups learn to tolerate the door shut at least as long as they have something to munch.

5. **Extend Crate Time.** Over a week's period or so, increase the length of time that puppy stays inside the crate with the treat toy. In between training periods, just leave the door open. You'll be surprised how often a worn-out puppy might seek out crate time on his own for a nap—or to get away from the cat.

Once your puppy accepts the crate as a fact of puppy life, you can move the crate to a more acceptable spot in the house. A place next to your own bed will let the puppy sleep in his own spot but near your familiar smells and presence. That also offers you a more private area to seclude him, when necessary, from activities in the living area or kitchen that might keep him over stimulated.

HALTER AND LEASH TRAINING

Leash laws may require your puppy to walk nicely on a leash and know how to heel when off your own property. Even if they don't, it's simply polite puppy behavior to know leash etiquette. Proper leash manners allow puppies the freedom to safely explore the world beyond your front or back yard.

Large breed puppies can grow into power-boat tuggers able to pull the leash from your hands, or drag you all over. That's not just doggone ruled, it's dangerous for you if bowled over and dangerous for them if they run into traffic or become tangled far beyond your reach.

Even friendly puppies can get scared and a leash provides security and a comfort level when a trusted owner offers guidance through a crowd of strangers or scary situations. But puppies won't automatically know how to politely walk on leash. When you pull, dogs instinctively pull back and if you allow the pup to win that can make it even more difficult to overcome the urge.

It's much easier to teach a small puppy than a powerful adolescent or adult. Now is the perfect time to teach your puppy to walk nicely on a leash, so begin immediately when you bring Junior-dog home. Here's how.

1. Many purebred puppies wear temporary collars (or color coded ribbons) from birth to help identify them from litter mates. But if a collar is new to your puppy, give him some time to get used to it. A flat nylon collar with a metal buckle, that you can fit two fingers beneath, is ideal. You very likely will need to get larger ones as the pup grows, so inexpensive ones at first work fine.

2. For powerful pups that might be tempted to pull you off your feet, use a no-pull harness. These training tools work especially well for older hard-headed pups because it self-trains them not to pull. The leash hooks to a clip on the front of the dog's chest, so that when she pulls, the harness turns her back toward the person holding the leash--and effectively, the dog trains herself not to pull.

3. Before attaching the leash or putting on the harness, encourage your pup to sniff them. Smell is an important way puppies communicate so a good sniffing is important. But it's not a toy, though, so don't allow him to chew or play tug with the leash.

4. Choose an appropriate style of leash for your size puppy. Lighter weight nylon leashes work well for small pets while heavier leather leashes may be more appropriate to larger pups. I'm not a fan of the "retractable"

leashes since these can teach pups to pull and reward jumping up, but may be fine for Toy size dogs. A six-foot length typically gives enough puppy freedom without owners losing control.

5. Don't worry about "heel" at this point. The "heel" position is walking alongside you on your left side at knee-level, while stopping and starting when you do, and sitting when you stop. At this point, just aim for your pup to not surge ahead or drag/pull behind, but simply walk nicely on either side on a loose (not tight) leash. That's actually counter-intuitive for most puppies that want to go-go-go! And if you keep the leash tight, he'll naturally pull against it so avoid tugging or trying to drag him. Simply hold the leash in your right hand, doubling up the extra slack so it doesn't drag, and hold that right hand at your belt buckle level.

6. Have treats or favorite toys or other rewards (a sniff of something stinky for nosy pups!) and dole out with your free hand. You may also wish to use clicker training to communicate with your puppy. Show your pup a treat as he sits or stands at your side. If you plan to eventually compete in obedience trials or other dog sports, it's traditional to have him walk on your left side. But if you don't care about competition, it really doesn't matter which side as long as you're consistent.

7. Wait until the puppy focuses on the reward. Then say, "let's go!" or another verbal cue such as "heel" that you use consistently. It's important that you talk to the puppy in a manner he understands so review the article how to talk to puppies. Hold the treat right in front of his nose as you begin to walk, luring him to keep pace.

8. He should not be jumping up for the treat or toy, so lower the position if he's trying jump up. You can also use a long wooden spoon with a sticky treat, or a commercial "treat stick" designed for that purpose so you don't have to bend over.

9. After a few steps, stop and have your puppy sit. Reward him with the treat.

10. Repeat the leash walk exercise, with the lure. Stop every few steps and place your pup in a sit or down, and reward him. The pup quickly should understand that "heel" or "let's go" (or other consistent command) means to walk at your side--and you will pay with a reward when he sits as you stop.

11. When he's performed several exercises, your dog won't need to be lured, but will want to know you have rewards handy. Increase the pup's attention and anticipating by eventually offering the reward intermittently--rather than every time, pay every second, third or fourth time. This teaches your dog that he should always obey since he never knows when a treat will be produced.

12. Once he pays attention for you to give the "heel" command and anticipates the "sits" when you stop, increase the several steps to a dozen or more of the "heel" exercise. Try heeling your dog around the entire perimeter of the yard, or do laps outside the house.

13. After the puppy understands the concept of loose leash walking and heel, change up speeds. You want your dog to maintain the pace at your side, whether you walk, trot or run. Also practice changing directions. When your pup walks on the left, a turn to your right or an about-face to the right should be pretty easy for the dog to follow. Turning to the left may require luring with the reward, at least initially. Turn it into a game so that once the pup understands he must pay attention, you can praise extravagantly when he's not fooled by a change of pace or direction.

14. Eventually move the practice times to areas that have more distractions. After all, leaving your back yard or living room will be necessary when you go to the park, or take a car ride to visit Grandma, and you want loose leash walking to be a default behavior wherever you go. For instance, practice in the front yard during morning rush hour or when your spouse tosses a ball on the other side of the room.

TEACHING COME

Training a recall--how to train a puppy to come--is a basic puppy training command all dogs should learn. It not only promotes polite behavior, it can save your puppy's life.

Curious puppies get into trouble without constant supervision. Even when you watch the baby, that teasing squirrel can tempt him to run into oncoming traffic before you can stop him.

A recall—coming when called—allows owners to prevent trouble even from a distance. For example, maybe your child opens the door for the mailman, and the puppy dashes out. Or the little guy decides to make friends with the black and white stinky visitor—skunk!—and you notice too late in the back yard. Even tiny puppies travel faster on four pudgy paws than people, so there's no way to catch him—and in fact, chasing a puppy becomes a racing game you won't win. Teach "come" and your new pup will stay safely within reach, even without benefit of a leash.

Puppies refused to come when called for several reasons. New puppies may not know their names. You might as well be shouting gibberish.

In most cases, though, puppies don't know what the command means. It's important to explain the term in language your puppy understands. After all, if you don't speak French, it's not fair to expect you to understand that foreign language—and it takes a while for puppies to learn "human." Clicker training is a great way to communicate with your puppy.

Another reason puppies ignore the recall is there's no benefit to them. Why should your puppy forget chasing that butterfly, or running across the street to meet the kid with a ball, and instead come back to you—BORING! Coming when called needs to trump whatever alternative behavior entices the puppy to ignore your command.

1. Figure out what reward—treat, squeaky toy, tug game—your puppy likes best. Be sure it's irresistible and much more exciting than anything else in his puppy world. Reserve that for training exercises. Treat rewards are more about fun attention as the food, so it should be tiny, smelly, and no bigger than the tip of your little finger.

2. Find a time when the kids aren't around, the house is quite and the other pets take a nap. Avoid distractions so puppy has only YOU for attention. Call his name, get his attention, and go to him if need be to show him the treat or squeaky toy.

3. Once he's focused on you and the reward, say "Name, come!" Then turn around and RUN in the opposite direction. This uses his instinctive urge for social play. Puppies can rarely resist the urge to chase.

4. Let him catch up to you, and hand or toss him the reward. Praise him for being such a smart doggy. Give lots of petting and happy talk, so he knows without a doubt that he's pleased you.

WARNING!
One of the most common—and worst—training mistakes is to punish the puppy once he finally does come. Sure, you're irked that he ignored your frantic screaming his name to come. Maybe chasing him made you late for work. But you teach the wrong lesson by acting upset. He learns that when he finally comes he'll be chastised, so he's even less likely to obey the next time. Never punish when your puppy comes no matter how long it takes him to respond. Here's how to teach your puppy to come on command.

5. Repeat the chase game several times in a row. Leave him wanting more, so stop before he gets tired of the game. Practice the "come" command in this way once or twice a day for a week.

6. After a week, try the exercise while standing still. Make sure the puppy isn't sleeping, eating, or concentrating on something incredibly interesting. Say "Name, come!" and show the squeaky toy or treat. When he arrives, throw a huge puppy-party with the treat or toy reward.

7. Once he understands what "come" means and routinely obeys without distractions, challenge him. Try calling him away from interesting pastimes like chasing that butterfly. Practice "come" in new locations—not just in the living room, but also outside in the yard or at Grandma's house.

8. Any time your puppy comes to you, no matter how long it takes, be sure to praise and reward. Above all, you want the puppy returning to you to have only positive associations so he'll never fear returning to you.

TEACHING SIT

Teaching your puppy to "sit" on command is a great tool you can use in many ways. This is an easy command to teach, and helps your new puppy feel like a winner when he gets praise for the natural behavior.

Once she knows how to "sit" on command, you can use this as a default behavior the way children are taught to say "please and thank you." For instance, giving the command to "sit" is a terrific technique for you to control those rambunctious puppy bursts of energy. As long as her tail stays on the ground, she can't get into more trouble nose-poking into off limits areas.

Your puppy will learn to use this default behavior as a way to pay for bigger rewards. A sit becomes puppy currency to ask for (and receive) benefits, because she needs to know that only by following the rules of the house will she get what she wants.

Here are some examples. To go out the door, she should pay with a "sit" first. At mealtime, a "sit" becomes a polite request and her reward is getting the bowl placed before her. When the puppy brings you a toy for a game, teach that she must first "sit" and then she'll be rewarded with the game.

This isn't mean—just imagine the chaos of that blustering pushy puppy once she reaches adult size! Teach the default sit now. That places you in control, while it reinforces your puppy's social position in the family. She learns from the very beginning that as a part of the family, she has to get along with humans and since you control the resources—the food, opening the door, games—she must be polite to you.

There are several training techniques available today. **Lure training** uses a high value reward like a favorite treat or toy to gently lure and guide your puppy into the sit position.

1. Stand in front of your puppy and say, "sit." Be sure to speak to her in a firm, calm voice.

2. Hold the lure just above her head but in front of her nose, and lift the lure upward over the top of her head. To follow the movement of the toy or treat, she has to lift her head, and that puts her off balance. As her nose follows the treat, her furry bottom must touch the ground to keep from falling over.

3. As soon as her ass-ets touch down, give her the treat or toy reward.

4. Set up a puppy routine and repeat this exercise several times each day. If you're working with treats, be sure to schedule the training before meals so she's a bit hungry. Within a short time, your puppy learns she can shortcut to the treat by simply planting her bottom as soon as you say "sit" rather than waiting to be lured.

5. Once she knows what "sit" means, partner the word command with a hand signal. Decide on what signal to use—like a closed fist—and use it every time. By using the word command with the same hand signal each time, and without the lure, she'll begin to associate the hand signal with the command. Your goal is for the puppy to recognize the hand action and word, perform the behavior, and then be rewarded with the treat or toy.

6. At first be sure to reward with the treat or toy EVERY SINGLE TIME. Be sure you use a reward that the puppy ONLY gets during these training drills so she looks forward to the lessons.

7. Eventually, ask for the "sit" without rewarding (other than verbal praise) and offer the treat/toy reward only every second or third time. This is called "intermittent rewards" and is a powerful teaching tool. Your puppy learns that she might get a goody, and she never knows

when, so she's more liable to be faithful. The goal is for her to learn to recognize the command and perform the action with or without seeing a reward.

Clicker training shapes a natural behavior. Rather than luring the puppy into position, or pushing/prodding or otherwise placing her into a sit, clicker training and shaping lets the puppy do her own thing, and then rewards her for the action you like—in this case, a "sit."

It takes a bit longer, but once the light bulb goes off, your puppy will nearly turn back flips to "discover" what else you want her to do. Clicker training is great fun for puppies and teaches them how to learn, and how to please you. Use tiny smidgeons of treats, so it's more just a taste and smell than anything to fill up the tummy.

1. Gather your treats and clicker, and set the treats aside so the puppy doesn't focus on them. Then simply watch for your puppy to sit on her own—and click as soon as her bottom touches down. Then toss her the treat. Note: Timing is key and it's important to CLICK exactly when the tail makes contact. That's how you communicate to her "sit" CLICK! is what you like. The treat follows to reinforce the behavior.
2. She'll probably look a bit confused but grateful as she gobbles up the reward. Now she knows treats are handy, and she wants another one. This is when puppy brains kick into high gear, trying to figure out how to get another treat. Don't talk, don't lure, don't point or offer other guidance. Let her figure it out on her own. Puzzling out how it works teaches the most powerful lesson. She'll know something prompted the "click-treat" but it may take several mistakes before she happens to repeat the sit—and you immediately click-treat.
3. After this second or third treat, she recognizes she's on to something! You can nearly see the wheels spin as she starts offering all kinds behaviors that led up to the click-treat. Maybe she paws your leg, barks, grabs a toy, scratches and falls into a sit by accident (click-treat!).
4. When the light bulb goes off—if I "sit" that click sounds and a click means a treat—your pup may offer half a dozen or more sits in a row. Quite while she's still excited so you don't wear out her enthusiasm. Several short fun sessions teach more than a single marathon one that wears her out.
5. Once she realizes the behavior prompts the click-treat, you can start associating the command with the action. As her bottom hits the ground, say "sit" at the same moment you click, and then give the treat. That way she figures out the word identifies the action.

By teaching your puppy a default "sit" command, the whole world of possibilities open up for you both. Everyone loves a polite puppy. You'll be amazed at how your dog will figure out many ways to "ask" for privileges once she knows this doggy please-and-thank-you behavior. Once your puppy has learned this default you can progress to teaching her to sit and stay with these tips.

TEACHING DOWN

Why is it important to learn how to train a puppy to lay down? Dogs use certain postures naturally as ways to signal intent. Puppies are no different, and it's helpful to understand what your puppy's body language communicates.

Dogs communicate as much with body language as they do with whines, barks or growls. You may have heard of calming signals that dogs use to diffuse tension in themselves and other creatures. These include yawns, averting their eyes, and licking the nose--and also assuming a "down" position.

Lying down not only tells other dogs that he's no threat, it also helps relieve her own stress and tension, relaxes her, and helps her think. In other words, placing your puppy in certain postures can help with his puppy attitude. A dog in a "down" (reclining) position is a calming signal that tells other dogs that he's calm and means no harm.

Lying down also helps your puppy to calm himself. It's a great exercise in relaxation for an over excited baby dog, and a positive way for you to help your puppy practice self-control. Learning the "down" command keeps the puppy from jumping up on visitors, pestering the cat, or chasing the kids and becoming an unwelcome aggravation.

There are a couple of training techniques to teach your puppy to lie down on command. Here's how to do it using **lure training.**

1. Show your puppy his training reward of choice—that can be either tiny smidgeons of a strong smelling treat, or maybe a favorite toy. Remember that he should ONLY get these favorite rewards during training, so he's more eager to interact.
2. Place your puppy in a "sit" position. Once he's in a comfortable sit, and paying attention to you, give the command, "down."
3. Hold his reward in front of his nose, and lower to the ground and slightly ahead of him, so that he must follow. For tiny pups you can teach this on an elevated surface like a coffee table, and lower the treat/toy just below table level. You use the reward to lure him into walking his front legs forward until he's in a down position. Be sure his nose stays in contact with your fingers and treat, all the way down.
4. Once he's in position, give him the reward. Praise!
5. Practice the command and behavior several times, so he understands the concept. Generally it's best to train in several short sessions of 10 minutes or so throughout the day, instead of one long marathon session that wears the pup out. Quit while he's still interested. You want the

puppy to be eager for the next session, and not dread training. It should be fun for you both.

6. Remember that pups learn by making mistakes so a mistake is just a chance for a do-over. End with success! Praise along with the treat or toy and throw a puppy party to celebrate how smart he is.

7. After he's learned to "down" from a sitting position, practice having him "down" from a standing start.

With **clicker training**, the puppy trains himself almost by accident. Basically the sound of the CLICK signals the puppy that the behavior (in this instance, lying down) is what you want—and then you reward the puppy with a treat or toy. When you've already taught him to "sit" on command using the clicker, he'll know to offer you different behaviors to see if he can turn you into a treat machine. Instead of luring, pushing or positioning the puppy, you wait for him to assume the position on his own. Here's how.

1. Have treats and clicker ready, and watch your puppy until he assumes the "down" position on his own. Click at the EXACT moment he goes down, and then reward the behavior with his favorite treat or toy.

2. When this is the pup's first experience with a clicker, it may take him several minutes to accidentally assume the position again. Repeat the CLICK and reward. Don't offer any other verbal encouragement or guidance, you want the puppy brain to percolate on its own and process the cause-and-effect of his actions and getting the treat.

3. If the puppy already understands through previous training that the CLICK signals he's performed what you want, he won't take nearly as long to repeat the "down" when he connects the dogs. Once he's "got it" you can begin using the command "down" at the same moment you click. Your pup will very soon associate the action with the word.

4. Add in a hand signal with your verbal "down" command. Choose something that won't be confused with any other and use that same signal with consistency. For instance, you could hold your horizontally (palm down) toward the pup and make a downward sweeping gesture as you say "down." Click and reward when he complies. Used with consistency your puppy will learn to respond to the verbal and/or silent hand signal command. What a smart baby dog!

Once your puppy understands and complies with the "down" command, you'll have a new tool for controlling those rambunctious puppy moments. That helps him be a polite family member, and welcome guest if you visit others. You'll both get all kinds of praise and admiration for being a great trainer of a genius puppy.

TEACHING WAIT/STAY

Learn how to teach a puppy to stay to prevent your puppy from becoming a door-dasher, injuring others or hurting herself. Some puppies think they're always on the wrong side of a door, and try to dash out any time it opens.

That's not just a nuisance and bad manners on the part of your fur-kid. It's also potentially dangerous for the pet when he escapes the house when visitors arrive—like when Halloween trick-or-treaters arrive or folks come to visit for the holidays. It's also scary and dangerous for people who become startled or knocked down when puppies jump up on them. Puppies don't have to be big to bowl you off your feet, especially if stairs or ice and snow are involved.

Dealing with door-dashing pups is particularly frustrating for owners. Even when the fur-kid understands that a particular location (the doorway) is forbidden, she may avoid the place when you're looking but making a zooming escape as soon as visitors arrive and the door cracks a whisker-width open.

What can you do? Recognize you will NOT stop a pup's urge to see on the other side of the door or beat you outside. You cannot change instinct, but you can modify some of these irksome behaviors.

The command "stay" more often is used in obedience training and means "don't move from this position." In other words, once the puppy sits, stands or lies down and is told to "stay" the pup is not to change position until released. That can be a difficult lesson especially for a youngster to learn. It's a vital command to learn for dogs that will compete in various sports or trials.

But for pet dogs I like the "wait" command for everyday polite behavior around the house. The "wait" command can save your puppy's life. For instance, if one of the kids leaves your gate open, telling her to "wait" can keep your puppy from chasing a stray cat into the street.

While "stay" freezes all doggy action, a "wait" simply stops forward movement. A "wait" is perfect for stopping door-dashing dogs. As the puppy approaches the door you tell her to "wait" so that she pauses. That lets you go out first, or allows guests to enter. The "wait" still lets her stand, sit, or down—or even back up—as long as she does not cross that invisible boundary.

You can also use the "wait" command to stop your puppy from leaping forward in a rush to reach the dinner bowl so she must "wait" politely until you place it on the floor. Then you give her permission to come forward and eat.

An effective and quick way to teach your puppy "wait" is to use the door as a training tool. You won't need any sort of reward, either. Getting to go through the door rewards the puppy better than any treat or toy. Here's how it works.

1. Walk to the door as usual. When your puppy comes along, tell her "wait."
2. Place your hand on the doorknob. The pup likely will dance around seeking to get between your legs and the door as you open the door but just a crack.

3. When she starts to push ahead of you to go through, say "WHOOPS!" (or "YOU BLEW IT" or a similar cue) and shut the door.

4. Just wait a moment. When she finally makes eye contact, again tell her "wait" and reach for the door. When she moves forward, pull your hand away once again and say WHOOPS!

5. Once again wait until she's calm and looks at you. Reach for the door. If she remains calm, begin to open it and continue as long as she waits and doesn't move forward. It may take many repeats before your puppy makes the connection. But sooner than you think, she'll realize the door only opens if she remains still.

6. Reward her for a short three to five second "wait" by giving her a release command—"okay!" in a happy voice, and throw open the door so she can sprint outside. Remember to choose your commands with care and use the same words each time so the consistency helps her learn what "wait" and WHOOPS mean.

When a puppy consistently waits for five-seconds when asked, you'll know that she at least understands what you want. At that point, practice extending the amount of time she waits to ten seconds, fifteen, thirty seconds and so on. She should eventually be able to contain her exuberance and wait—even when the door remains open—until you give her the happy release word.

Practice at a variety of doors in the house so that she understands the command applies no matter where it's given. Baby gates, car doors, front and back doors, gates in the outdoor fence, and just the ringing of a doorbell can all be used to train consistency to ensure your puppy grows up to be well behaved—and safe.

15: Understanding

Puppy Mistakes

Puppies don't make mistakes on purpose. They are not vindictive. Dogs do not set out to get back at their owners out of pique. Bad behavior is the number one reason puppies lose their homes and their lives.

It's vital to understand bad puppy behavior (which usually is NORMAL for the baby) if you are to preserve your loving bond. To help you do this, you can use the P.E.T. test to figure out what's causing the problem and heal your relationship. Only then can you choose the best plan to fix the problem. P.E.T. stands for *P*hysical health, *E*motional issues, and *T*raits of personality and instinct.

THE P.E.T. TEST

Physical Health
Sick puppies tell you they feel crummy with bad behavior. For instance, an upset tummy prompts a bathroom deposit on your carpet or a sore spot causes a reflexive grown and bite when she's petted. Any sudden change in behavior is a wake-up call that your pup needs your help. Before anything else, have her health checked by the veterinarian.

Emotional Issues

Emotional issues caused by stress also impacts behavior. For instance, a change in routine (such as your work schedule) increases her chewing items that smell like you, because the scent makes her feel more secure. She may display separation behaviors. Social hierarchy issues between pets also cause stress-related bad behaviors. She may squat-and-pee to show deference when the older dog simply approaches to sniff her, or a shy pup might snarl out of fear.

Traits of Personality and Instinct

These traits include a puppy's individual personality, as well as inherent behaviors that are hard-wired into every canine brain. Puppies naturally chew, poop, and cry—you can't stop instinctive behaviors. Herding dogs naturally nip at heels and chase cars or bikes—or kids. Terriers were bred to dig, and my target your sofa. Personalities also vary, from wired in-your-face energetic puppies to the sedate or even shy canines.

People who have never shared their life with a puppy may have inaccurate notions what to expect. A puppy's behavior varies greatly from your friend's adult nine-year-old Labrador who sleeps most of the day away.

Also, our memories of beloved childhood pets filter out the negatives and paint rosy portraits of Saint Spot who could do no wrong. New puppies suffer in the comparison. You must have realistic expectations about your puppy's instinctive, natural behaviors. Once you understand why they behavior in certain ways, you can train puppies to use legal alternatives by employing positive rewards.

Your new baby is not a saint. She's not a stuffed toy, either. It is unrealistic to expect her to be perfect, especially when you both have very different ideas about what you want—and need—out of the relationship. Above all, your new pet needs your love, support, and permission to be a normal puppy, with all the intrinsic canine frustrations that may bring. After all, your baby dog accepts you with all your imperfections (even when you insult her by spurning a nasty saliva-soaked tennis ball!). Owners learn to accept, and even to cherish the unique canine foibles of their puppy friends.

Rules of the House—Set Limits and Enforce Them

It's hard enough for you and your puppy to understand each other without further muddying the water with inconsistencies. Figure out ahead of time what rules matter to you. Make sure that everybody in your household understands the set limits, so that your puppy isn't confused with mixed signals.

It's not fair to her, or to you, to be wishy-washy when enforcing the rules of the house. Your puppy won't understand why "sometimes" she can jump on the furniture and get a laugh (from your son), and the same behavior another time prompts anger (from you).

Biting and grabbing pant legs, jewelry or other "illegal" targets may seem cute in a puppy, but turns dangerous in a grown-up dog.

When devising your rules, build in some wiggle room, particularly in areas where the puppy's innate personality or instinctive behaviors are likely to clash. For instance, your Basenji puppy is an active breed that loves scaling the heights, so forbidding her access to the back of the sofa perches will drive you both crazy. Be realistic. Offer some legal opportunities for her to do the right thing.

Almost all misbehaviors arise from misunderstandings about what constitutes a realistic expectation. Puppies chew. Puppies play. Puppies cry, and bite, and poop. These are normal behaviors you cannot—you SHOULD not—even attempt to stop. Understand why they do the things they do, so you can offer them alternative outlets. That keeps them happy and healthy, and keeps your love alive.

If you're both lucky, you have ten or more years together to share. Toy breed puppies may even live into their twenties. Strong relationships are built on mutual trust and to a degree, on compromise. Believe me, your puppy will never stop trying to "train" you to conform to her own canine ideal. She won't give up on you, even when that perfect vision never comes true. Nor should you consider giving up on her.

Work it out. To be fair, set realistic rules of the house. Decide what's important to you, while keeping in mind what's important to your puppy. Then consistently enforce the rules. Don't change the rules mid-stream. And be sensitive to your puppy, should she make a mistake. Be a "pet detective" to figure out why she lapsed, so you can correct the problem without risk of making it worse.

Effective Puppy Corrections

I hate the word *punishment* which smacks of retribution and much prefer to talk about corrections. The best way to deal with puppy misdeeds is to interrupt the behavior with a humane correction, and offer the puppy a better opportunity.

A correction works to interrupt the behavior by startling the puppy so she stops what she's doing. It doesn't take much to break her concentration. Once that's done, you have a few seconds to engage her attention and direct it in a more positive, acceptable behavior. After she's re-targeted the behavior, you reward her. For instance, *interrupt* the puppy from chewing the chair leg, *redirect* her teeth onto the legal chew toy, and *reward* her for gnawing the right target.

W.A.G.S. System

The most successful plan for fixing problem behaviors includes four key elements. If you miss one, you're likely to fail. These are easy to remember, if you just think of the acronym W.A.G.S. It stands for *W*atch for problems, *A*ct immediately, *G*ive better targets, and *S*upport with praise.

- *W*atch for problems so you can interrupt and stop the behavior right when it's happening—not after the fact. Not every correction works for all puppies, so you must define the ideal puppy correction for your pet. Pups that practice bad behavior are more likely to repeat the mistake.

- *A*ct immediately and interrupt bad behaviors once you understand the problem. Educate yourself about what motivates puppy behavior so that you have realistic expectations, and know how to answer puppy needs.

- *G*ive your puppy a more appropriate target that's legal so she can indulge in normal puppy behaviors without getting into trouble. You cannot stop normal puppy behavior. But you can modify the behavior and give your pup an irresistible alternative.

- *S*upport your puppy with praise and good training techniques. Do that by immediately praising her cessation of the "bad" behavior, and rewarding her to do the right thing. Look for ways to catch her in the act...of doing something RIGHT so you can praise.

Using Good Sense

Every puppy and dog is different—where have you heard *that* before? Seriously, what works to correct one puppy may not faze another, so you'll need to experiment a bit to find the perfect puppy correction.

Scent corrections either repel or attract the puppy. For instance, Vicks VapoRub has a strong menthol odor that keeps the puppy from chewing dangerous items like electrical cords.

Noise corrections typically are used to startle the puppy enough to stop an objectionable behavior midstream. These must be sudden, out of the ordinary, and used sparingly or your pup will lose her "startle" reflex. An empty metal coffee can filled with pennies to shake is one such interruption.

Tactile corrections come out of nowhere to physically startle the puppy. One very effective example is the squirt gun. Dogs not only dislike the unpleasantness of getting wet, a zap with a stream of water on their furry tail is a mysterious force when it comes from across the room. However, some puppies LOVE to get wet so this may turn into a reward rather than a correction.

COMMON COMPLAINTS

Puppies are nothing if not inventive. I once was asked how to stop a puppy from swiping dirty underwear and presenting it to guests, including the visiting minister. Stop the puppy? My goodness, that baby deserves applause!

The most common complaints, though, are more serious. I'll walk you through them, and show you how to evaluate the problem with P.E.T., and how to correct it with W.A.G.S. With patience, you can turn bad behaviors into positives and keep your bond intact.

BITING

Use the P.E.T. test to determine if the biting stems from a physical, emotional, or innate puppy trait. A health problem may prompt your puppy to bite, either in reflex from pain or out of stress from fear or defense. Most puppies bite, however, just out of normal exuberance when they play, so biting shouldn't be unexpected. Socialization helps temper the biting, and you'll need to teach your pup some limits if Mom-dog fell down on the job.

How do you do that? Remember W.A.G.S. *Watch* and then *Act* with prompt interruption, and that means *right* as she chomps your ankle, or nails your hand.

All dogs bite and chew, but it's important to teach bite inhibition and stop puppy biting before it gets out of hand. What's baby-cute or aggravating in your new pup becomes dangerous once he grows up.

Needle-sharp puppy teeth easily rip clothing and tear flesh, but an adult dog's jaws also can break bones or worse. Even friendly dogs cause terrible injury if not taught how to pull their punches. One accidental bite could label your puppy as a "dangerous dog" and result in an expensive lawsuit, increased insurance rates, and costly medical bills. Teaching bite inhibition not only protects people and prevents heartbreak, it could save your puppy's life.

Dog Bite Behavior

All dogs squabble (just like people do), but proper training prevents dog bites. Dogs have exquisite control of their jaws and know exactly how close they can snap without making contact. Adult dogs don't miss unless they mean to, and air-snaps and bites that DON'T break the skin are calculated canine warnings.

Dogs mouth objects, other pets and people during play or other social interactions using a soft or "inhibited" bite that causes no damage. Learning to master the power of their jaws—bite inhibition—allows dogs to make important points and resolve differences without hurting each other, or you. Don't expect to stop mouthing altogether, but do teach your puppy the legal limits.

Puppies must learn bite inhibition technique while young. Other dogs are the best teachers and puppies learn by interacting with Mom and siblings. The other pups yelp and bite back if the youngster chomps down too hard, and Mom-dog stops the games if he's too rough, so Junior learns limits.

Orphan puppies, singleton pups without littermates, or puppies taken very early from their mother may not learn these lessons. Pups also can get over-excited or tired, and chomp down too hard during play, even when they know better and mean no harm.

Pups that are startled or fearful may lash out instinctively. When the scary object (other dog, child, mailman) goes away, they feel rewarded and thereafter may bite first to get their way. By teaching your puppy bite inhibition, you can prevent a host of potential behavior problems. Here's how to teach bite inhibition.

How To Teach Bite Inhibition

Teaching requires effective communication. Puppies simply don't know their teeth hurt. Yelling or physical punishment won't explain what's wrong and can make biting worse. Grabbing, pushing, hitting or other contact with a biting pup makes him think you're just playing rough, too--and hurting him can damage the bond you share or prompt him to retaliate even more. Yelling can be interpreted as you're "barking" just like him, and escalate his excitement.

- Explain in terms your puppy can understand. While he won't know specific words, use exaggerated body language, facial expressions, and tone of voice to get the point across. Puppies don't want to hurt you, and they don't want the games to stop, so use this to teach a powerful lesson.

- Instead of yelling when the biting becomes uncomfortable, say "oooooooooh" in a gentle tone of voice, and then pout. Say, "I don't like that you hurt me!" with as much emotion as possible. Whimper if you can manage. This works especially well with tough pushy puppies.
- If the mouthing hurts, YELP!!! just as another pup would announce pain. Don't pull away from him as that encourages a game of "tug" that you won't win. If the YELP!!! doesn't make him let go, push IN toward his mouth to prompt his gag-reflex so he'll release.
- Immediately after your YELP, give the pup a time-out. Thirty-to-sixty-seconds is long enough for him to get the message. Confine in a small room out of sight before giving another chance and resuming the game. If he again bites too hard, repeat the yelp and time-out to teach the lesson that BITES make the fun STOP.
- It may take several repetitions before he figures out the cause/effect that HE controls the game and can keep the fun going by acting like a gentleman. Once the pup mouths gently, praise him and allow the attention to continue.

Practice "Good" Bites

Once your puppy develops a soft mouth, teach him to stop mouthing on request and never to initiate mouthing. Periodic training sessions are essential throughout his life. A good drill might be to allow the pup to mouth for 15 seconds, then say "off" and offer a food reward or toy. He must stop mouthing to get the reward, which also pays him for stopping. After he takes the reward, he can resume mouthing for another 10 to 15 seconds if he likes, then repeat the exercise.

Bite inhibition doesn't mean stopping the mouth behavior altogether. That's too much to ask, and would be equivalent to tying your hands behind your back. Any dog may bite if provoked. But a dog with good bite inhibition that bites will *cause no harm*. And that's a comfort zone owners owe to themselves and to their dogs.

BARKING

Crying is one of the most common complaints of puppy owners. Be aware that just like human infants, crying is natural behavior for baby dogs. I hear it again and again, "She cries all the time, what does she want?" Or they'll complain, "She wakes me at 4:00 a.m. every day and won't stop crying until I feed her. How can I make her stop?"

WARNING!

Shock collars are NOT effective or humane for bark training, no matter what the sales copy may say. They can damage your relationship with your puppy. Because every pup is different, not all the techniques listed above work for every pup—most require an investment of time. If you haven't seen improvement in three to five days using one of the anti-bark techniques, try a different approach.

In answer to the first question, she wants your attention. She may not even know what she wants. It may be the pup's way of saying, "I'm bored. Entertain me!" The more you try to give her what she wants, the more she cries the next time—heck, you've trained her to pester.

Puppies also cry, squeal, scream, or otherwise make sudden sharp sounds of distress if they're hurt or frightened. As you get to know each other, you'll learn to hear the difference between a distress call, and a more mundane puppy complaint, such as she wants you to wake up and play with her.

Puppy barking drives owners and neighbors crazy—it can't be totally eliminated so don't expect to stop it. Dog barking is one of the most common behavior complaints but this normal puppy communication becomes a problem only if puppies aren't taught proper limits.

Puppy barking serves many purposes. Puppies bark when they play, to greet you (or the cat), or defend against scary or intimidating interlopers. Consider your puppy's bark as a doggy fire alarm to warn about anything unusual, interesting or exciting—a friend or stranger's arrival, a sudden sound, or the unexpected sight of you wearing a hat.

Puppies want to be your protector, so don't discourage the behavior. You wouldn't want Junior-Dawg to ignore the burglar, would you? Instead, teach limits. Rather than quashing the barks, figure out why the pup barks and teach him the difference between appropriate barks and problem barks using these tips.

- **Don't bark back.** Talk to your puppy with tone of voice and body language—not just the words—to make sure he doesn't misunderstand. Barking is also a joyful expression. Use a calm voice or else yelling makes King think you're joining the chorus, and he barks even louder.

- **Give your puppy a "bark limit."** Maybe he's allowed to bark three times, or five times—until you acknowledge his warning so he knows you can take over for him. After the designated number of barks, praise your puppy—"GOOD bark, GOOD dog, now HUSH" and give him a treat as you praise. It's hard for dogs to bark while chewing so this actual serves a dual purpose.

- **Watch for triggers.** Barking at the mailman teaches pups to repeat the behavior when your two-pound terror thinks, "My ferocious bark chased him away—I'm an awesome guard dog, beware!" You may want to enlist your mail carrier's help—ask him/her to feed King a treat after he's barked, and praise for being quiet.

- **Remove the audience.** If she barks and you come running every time, you reward the behavior. Instead, thank her then say, "HUSH." When she stops, praise and give her a treat. If she keeps barking, *Act* immediately. Turn your back and leave the room. Most dogs want company, so leaving tells her she's doing something wrong. She'll learn to be quiet if she wants you to stay and give her attention.

- *Give* **door drills.** Ringing the bell, knocking on the door, and arrivals or departures excite puppies or sometimes scare shy babies, so associate the location and sounds with good things for the puppy. Stage arrivals at the front door with an accomplice "visitor" loaded up with treats to toss the pup to help her stop seeing visitors as threats.

- **Relieve the boredom.** Many pups bark because they're lonely or bored. Even if the pup has nothing to bark about, talking to himself may be better than listening to lonely silence. Chew toys that reward the puppy's attention with tasty treats also fill up the mouth—he can't bark and chew at the same time. Puzzles toys can be stuffed with peanut butter or kibble treats that Fluffy must manipulate to reach the prize.

- **Block scary sounds.** Inexperienced pups hear lots of "new" stuff that may inspire barking. When barking arises from fear, the pheromone product Comfort Zone with D.A.P. may help relieve the angst. White noise machines are available to mask sounds, or simply turn the radio to a normal volume and tune it to static.

- *Support* **with training.** Tools such as Gentle Leader and Halti can work wonders. Pulling on the lead gently presses the pup's mouth shut for the few seconds of pressure and signals her to be quiet—and you don't have to say a word. The halters are available from pet products stores and veterinarians.

- **Try a new tone.** Tone collars emit a loud, short tone at the first "woof." That's often enough to make Fluffy stop, and search for what caused the tone—and eliminates boredom and the barking, often within minutes. However, the collar must be adjusted properly or can "punish" the wrong dog if a canine friend is barking nearby.

- **Curb barks with scent.** Researchers at Cornell University in New York found citronella collars to be much more effective in bark training. Citronella collars give a warning tone first; additional barking prompts a squirt of scent that stops the barking. Some of these collars have remote control activators.

Provide your puppy with "legal" chew targets, so he won't be tempted to gnaw your shoes.

CHEWING

You can't stop puppy chewing, because it's normal dog behavior. Puppies don't chew your prized possessions because they're mad at you. They instinctively use teeth the way human babies reach out with tiny fists. Your puppy chews to explore the world, to manipulate objects, to relieve boredom, and because it feels good.

Destructive chewing still makes owners howl. Years ago I hobbled for weeks when my pup gnawed a quarter inch off just one of my high heels. He also chomped my husband's favorite property—the TV remote. He targeted items that smelled like us to feel closer to us, and soothe puppy loneliness, but we still didn't appreciate the compliment!

Chewing gets pups in trouble when they aren't provided with legal chewing opportunities, and forbidden objects are left within reach. Puppy chewing can break teeth, result in dangerous swallowed objects, or burns and electrocution if Junior bites an electrical cord or eats a poisonous plant. Teething increases the urge to gnaw because it relieves sore gums, but dogs usually continue the habit into adulthood.

Don't try to stop it. Instead, prevent puppy chewing problems by *Watching* for temptation, *Acting* to prevent and remove them, *Giving* lots of better (legal) opportunities, and *Supporting* with positive training techniques and praise. Refer to these 8 tips to manage your puppy's gnawing habit.

- **Puppy-proof the House.** A new puppy forces us to become better housekeepers. Keep tempting objects like shoes, handbags, tissues, and your child's favorite stuffed toy safely out of reach.

- **Confine the Pup.** When you can't supervise, provide a "safe" room that has no dangerous or forbidden temptations. Baby gates work well to control puppy access, and can block off a hallway, stair, or room.

- **Use Repellants.** Products that taste nasty can keep puppy teeth at bay. Bitter Apple applied to electrical cords helps train pups to leave dangerous items alone. Many dogs find the scent of Vicks VapoRub offensive. Paint Vicks VapoRub on wooden baseboards or apply to cloth draped over other forbidden targets to keep puppy teeth at bay.

- **Don't Confuse Him.** Puppies can't always tell the difference between your new designer sandals and the "legal" old slipper. It's best to offer chew toys that he won't confuse with forbidden objects.

- **Make A Trade.** Chasing a pup to retrieve your stolen wallet becomes a great game of keep-away, and can teach your smart-aleck pup to swipe things to invite a tag marathon. Instead, when you catch your pup chewing a forbidden object, tell her "no." Offer an irresistible legal chew toy (maybe filled with liverwurst?) as a trade.

- **Offer Puzzle Toys.** Rubber chew toys with openings stuffed with healthy treats keep puppies interested and on target. Some are mint or peanut butter scented to be more appealing. Goody Ship, Buster Cube and Kong products are examples of a wide range of outstanding puzzle toys that can be filled with soft food, peanut butter or commercial treats designed just for puppies.

- **Provide Chewies.** Rawhide chews or edible "dental" chews come in all shapes and sizes, complete with a variety of strong scents and flavors. Soak rawhide in warm water and zap with the microwave for ten seconds to soften the leather and make it more pungent for tiny puppies. Monitor rawhide fun, though. Larger pups are able to gnaw off and swallow pieces, and eating too much rawhide spoils appetites and may prompt constipation or even blockage.

- **Rotate Toys.** Puppies get bored with the same-old every day. Provide at least three to five "legal" options for your chew-happy baby and rotate a couple of times a week. That keeps puppy happy, your precious belongings undamaged, and your fur-kid safe despite himself.

EATING POOP

Most new owners are delighted by puppy antics but puppies eating poop prompts anything but smiles. My own darling Magic indulged when he turned six months old. He'd make a beeline to visit his horse buddy next door and find the nifty treats she left on the ground. After these nasty snacks Magic always tried to kiss everybody on the lips, yuck! Then Magic started to bring his own "creations" into the house.

Dogs commonly eat their own or another animal's droppings (coprophagia). This is normal behavior for mom-dogs that must clean up after their babies, and some of the pups may end up mimicking this behavior. It first appears in pups at about four to nine months of age.

When we wave our hands, shout with disgust, and chase Puppy all over the yard, that's great puppy entertainment. Chasing him can actually reward with behavior and encourage your puppy to play poopy-keep-away. And then he'll run over and want to kiss your face, ewww!

Eating other animals' waste may have to do with taste. Cow and horse manure may contain undigested corn or other ingredients appealing to your pup. The cat's litter box may as well be a puppy snack bar. Cat food contains more protein than dog food, and as a result, feline waste tastes good to dogs. The nasty habit is not only unsanitary it puts Sheba's tail in a twist to have a dog messing with her toilet. Cats pestered in their bathroom look for another place to "go" such as behind the sofa.

Other times dung eating stems from boredom. Pups left out in the yard alone have little to do.

The frequency increases after one year of age. The good news is most pups outgrow the habit. The bad news is, some dogs hang on to the nasty practice their whole life. Shih Tzus appear to be more prone to the behavior.

- Puppies may eat waste to get your attention, which means even yelling rewards their behavior. Remember W.A.G.S. *Watch* to prevent his munch, and *act* promptly if he gets to the treat first. Don't make eye contact or speak to him, but shake a can full of pennies or clap hands to make the noise interrupt him. When he stops, praise him.
- For bored pups, increase playtime to a minimum of 20 minutes aerobic exercise twice each day. Increase the number of toys to keep your puppy

busy when you're away if he's left in the yard. A treat-spiked toy such as a Kong filled with peanut butter offers a tastier, healthier alternative.

- Prevent access by walking your puppy on a leash and leading him away once he's done. Reward him for leaving stools alone. Teach him to "come" and sit in front of you after each bowel movement—his or the other dogs'—and give him a fantastic treat while you pick up the waste.

- Some dogs may eat their own stool when it hasn't thoroughly "processed." A more digestible food may help. Ask your veterinarian for a recommendation. You'll need to make a gradual change in the food or the sudden change could prompt

- Make the stool unappealing by adding a spoonful of canned pineapple, canned pumpkin, or spinach to the pup's meal. Include a dash of MSG in the food, which changes the consistency so dogs won't find the waste as appealing. Commercial products such as For-Bid may help.

- Scoop and clean the cat box as often as possible. Leaving droppings any length of time asks for trouble. Automatic cat boxes sweep the feces into a bin within ten minutes of the cat's deposit.

- Place the litter box on a table or counter out of doggy reach. If the cat doesn't object, a covered litter box might deter the dog but allow the cat access and privacy.

- Use a baby gate to keep the dog out of the cat's domain. Some cats can jump over the standard gates, or you can install it a couple of inches off the ground so Sheba can slink underneath while the jumbo-size pup can't get through.

- Add a tablespoon of vegetable oil to the cat's food so her waste becomes softer and less attractive to snacking dogs. A spoonful of canned pumpkin added to her food also changes the taste or consistency of her stool to make it less appealing, and many cats relish pumpkin as a treat.

- Finally, if you can't be around to supervise, muzzle the miscreants.

In our case, walking on leash away from the horse, a baby gate to keep him from the cat box, and rewarding Magic with a treat after bowel movements did the trick. He's an adult now and hasn't "indulged" in more than eight years. Good boy!

If you don't want a pock-marked yard, offer digging spots for your puppy.

DIGGING

Puppy digging can turn your yard into a moonscape. Puppies—and especially terrier breeds—just can't escape the lure of kicking up dirt. Terriers were bred to "go to ground" after burrowing critters, and they can't help themselves since it's an inborn trait. (Remember the P.E.T. Test!). If not allowed an outlet, they may dig through your sofa or carpet.

But he doesn't have to be a "holy terrier" to indulge in diggidy dog behavior. Puppies of any breed may notice you working in the garden and want in on the fun and copy your digging. They dig up plants, tunnel beneath fences, or dig out of boredom.

They also dig to cool off or stay warm. Hot dogs instinctively scoop out holes to rest their tummies against the cool soil. In the winter, dirt is great insulation and a hole is a warm place to rest. Understanding why pets dig can help you figure out ways to stem the excavation.

- **Tell Him No.** Ideally, you want to interrupt your dog's digging habit by first telling him to stop. Use an air horn, handclap, or short, emphatic NO! Then praise when he stops digging, and give him a toy or treat to replace the forbidden activity.

- **Give More Attention.** Dogs that dig out of boredom need more one-on-one attention from the humans they love. Spend more time with your pup and when he's in the yard, give him something better to do.

- **Tire Him Out.** Exercise tires out puppies and reduces digging—a tired pet is generally a much better behaved pet. Twenty minutes aerobic exercise twice a day is a good rule of "paw" for pups over four months of age. Just make sure both you and your pet don't over-heat when playing fetch.

- **Cool Off Hot Dogs.** In hot weather, give outdoor pups plenty of shaded, cool damp places to rest with lots of available water. That will prevent the urge to tunnel for cool resting spots. Better yet, bring him inside to cool off to prevent heat stroke.

- **Keep Pup-cicles Warm** In cold weather, provide a warm place sheltered out of the wind and wet. Refer to these cold weather tips to keep puppies safe and prevent the need to dig.

- **Fix Your Pup.** Spayed and neutered dogs have much less incentive to escape a fenced yard in search of company.

- **Provide A Puppy Pastime.** Puzzle toys such as the Goody Ship, Buster Cube, or Kong toys can be stuffed with peanut butter and other goodies. Rex will be much more inclined to work at getting the treat out and forgo the pleasure of pock marking your yard.

- **Make Temptations Unattractive.** Placing chicken wire an inch below the topsoil, or scattering cut up rose trimmings, holly or other prickly mulch helps keep puppies from digging in gardens. Sticky Paws for Plants works well to keep indoor plants safe from your puppy's digging behavior.

- **Barricade Openings.** Sometimes it's helpful to cover over the holes with canvas, chain-link fencing, bricks, or other impediments. But some dogs will not be denied, and simply dig around the obstacle.

- **Give Him His Own Digs.** For hard-case puppies, build a sand box for his legal excavation. A shaded area about three feet wide, six feet long and two feet deep will satisfy most dogs. Let him see you bury one or two of his toys (very shallowly) and then encourage him to dig them up. Get down on your hands and knees and show him by pawing the sand with your hand.

Forget about what the neighbor's think! If a doggy playpen can save the rest of your yard, and preserves the love you have for your puppy, isn't it worth it?

JUMPING UP

A puppy jumping up aggravates and even terrorizes people. His paws muddy slacks; her claws snag pantyhose. Being tackled by a dog is an unpleasant, dangerous surprise. It's also rude behavior that should not be allowed in polite human/canine society.

It's not the pup's fault. Dogs instinctively lick each other's faces as a greeting display, and a submissive pup aims attention at a dominant individual's eyes and mouth. Jumping up is a type of doggy communication and licking the owner's face is a polite canine "howdy!"—a way for him to acknowledge you are the boss, and to solicit attention. Since puppies don't stand eye-to-eye with owners, they tend to jump up toward people to compensate for their size.

Many people consider jumping up to be cute when the Saint Bernard is a puppy, but the attraction tends to fade as the dog matures. It becomes a safety issue around children and elderly people who can be seriously injured by a jumping dog. Your circle of friends may include folks who (gasp!) dislike or are even frightened by dogs of any size.

Teach your pup a more appropriate way to greet people. Once she realizes her behavior offends you, she'll strive to find another way to say hello.

1. Don't step on her toes, and don't knee her in the chest. Either action can be painful, which tends to prompt avoidance behavior or even aggression. Instead of teaching your dog to greet you appropriately, such actions tell her to avoid greeting you altogether—and that's no fun for anybody.

2. Do NOT reward the jumping up with petting or playing or any sort of reciprocal greeting. That's what she wants, after all. Instead, teach her that she only gets attention when she SITS on command.

3. Have a family member help you with the training. As Pete enters the front door, he should stand still and greet the dog with, "Cricket, COME!" followed by "Cricket, SIT!"

4. When Cricket sits as requested, Pete should offer his hand for a sniff (very important to dogs in greetings). Once Cricket sniffs the hand, Pete can stroke her cheek or neck, saying "Goooood Cricket," to reward the behavior.

5. If the dog still insists on jumping up, Pete should step backwards so the dog's feet miss—and at the same time, turn away from her. That interrupts the canine "howdy" because a dog can't properly greet a person's back. Cricket learns that if she wants to receive a greeting, she must keep all four feet on the ground and plant her furry tail.

6. Once the pup's paws hit the floor, again give the "sit" command and repeat the exercise. After this social greeting has been exchanged, Pete can then walk into the house and take a seat. The puppy will likely follow—have other family members waiting in the room to reinforce her good behavior with "good dog!"

7. Drill with your dog, until a sit prompts more attention for her than jumping up ever did. If a wet slurp across the mouth doesn't offend you, then you kneel down on your pup's level to put yourself in range of her kiss so she doesn't have to leap.

8. And remember, there's nothing to stop you from training your extremely well-behaved dog to jump up—but only on your command.

When your puppy reaches adolescence the dog often becomes rude out of testing limits (just like a human child), or the clueless baby doesn't understand how to control impulses. Adolescent jumping up can turn into "nose boinking" behavior which can lead to broken glasses or even a bloody nose. Jumping up often combines with mouthing behavior where the pup bites and grabs at your hands, clothing or even (ahem) your buttocks in a drive by grab-tag game.

In most cases, the puppy doesn't mean to be bad and it's simply how he plays. Each dog is different so not all work with every pup. Here are some of my favorite.

- **Keep It Low Key.** Homecomings and departures are a prime time for jumping-up because puppies want to greet or stop you from leaving. Turning your back on some of these dogs actually revs them up even more, so instead try ignoring the bad behavior. "Ignore" means you make no eye contact, say nothing, and stand still like a boring zombie and offer no reaction for idiot puppy behavior.

- **Dance Your Dog.** When your puppy jumps up, grab her front paws and dance her around the room. Some pups hate this so much that's incentive enough to stop jumping. However, with other pups that enjoy the "dance" it could reward the behavior. If this causes more intense mouthing and biting of your hands, try a different tip.

- **Play A Game.** Teach your puppy a conflicting behavior such as "fetch your ball." She can't jump up if she's running to bring you her ball or other favorite toy. Just the name of a special game or toy—"go get your bear!"—can change the dog's focus and redirect the behavior long enough for you to evade the jumping. With enough repetitions, your puppy will begin to associate your home-coming with "go find" instead of jumping up.

- **Hide A Toy.** For pups that ambush you and bite your ass-ets while playing outside, hide a toy or two in the back yard and ask them to "find" the toy. Bad weather can give puppies cabin fever when they don't have adequate time outside to run off the energy. Mental stimulation can wear them out, too. Show your puppy a favorite toy and then roll it up inside an old towel and knot it to make a puzzle. Encourage the pup to un-ravel and get the toy. You can even tie the first toy-in-the-towel inside a second one for more of a challenge for relieving boredom on days.

- **Practice Commands.** A conflicting behavior—like "sit" when you come home—helps enormously. You'll need to practice your puppy's "sit" during calm moments first, and then ask for this polite behavior before you leave and when you arrive home. Guests will appreciate a polite "sit" when they arrive, too, and won't appreciate your puppy leaping around and mugging them for attention.

- **Cry and Yelp.** Many puppies don't know their own strength. When they jump up and you wave your arms and try to push them off, they may think it's a game and grab and bite harder. Tell them it hurts the same way another puppy would, with a YELP! Lay it on thick, over act, and cry and sob like the pup has done major damage. Some tough dogs really get the message using this. For the out-of-control grabby ambush type of dog play, give him a taste of his own medicine and SCREAM (very loud but very short), and fall over "dead." Don't move, don't say anything. Play dead for at least 15-20 seconds. The shock value may be enough to send a permanent message that such games stop all interaction, plus they hurt you—and playing dogs really aren't interested in hurting you and won't want you to cry.

- **Body Block Noise Boinks.** An anxious or playful pup may leap high and very rapidly and suddenly "poke" at your face with their nose. That can be triggered by leaning over top of them especially when they're in a high-arousal situation like a homecoming or around other dogs. It may be a way for stressed pups to relieve their anxiety so be aware of situations that cause these behaviors. Dogs control each other's movement with their body language. Think how a Border Collie makes sheep move just by getting close. You can stop your pup's jumps by stepping close to him just before he leaps. Cross your arms, and step into the pup's personal space before he crouches to leap.

- **Use A Drag-Line.** This is a long leash that the pup can "drag" along the ground. When the pup approaches, before he can jump simply step on the line. That prevents him from jumping up. While you step on the line, don't make eye contact or give attention until he stops trying to jump.

- **Employ A Tie-Down.** With a tie-down, you simply attach your drag-line to a fixed object like a fence, stair rail or other immovable object like an eye-bolt into the wall. This exercise uses the same principles as teaching the "wait" command only instead of closing a door or gate, the pup is confined by the leash. That keeps you safe from mouthing and claws, and prevents the pup from jumping up and grabbing. Practice puppy sits and downs, while you stay out of range. The puppy only gets rewarded with contact from you when he stays calm with all four feet on the floor.

- **Recruit Help.** Practice the tie-down exercise with several friends. Have them approach, one after another, and the pup only gets to be petted if he doesn't jump. If he tries to leap, back out of range and say, "You blew it! Whoops! Too bad!" or something similar. Repeat the exercise ten to twenty times in a row, and the pup will learn the lesson.

NOISE PHOBIAS

Scary noises from storms, or even 4th of July fireworks can turn the bravest canines into scared puppies. Even fireworks noises for New Years, cars backfiring or gunshots during hunting season also create dog fear, and happen throughout the year.

Up to 20 percent of dogs suffer from noise phobias. For fireworks celebrations, owners can predict events and take steps to sooth upset doggy feelings. But unexpected storms can be difficult to manage. Frantic pups pull down window blinds, collide with screen doors or crash through windows, while others simply shiver and moan. It's important to puppy-proof your home so the frightened pup isn't injured, and a secure fence should withstand even a puppy panic attack.

Behaviorists recommend pups be counter-conditioned to the scary noises by exposing the fearful dog to recorded sounds of scary noise played at a very low volume, and rewarding him for staying calm. Gradually, you increase the noise level, to help the pup "get used" to the noise—desensitize him—so he can learn to tolerate it.

Desensitization programs can take weeks and sometimes months to work, though. Pups suffering from storm phobias also may react to the sounds of rain. Even to the sensation of humidity or barometric pressure can trigger behavior problems, and you can't do much to control humidity or barometric pressure. Use these tips to dial down the noisy fear factor.

1. Fearful dogs may instinctively look for tight-fitting places to hide. They often squeeze between furniture and the wall, or hide your armpit. This applies a comfortable "hug" pressure sensation that seems to calm them, so let your pup seek his own shelter.

2. Avoid offering sympathy. Coddling your pup when he's fearful can reward the behavior. Instead of saying, "poor baby are you scared?" use a matter of fact tone, "wow, that was a loud noise--but we aren't scared."

3. Some puppies benefit from the Storm Defender that reduces static electricity that prompts some behavior problems. Another option is the Anxiety Wrap that applies even pressure to the dog's body and helps him better manage his stress. A similar product that applies pressure is the Thundershirt. In addition, the Calming Cap seems to help some pups through stressful, anxious situations by hiding their eyes.

4. Avoid giving your puppy a sedative, because it won't reduce his fear. He just won't be able to do anything about it, which can make his anxiety even worse. Your vet may prescribe anti-anxiety medication based on your individual pup's needs.

5. Ear plugs that mask the sound may also help. My veterinarian Dr. John Brakebill says when a client's dog went crazy after they moved near a gun range, the phobia calmed during treatment for an ear infection because the thick ointment muffled the sound. He suggests cotton balls or ear plugs as a temporary solution to help muffle the noise. Ask your vet to show you how to safely place anything in the dog's ears, though, so you don't damage the pup's hearing and plugs are easily removed after the upsetting sounds subside.

6. A natural supplement of melatonin may help--a substance similar to a chemical produced in the brain that helps regulate sleep. Melatonin

helps reduce the panic attacks in noise-phobic dogs, but it won't sedate the pup. Melatonin lasts several hours and may be cumulative over several days so you can plan ahead for known scary events like 4th of July. Melatonin can be found in health food stores, pharmacies, and some supermarkets. Always check with your veterinarian for the proper dosage for your size and breed of dog.

7. Another option includes pheromone products that ease the fear. Plug-ins, sprays, and infused collars are available at pet products stores. It helps a dog put a damper on fear long enough to "think" so that your behavior modification/training techniques can work. When the weather report indicates storms or fireworks displays are in the offing, be prepared. The infused collar works more immediately. The spray can be used every one to two hours on bedding or a bandanna the puppy wears.

8. Dogs can't panic when using their brain for something else such as "work" so give your pup a job to do just before and during the thunder and lightning display. Drill him on obedience commands and special tricks, or ask him to play fetch and carry around a favorite toy. That engages his brain into productive activity rather than thinking about the scary noises.

9. Giving him treats and positive rewards for remaining calm also reinforces the benefits of controlling his emotions. Each time the wind blows, or thunder booms, try saying, "Wow, what fun!" to jolly him along and show there's no reason to fear, and then give a treat.

10. Turn a radio to static to create white noise that muffles scary noises. Certain types of music can prove calming, too, by "entraining" the dog's heart, respiration and brain waves to slow down and match the soothing rhythm. Harp music can be especially calming.

SEPARATION BEHAVIORS

Puppy separation anxiety isn't uncommon. According to veterinary behaviorists reporting at the Western Veterinary Conference, about fourteen percent of pet dogs seen in veterinary clinics suffer from problems being left alone. Puppies adopted before eight weeks of age, mixed breeds and pups adopted from shelters are at highest risk.

Affected puppies feel over-attachment to one or more family members. Problems develop when the amount of time you spend with the pet changes. Puppies learn to become comfortable with their new routine, and a change in routine perhaps due to kids returning to school, your new job, new dog introduction or baby can cause puppy stress.

Animal behaviorists use different terms to describe the condition. That's because not all dogs become anxious when left alone, although they do act out. *Separation distress* doesn't necessarily mean the pup feels anxious and probably is a more accurate description of dogs displaying separation behaviors.

Separation behaviors encompass a whole range of activities that might take place as a result of the puppy being left alone. Many times, dogs act out because they're stressed or anxious at the owner's absence.

These puppies tend to follow you around the house and becomes increasingly upset as you prepare to leave. When left alone, affected pups act anxious or distressed, often become extremely vocal, and sometimes forget house training. They may destroy property either to escape or as a way to relieve stress.

Many pups with separation anxiety target personal items. For instance, they chew up your shoes or a favorite purse. They aren't retaliating for being left alone. Because these items smell like you, that can trigger anxiety that prompts destructive displacement behaviors. Puppies may also seek out objects that smell like you because your scent comforts them.

In a similar fashion, pups may forget potty training. Older pups might even decide to mark with urine or defecate on something that smells like their owner. This isn't to get back at you, but instead is the pup's attempt to self-calm.

But some behaviorists suggest that separation behaviors such as emptying your sock drawer or chewing up the toilet paper may arise out of boredom. This could be the canine equivalent of a teenager left alone by parents, and throwing a party. About the only way you can tell the difference is to set up a video camera while you are gone, and have it looked at by a behaviorist to see if the dog shows anxious behavior or simply appears to have a good time disemboweling the sofa cushions.

Pets should never be punished for any anxiety-based behavior because punishment makes it worse. If your puppy exhibits destructive separation behaviors, you can take steps to reduce the problem.

- Your veterinarian may prescribe drug therapy that relieves the angst, such as Clomacalm (clomipramine hydrochloride), or Reconcile (Prozac or fluoxitine). But drugs alone won't be a magic wand.

- The most intense acting out happens within the first twenty to thirty minutes after you leave, and how long you're gone doesn't seem to matter. So if you can distract the puppy during this critical period, much of his upset feelings will be relieved, and destructiveness may be eliminated.

- Desensitize the puppy to the triggers of departure. Pick up your car keys fifty times—but then don't leave. Put on your coat or open the door a dozen times, then stay inside. Repetition of these cues makes them lose meaning so the pup doesn't get upset, and remains calmer when you actually do leave.

- Stage absences to build up the puppy's tolerance level. Leave for one minute, two minutes, four, ten minutes and so on. Do this ten or fifteen times in a row so that (just like with the keys) so the repetition makes it less important to the pup.

- Make sure the puppy gets lots of exercise before you leave, and after you return home. A tired pup is a better behaved pup. If he's worn out, he'll snooze rather than chew up the cushions.
- Soothing music can also help calm anxiety. I like to use harp music, which acts like a natural sedative and keeps anxious dogs peaceful.
- Bach Flower Essences also can help dogs with anxieties. You can add the drops to the puppy's water bowl for all day sipping.
- You can also offer puzzle toys filled with tasty treats, and hide them around the house for the puppy to find. When he's thinking and hunting for treats, he can't worry or develop a full-blown panic attack.

PART FIVE

CANINE FASCINATIONS

16: Favorite Legends

In the Beginning

The dog was arguably the first creature to be domesticated—to cross that human ring of firelight and stand beside us as defender, helper and friend. As the "wolf in the parlor" the dog's sensory ability to hear the un-hearable and sniff out prey, herd and stalk, and capture with incredible physical prowess and stamina, left our ancestors in awe. Of course, the dog's incredible loving nature and sociability made them fit right in with their human "pack" families.

People of the past sought answers to their questions about the dog's amazing abilities and often devised delightful, eloquent myths to explain the inexplicable. Ancient civilizations honored both wild and domestic canines with paintings in caves and on canvas, celebrated them like gods, and were mystified by their weird and wonderful behaviors.

Today, that puppy snuggling on your lap has become a beloved companion. But when Junior-Dog howls at the moon or alerts to things we can't detect, his puzzling behavior still can shiver your spine.

Creation Stories

In South America, some Inca tribes believed that human life was first released from the underworld by a dog scratching up at the earth from below. Asians were especially partial to dogs, and believed that the Dog of Many Colors had created the world.

Native American people cherished dogs. Shawnee legend says that Our Grandmother and her dog live close to the Land of the Dead where she weaves a basket--when it's finished, the world will end; but each night while Our Grandmother sleeps, her little dog unravels the day's work and buys us more time.

According to Navaho traditions, Coyote is a master trickster from whom not even the gods are safe. During the creation when the night sky was made, instead of carefully placing the stars, Coyote haphazardly flung them in one mass and created the Milky Way.

Ghost Dogs

Leeds Castle, a medieval fortress in the Kentish countryside near Maidstone, England, has at least three ghost dogs. The fierce "Black Dog of Leeds" dates from the 15th century and is considered a portent of doom, thought to be the ghost of Henry VI's aunt who was imprisoned for practicing witchcraft.

But one of the other dog ghosts actually saved a life. A visitor perched in a bay-window seat in a room located high over the moat, and saw a black dog walk across the room. She thought it was a real dog until it disappeared into the wall. The surprised woman rose from her seat to investigate; abruptly the bay window cracked and fell apart, dropping in the water below with a crash. Had she not risen to follow the ghost dog, the woman would have plunged to her death.

Werewolves and Dog Men

During the Middle Ages, only the wealthy minority could afford to keep dogs, and the war dogs abandoned by solders wandered cities, living on garbage and roaming in packs. Many survived by reverting to a semi-wild state and copied their ancestors' proclivity for digging up and feeding upon corpses.

As a result, many people believed the legends of devil dogs, werewolves, dog-headed dragons and other hideous creatures. In 1685 Germany, a dead burgomaster was said to have ravaged the countryside as a werewolf. Even the unpopular King John of England was reputed to have become a werewolf after he died.

Kludde is an evil Belgian goblin and is feared as a werewolf or large winged black dog that walks on his hind legs. He plays brutal tricks on people, usually around twilight, knocking them down. One can hear the chain about his neck clanking and can recognize him by the two small blue flames that hover about his head.

Fearsome creatures known as Cynocephali were monster men with the heads of dogs who populated medieval legends. They were thought to worship Hecate, the goddess who could pacify the cruelest of dogs. St. Andrew had been instructed to preach the Gospel to these dog-men, and Cynocephali appear again and again in church manuscripts of the eleventh and twelfth centuries.

Among the pantheon of early Japan was Omisto, the god of suicide. Omisto had the body of a man with the head of a dog, and rode a charger with seven heads. Omisto promised eternal joy to any man who killed himself in Omisto's honor.

Similarities between the social behavior of wolves and humans have promoted many stories of children being raised by wolves. One of the oldest and most famous of these myths celebrates Romulus and Remus, brothers who later founded Rome.

Gods, Demons and Dogs

The ancient Chinese believed that demons feared black dogs; for that reason many black dogs were sacrificed so that their blood could be sprinkled to exorcise demons. During the Middle Ages in Europe, a similar belief fostered the practice of smearing the blood of black dogs on the walls of the home to protect the householder from demonic possession. In Brittany, elaborate rites supposedly forced wicked souls into black dogs, which were then ceremoniously destroyed.

The Celts who settled in Gaul (France) in the fifth century B.C. followed a Gallic religion in which their god Smertulus was the "devouring dog," a symbol of destruction and death. They also believed the horned nature-god Cernunnos was often accompanied by a wolf. The ancient Greeks considered Apollo a wolf-god, and the Arcadians worshiped Zeus as a wolf-god. Odin, god of Norsemen, also had a wolf as companion, and the Norse underworld also was inhabited by a god known as Fenris-wolf who symbolized chaos and the everlasting ice fields that would one day return to engulf the world.

Although ancient Egyptians worshipped cats, they adored dogs as well. About 4240 B.C. the upper Egyptian culture worshipped Set, a Greyhound figure with a forked tail. Another god of ancient Egypt, Anubis, was conductor of the souls of the dead—the cleansing god, and the guardian of the gates of the underworld. Dogs were never considered subordinates by the Egyptians— they were hunting dogs, war dogs, even temple dogs, but always equals, and killing a dog was punishable by death. Only slaves or children acted as shepherds of livestock, an occupation considered too lowly for the dog. After death, the dog was embalmed and his remains placed in a sarcophagus; the dog's human family mourned his passing with weeping and by shaving their entire bodies.

Supernatural Guard Dogs

Vulcan, the Roman god of fire and metal, forged a bronze dog that slowly came to life under his divine breath. From this dog was born Cerberus, the watchdog of Hades. Cerberus lay chained to the gates of Hades, where he fawned on those who entered and devoured those who tried to escape. He had three heads: a lion, wolf and dog, with a mane of writhing snakes, a dragon's tail and a mastiff's body. The ancient Romans placed a cake in the hands of their dead to pacify Cerberus.

The Icelandic goddess of the dead is Garm, the Dog of Hel. It's said that anyone who fed the needy while on earth will find bread in their hand to bribe Garm for safe passage. The Avesta, sacred book of Ancient Persia's Zoroastrian religion, tells of a rainbow bridge guarded by a yellow-eared dog whose bark drives out the fiend from the souls of the good.

Dogs and the Hereafter

At one time in Greenland, the children who died were buried with the head of a dog—a trustworthy guide into the next world. Aztecs believed their dogs were spirits sent by the god Xolotl—god of fire, lightening and death—to guide them in life. They also believed when a human died, a dog would lead the soul of its dead owner through the underworld, so a dog was sacrificed at every burial for this purpose.

South American lore tells of dog-demons that sit in judgment of human souls. Tezcatlipoca is the Aztec Prince of the underworld in the Mexican Book of the Dead. He has powers over both life and death, is a bringer of disease and pestilence, and often appears as a dog or coyote. Zotz is a huge winged creature with the head of a dog that lives in the darkest regions of caves, according to ancient Mayan scriptures. Condemned souls must travel through the House of Bats, so that Zotz may receive his daily allotment of blood.

Shawnee legend says that Our Grandmother and her dog live close to the Land of the Dead. There each day she continues to weave a basket. When the basket is finished, the world will end. But each night while Our Grandmother sleeps, her little dog unravels the day's work and buys us a little more time. No wonder our dogs are indeed our best friends!

17: Fun Canine Foibles— Explained

Rolling in "Schtuff"

It never fails—after giving your dog a bath so he looks and smells lovely, he ends up rolling in poop or dead animals. We love them and enjoy cuddling with our dogs, but the behavior can really make it a challenge to get up close and personal. Why do our dogs insist on seeking out the stinkiest stuff and rolling in it?

Dogs live through their noses. Pungent scents prompt rolling behavior in some dogs. This scent ecstasy is similar to what cats experience when exposed to catnip. But when it comes to canines, the doggy indulgence is a good bit more noxious, and tends toward offal.

When a dog finds what he considers an attractive odor, he rolls to rub his shoulders, back and neck into the offering. He spreads the scent over himself as though it's doggy cologne.

Nobody knows for sure why dogs roll in nasty things like rotting garbage, dead animals, or feces. I grew up next door to a river, and our dogs always considered dead fish to be particularly attractive--eww!

Puppies enjoy puddle-jumping, rolling in mud—and other noxious substances.

We know that our dog's sense of smell is many times more sensitive than our own. Maybe they detect subtle nuances that the human nose simply can't appreciate.

This may actually be an evolutionary trait that helped communicate with the family group when wild canids roamed the earth. "Perfuming" himself with such scents may allow the dog to carry the smelly message home, so other dogs can "read" all about the discovered food source.

Eating Grass

When dogs eat grass owners are puzzled because they often vomit. But eating grass seems to be a natural behavior for many dogs and isn't as odd as some of the other strange stuff puppies eat. But if it tastes so good, then why do puppies eating grass later vomit?

Dogs need a balanced diet and are considered are omnivores, which means they can eat nearly anything, including vegetables or fruits. Puppies actually can safely eat many people foods. Wild canids like coyotes typically eat vegetable matter found in the stomach and intestines of prey animals. They also may eat roots, grasses and even fruit.

Your puppy probably also begs for and enjoys snacks of raw vegetables like lettuce, green beans and carrots, or even apples. These can help keep your puppy's breath fresh and teeth clean, too. Maybe he also likes the flavor of munching on grass, but that still doesn't explain why he gets sick.

Most pet dogs occasionally eat grass, which may be used as a natural emetic to stimulate vomiting when the dog feels unwell. When the puppy has a gassy tummy, gulping mouthfuls of long, tickling strands of grass prompt her to "whoops" out whatever upset her tummy.

However, grass eating does not always result in vomiting; some dogs may simply relish the flavor or texture. Some speculation exists that grass grazing may provide trace elements of vitamins.

Indoor dogs may indulge their urge to graze by nibbling houseplants which, depending on the plant, may be dangerous or even poisonous. Occasional grass eating isn't a cause for concern. You can even provide some healthy wheat grass for your dog to gnosh. Pet supply stores often have grass or herb growing kits available.

However, if grazing becomes a habit, and especially if grass eating prompts vomiting more than two days in a row, your pup should be examined by a veterinarian to rule out a health problem. An upset tummy that becomes chronic should be diagnosed to rule out intestinal parasites like roundworms or something more serious.

Pica—Incredible Inedibles

Your puppy picks up objects and explores the world with their mouth. Chewing up, mouthing and sometimes swallowing stuff can get them into trouble, and even lead to blockages or poisoning. Other times, the strange stuff puppies eat doesn't necessarily hurt them—it just puzzles their owners.

Eating non-edible stuff is called pica. Puppies often accidentally swallow pieces of toys, but pica refers to almost an obsessive urge to eat rocks or gulp mouthfuls of dirt, sticks, sand or other nondigestible objects.

Eating non-edible objects can become tempting with the object is flavored or scented and becomes irresistible. Common problem objects include grease-covered items from the kitchen, milky baby bottle nipples, and used tampons or soiled diapers. Most items tend to smell like you—such as worn socks—so keeping these items out of puppy mouth-reach is important. Refer to Chapter 11 for first aid tips if your puppy swallows dangerous objects.

Some puppies seem to be drawn to come kinds of dirt, or even want to chew rocks. Wild animals occasionally target soils such as clay that absorb toxins. Parrots in the wild, for instance, eat mineral-rich dirt to supplement their diet. We don't know if that's behind the puppy's urge to target dirty delights.

Probably the smell plays a role in the attraction, especially if some other critter has urine-marked the area. Puppies may taste the dirt to better understand what the message says. I've known of dogs that prefer specific areas, too, such as mulch piles that maybe have a mushroom-like aroma or taste. Dirt munching can stop up the puppy innards, but an occasional taste probably won't cause problems.

Drinking from Toilets

New puppy owners often feel disgusted but also curious and wonder why toilet dogs drink from toilets. After all, that's not the cleanest place to find water, and with the puppy's acute sense of smell you'd think that he'd realize that!

With tiny puppies, there's also a danger of them falling into the toilet and being unable to get out. Puppies can drowned in very little water so just be aware of taking safety precautions if this is an issue. It may be as simple as remembering to latch the bathroom door.

Puppies and adult dogs are creatures of habit, so once they find a "drinking fountain" they like, chances are they'll make a beeline for the commode whenever possible. But exactly why do they like it?

Smells Good. Part of the attraction may be the scent. After all, your own personal signature odor identifies you as the love-of-his-life, and nothing is more personal to you than the scent of elimination. What's nasty to us offers the puppy lots of important information so surrounding himself with "eau de YOU" when he dips his head into the tank may be the thrill of a puppy lifetime.

Cool Drink. The commode also keeps water cool. The porcelain container insulates and the larger water surface compared to a tiny puppy bowl also helps so it doesn't heat up as quickly. On hot summer days, water in the toilet may be more tempting just from a temperature standpoint. You may wish to invest in a water bowl that keeps the contents cool.

Cool Room. It's not only the water that's cooler. Human bathrooms tend to stay cooler than any other part of the house, because of the tile on the floors. For a hot, panting pup on a warm summer day this may be the best snooze spot ever. And he doesn't want to range too far from the cool nap zone to get a drink, so he just nips over a few paw-steps to take a slurp from the commode. It's not unusual for cats to follow you to the toilet, either, and puppies have some of the same reasons.

Fresh Drink. Water that sets in the puppy's bowl not only can become warm, it can get stale quickly. Every time you flush the toilet, a fresh flood of water—aerated for even better taste—floods into the holding area. Yum!

Tastes Good. Some kinds of water bowls hold odor or flavors, too. Plastic and metal containers may be off-putting to the pup, but the toilet container doesn't absorb these odors and the water stays clean tasting.

Oxygenation. Each time you flush, the water is refreshed, and the motion of the water churns oxygen into the liquid. That also improves the flavor. If this appeals to your puppy, why not invest in a doggy water fountain?

Cleaner Water. From the puppy's standpoint, water in the toilet may be cleaner than that found in his bowl. My dog Magic uses his water bowl to wash out his mouth after he's played tackle-the-ball in the grass and dirt. That means his first gulps of water leave grass and dirt in the water. The commode is a continual source of clean, debris-free water.

Instinctive Choice. Some experts speculate that drinking from constantly refreshed water instead of a bowl may hearken back to how dogs evolved to survive. Moving water—as in a rushing mountain stream—prevents the dangers of stagnation where all kinds of bugs like mosquitoes or molds and parasites like coccidia and giardia may be found. So dogs may be instinctively drawn to prefer "toilet water" to that in the bowl.

Of course, the "stuff" that ends up in the toilet (when puppy isn't drinking) doesn't provide the best water-fountain option. Aside from it being unappealing from a human standpoint, the cleansers we use in the toilet can be quite dangerous of the puppy ingests these toxic substances and could poison your puppy.

Dreaming dogs vocalize, twitch, and appear to chase dream-critters.

Dreaming Dogs

Yes, dogs (and puppies) do dream. We can only guess at what visions they see as their paws wiggle, whiskers twitch, and they woof as their tails thump with excitement. Perhaps he's chasing a ball, or teaching the neighbor's cat a lesson in manners. It's likely they relive in their dreams those events of normal dog life.

Dog dreams are born during the deep, rapid sleep phase—that means puppies dream more than adult dogs. Animals with the most highly developed brains tend to have the longest dreaming phase during sleep. People typically dream for up to two hours each day (whether we remember or not). Adult dogs spend at least that amount or more each day indulging in dreams.

Can Dogs See Color or TV Screens?

Can your puppy tell the difference between that red ball and the blue one? The retina at the back of the eyeball contains specialized cells called rods that detect shades of white, black and gray while cone cells detect color. Dogs have fewer cone cells than people do and see a dichromatic—or two-color system. The dog's cones are most sensitive to deep blue and green wavelengths. In comparison, people see a three-color system of red/yellow/blue. Dogs seem to be similar to people who are "color-blind" and unable to detect certain colors like red.

Dogs can be easily trained to tell the difference between certain colors even though they don't see them in the same way as people. Under normal light, dogs probably see green and blue as much brighter than red, because they have very few to no red-sensitive cones.

Like human eyes, the dog's eye can control the amount of light that passes into the eye. The specialized muscle called the iris—that's the colored portion of the eye—can contract the pupil to a round pinpoint in bright light, or open wide to allow in more light during low light. The lack of color sense is balanced by the dog having many more rods—light sensitive cells on the retina—than people do. The retinal illumination of the dog is about three times more efficient than ours.

Many of the short-nosed dogs like Pugs have high density vision cells arranged in a single spot on the retina, called the area centralis. The area centralis has three times the density of nerve endings as the visual streak found in long-nose breed dogs. Some researchers report this may be why short-nose dogs seem to react to the TV screen, or perhaps appear more sensitive to human facial expressions.

This may be why smaller breeds are cherished not only fit better on the owner's lap or for hunting or guardian abilities. Dogs able to see well in near-vision (lap-to-face) distances have the physical ability to be more responsive to our moods and emotions.

Magic, the author's German Shepherd, doesn't seem to care about the bright orange Paintbrush wildflowers surrounding him.

Dog Eye Shine at Night

Dog eyes also have the ability to "re-use" existing light to improve their vision in low-light environments. Many mammals, including cats and dogs, have a layer of highly reflective cells behind the retina that reflects back any light the eye captures. The *tapetum lucidum* enhances the light-gathering efficiency of your dog's eyes by nearly 40 percent and accounts for that eerie eye-glow you see at night. That means your puppy's eyes are more sensitive under low light conditions and have a better ability to perceive changes in motion than people. But the dog's visual acuity—how clearly they see—isn't particularly good under these conditions.

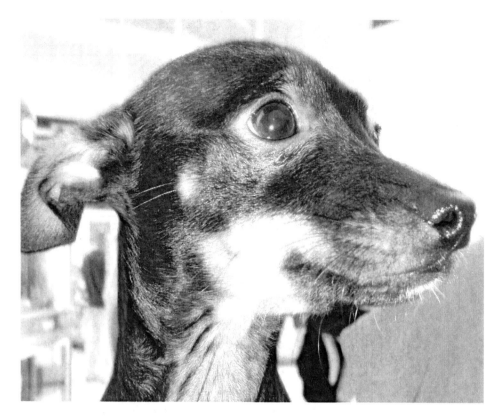

Dogs and puppies learn very quickly how to use body language and facial expressions to tug at human heartstrings.

Why Do Dogs Act "Guilty"

Do puppies feel guilty and do dogs show shame? Maybe you arrive home to find only empty Halloween candy wrappers, or perhaps the baby dog isn't yet reliably potty trained and "tells" you he's made a pile somewhere. When your puppy meets you at the door, head low with ears slicked back and eyes averted, is that a canine apology?

Certainly they can ACT as though they feel guilty. At least, the behaviors mimic what humans associate with feeling shame or apology. Whether or not this accurately reflects the dog's true feelings is open to debate.

Dogs do appear to care how humans feel, and not just when we're upset. We know from our own experience that pets often seem to sympathize when we feel lonely or sad, tearful or joyous. The puppy may solicit petting and snuggles that cheer us up, or spin in circles of happiness when we're happy. My dog Magic has learned what makes me giggle and smile, and chooses behaviors like a well-rehearsed comedian to garner the most laughs. And we know there are health benefits to keeping pets. In fact, some canine studies have shown that dogs feel empathy not only to crying owners, but to strangers who weep.

It seems dogs might in fact have the capacity to feel guilt. Or at least to anticipate that they may have done something wrong. I'm sure you've had the experience of walking back into the house where your pup—instead of greeting you with jumping up and wags for attention—slinks around and won't look at you.

Whereupon you ask the pup, in a firm tone of voice no doubt, "What did you do?"

And he looks even more guilty as you stalk about the house searching for whatever damage has been done. Maybe you find something he's chewed. Or perhaps he's been dumpster-diving and potentially swallowed some object that could cause intestinal blockage, so you're understandably fearful and concerned.

Your tone of voice and actions teach your puppy how to react the NEXT time, too. When dogs learn that you get upset if they scatter the garbage, they theoretically may "act guilty" after such behavior and tell on themselves even before you know something has happened. That's one explanation, anyway, but honestly, I don't buy it.

Your puppy displays these same apologetic behaviors when they've done nothing wrong. Often an owner walks through the door, and immediately the puppy acts guilty. So your voice goes into scolding mode as you search high and low for the infraction—but you find nothing wrong. However, Junior-Dawg still acts guilty. What's up with that?

You may have inadvertently taught your puppy to apologize based on certain body cues and context of the environment. Your tone of voice, the way you communicate with the puppy and "loom" over top of him, make strong eye contact in a canine-language challenge, all associated with the trigger of a home coming, can teach the dog to act contrite every time you return home, whether he's done something wrong or not.

Puppies quickly learn to associate your home-coming with a raised voice and your displeasure after only a couple of repeated bouts of you finding true infractions. But he won't necessarily connect your homecoming anger with having done something wrong because puppies have a very short memory when it comes to infractions. For them to connect the "bad deed" to your displeasure, you must catch them in the act so they associate digging up the potted plant is illegal.

After you've expressed your anger during homecomings a couple of times, the puppy learns to associate your arrival with you being angry. Even if he's done nothing wrong, he'll do his best to reduce your displeasure with his "apologetic" behavior.

Puppies do this with older dogs, too, to diffuse potential aggression. It's a way for them to tell the adult canine that "you're the boss." When your puppy slicks his ears down and grovels on the floor or even rolls over and wets—that's called submissive urination—these are all doggy signals designed to diffuse aggression. They're called appeasement signals, or sometimes termed calming signals.

Adult dogs do this to show other canines (and puppies) that they aren't all gruff-and-grumble and the fearful pooch has nothing to fear from them. They'll play bow to invite the other dog to play, for example. This is categorized as a "meta signal" that means other things like growls or wrestling that follow are meant in jest, sort of a doggy make-believe similar to a human dad playing "scary monster" to chase the kids (making sure they first know it's just pretend).

So does your puppy feel guilty when he empties the kids' Halloween sack? Is he ashamed for chewing up your new shoes? Does he apologize or "tell on himself" when he's done something wrong?

Honestly, nobody knows for sure. But it's clear that our dogs do pay exquisite attention to their human's behavior and emotions, and react accordingly to make us feel better and diffuse our upset feelings. How cool is that?! It's up to us, as caring and savvy pet parents, to do the same for the fur-kids that we love.

Tummy Rubs and Leg Kicking

When you scratch your puppy in certain spots, it seems his hind leg is wired to kick in response—and that's exactly the case. Irritations like bug bites or other itches activate nerves that signal the pup he should scratch to relieve the irritation. This scratch reflex is a reaction he can't control.

This reflex is so ingrained, that your veterinarian may use it as a test to help diagnose certain issues. Think of the puppy's scratch reflex like the knee-jerk response you have when the doctor taps your knee with his tiny hammer.

Where you scratch and which leg kicks in response varies between puppies. Typical areas include the back, both flanks and the tummy region. How hard you scratch also influences the reaction.

Most dogs and puppies enjoy tummy rubs, too, and may ask for one by rolling over and showing their tummy, so it must feel good. Just remember—rolling over also is a deference signal and depending on the circumstances, it may be a request for you to "back off, please, you're scaring me!" Watch what the rest of what the baby's body says, and if he moves away, let him.

Humping Your Leg

It's not unusual and actually is pretty normal for puppies to "hump" toys, each other—or your leg. Mounting, clasping and thrusting behavior appears first during puppy play between littermates and typically is done by both boys and girls. Adolescent male dogs continue to experiment, and often mount anything that doesn't move faster than they do—chairs, other pets, your leg, the family cat.

Castration during development decreases your pup's sexual interest, but even castrated dogs often continue mounting behavior. Mounting can be used as a challenge display, or a way to try and intimidate and achieve social status.

In addition, dogs that discover masturbation feels good may continue the practice, have erections and ejaculate even though they've been castrated. This can become a default response to stress or excitement, too, in which case you can try to control and anticipate situations that could prompt stress. Most times, the normal behavior can be managed by offering your puppy a different target—a stuffed toy, for instance—and confining him when you have guests to avoid any embarrassment. Your embarrassment that is, not his.

APPENDIX A:

Favorite Puppy Websites

I have found Internet resources invaluable for their educational impact—and for the fun they offer. Today, a computer and modem allows anybody to plug into the World Wide Web to visit nearly a limitless supply of puppy-related destinations.

I use online resources like professional websites to help research my books; electronic "bulletin boards" to ask and answer questions; memberships to Facebook and Twitter with expert friends and followers; and subscriptions to email lists or newsgroups that feature electronic communities of people with similar interests. The Internet has become one of my most important business and recreational tools. It keeps me connected to family, friends, and colleagues, and even allows me to conduct interviews with experts around the world.

It's important, though, to be able to separate the chaff from the wheat—the solid and reputable information from the "expert wannabes" that tend to crawl out of the woodwork. My list of favorites numbers far more than a dozen. But the ones I've featured here offer a good jumping-off place to begin your explorations. Most have multiple links that take you to other sites, in a never-ending chain of puppy delights. You should also try the search function on your browser. Simply type in your subject (puppies), and hundreds to thousands—maybe even millions—of puppy-oriented destinations are listed.

Puppy Care Plus!

Today nearly anyone can hang out a virtual shingle and declare themselves to be an expert dog trainer. The methods and qualifications are mixed, and just because someone has a TV show—or writes a book—doesn't make them the best fit for your puppy. The Association of Pet Dog Trainers (APDT.com) offers a search-able database to find qualified trainers, as well as good articles on what to look for in a trainer—and what all those "certified" initials mean. Here's a good article that explains what you need to know when you search for a trainer. (apdt.com/petowners/choose/certifications.aspx)   I am a certified member (cats and dogs both) of the International Association of Animal Behavior Consultants (IAABC.org)

Of course, when care issues and questions arise, the first place to look for answers is veterinary resources. The veterinarian who personally knows your puppy and can examine him is in the best position to answer specific questions, but many online veterinary sites offer general information on dog and puppy issues. WebVet.com is one of the best with content written by contributing writers that has been reviewed by veterinarians to ensure current and accurate information. PetMd.com also is a trusted online resource with veterinary information.

The American Holistic Veterinary Medicine Association (www.ahvma.org) is one of my favorite veterinary resources. Many people these days are interested in offering a wider range of care options, and this site offers a searchable database to find a holistic vet in your area.

Another link to bookmark is the FREE online version of the Merck Veterinary Manual. (www.merckmanuals.com/vet/index.html) You'll find up to date descriptions of diseases, conditions, signs and possible treatments for those who want to go the extra mile in understanding and caring for their new puppy.

Pedigree and Show Dogs

The folks who show and raise pedigree puppies take great pains to remain up-to-date and educated on everything there is to know about their particular dog breed. Type the name of any canine purebred into an Internet search engine and you're sure to find dozens and dozens of websites with lovely pictures and information. One of the best places to start is the American Kennel Club site (AKC.org) which links to an exhaustive library about dog breeds, sports and the fancy. The United Kennel Club (www.ukcdogs.com) also has great information in particular about hunting dog breeds and sports.

Puppy Rescue

Oh, there are so many wonderful rescue sites available! National animal welfare associations as well as many regional or privately funded groups host countless educational websites. They provide information on adopting homeless puppies and dogs, rescue operations, and uplifting success stories. Petfinder.com provides educational information as well as a searchable database for adoptable dogs (and cats…and other critters).

Puppy Fun

I've saved some of the best for last. You'll surely find more favorites as you explore the Information Puppy-Highway, but I came across these and just had to share them. Icanhascheeseburger.com

When you have a new puppy, health and behavior concerns are vital. But you can't call the puppy "hey, you!" forever, and the sooner he learns his name the better. Check out PuppyNames.com for a fun resource that offers hundreds of choices, top picks, and even the true "meaning" of a particular name.

Everybody loves puppy pictures. And you'll find thousands on the internet. One of my favorites is ICanHasCheezburger.com where you'll find hundreds of cute puppy pictures with creative sayings.

But heck, there are many sites that welcome your contribution. Don't be shy about posting pictures of your own precious baby. Social sites like Facebook, Pinterest, Tumblr and others adore puppy cuteness. And if you want to go all out, maybe you'd want to have an artist capture the beauty of your puppy in an original work of art. Again, there are many available.

APPENDIX B: Resources

Dog Associations

A dog association is a national organization that registers puppies, keeps records of their ancestry in pedigrees, publishes breed standards, sponsors dog shows and events, and determines who will judge them.

Kennels are individual establishments that strive to produce the "ideal" dog of a given breed. These dogs then compete in conformation and performance trials sanctioned by the dog association in which that dog is registered.

The goal is to determine which dog is closest to the standard of perfection in looks, temperament and/or performance. Depending on the dog association, the standard may vary somewhat. For instance, dog associations that register breeds in Europe prohibit cropped ears which may be required in the breed standard in the United States. Kennels and sometimes individuals hold membership in local or national dog clubs, which in turn are members of one or more dog association.

There are several kinds of dog clubs: All-breed clubs, Specialty breed clubs (a single breed), and Performance clubs. Performance clubs sponsor various dog trials, which are activities that test the dog's performance ability. Some of these trials are exclusive to one or more breed of dog, while others are open to any dog including mixed breeds. Trials may be specific to a breed's heritage-- what a particular dog was bred to do, like dig out varmints (Earth Dog trials). Other trials are just for fun, such as agility and flyball.

There are also a number of dog associations. Breed standards may vary from association to association, and not all dog associations recognize the same dog breeds. Be aware that registration does not guarantee the quality of a dog, only that both parents were the same breed. However, registered dogs can prove their quality by earning titles, and dog parents with titles usually produce high-quality puppies. If you are interested in learning more about dog show opportunities for you and your puppy, contact one or more of the following organizations located throughout the world.

American Kennel Club: AKC Customer Service, 8051 Arco Corporate Drive, Suite 100, Raleigh, NC 27617-3390. Telephone: 919.233.9767 AKC.org

American Mixed Breed Obedience Registry: P.O. Box 223, Anoka, MN 55303. AMBOR.us

American Rare Breed Association: 9921 Frank Tippett Road, Cheltenham, MD 20623, Telephone: 1-301-868-5718 ARBA.org

Australian National Kennel Council: http://www.ankc.org.au

Canadian Kennel Club: http://www.ckc.ca/

Federation Cynologique Internationale: Belgium. http://www.fci.be

Kennel Union of Southern Africa: PO Box 2659, Cape Town 8000, South Africa. Telephone: +27 21 423 9027, Fax: +27 21 423 5876 http://www.kusa.co.za/

Mixed Breed Dog Clubs of America: c/o Linda Lewis-Membership Secretary, 13884 State Route 104, Lucasville, OH 45648-8586. (740)-259-3941 http://mbdca.tripod.com/

The Kennel Club of India: http://www.kennelclubofindia.org/

The Kennel Club: United Kingdom. Telephone: 0844 463 3980, Fax: 020 7518 1028 http://www.thekennelclub.org.uk/

United Kennel Club: 100 East Kilgore Rd., Kalamazoo, MI 49001. Phone: 269-343-9020, Fax: 269-343-7037 UKC Website

Animal Welfare and Information Sources

American Humane Association
http://www.americanhumane.org/

American Society for the Prevention of Cruelty to Animals
http://www.aspca.org/

Animal Legal and Historical Web Center
http://www.animallaw.info/

Pet Partners
http://www.petpartners.org/
(human/animal interaction, service dogs, etc)

National Association of Professional Pet Sitters
http://www.petsitters.org/

Pet Sitters International
https://www.petsit.com/

SPAY USA
http://www.spayusa.org/

Recommended Books

Dog Facts: The Pet Parent's A-to-Z Home Care Encyclopedia

New Choices in Natural Healing for Dogs & Cats

ComPETability: Solving Behavior Problems in Your Multi-DOG Household

ComPETability: Solving Behavior Problems in Your DOG-CAT Household

Complete Care for Your Aging Dog

The First-Aid Companion for Dogs and Cats

Care Organizations

American Animal Hospital Association
http://www.aaha.org/pet_owner/

ASPCA National Animal Poison Control Center
http://www.aspca.org/pet-care/animal-poison-control

Animal Behavior Society
http://animalbehaviorsociety.org/

American College of Veterinary Behaviorists
http://www.dacvb.org/

American Holistic Veterinary Association
http://www.ahvma.org/

American Veterinary Chiropractic Association
http://www.animalchiropractic.org/

American Veterinary Medical Association
https://www.avma.org/Pages/home.aspx

The International Veterinary Acupuncture Society
http://www.ivas.org/

Canine Foundations

AKC/Canine Health Foundation
www.akcchf.org

Morris Animal Foundation
http://www.morrisanimalfoundation.org/

Drinking From Toilet, 308
Drowning, 209-210
Drunk Behavior, 212
Dwarfism, 16
Dysplastic, 174

E

Ear Mites, 32, 134, 139, 147, 164-165,
 182-185, 187
Ear Plucking, 134
Ear Position, 236
Ear Problems, 134, 183
Eardrum, 164, 236
Ears, 32-33, 37, 41, 62, 81, 117, 122, 124-
 126, 129, 133-134, 138-139, 142, 155-
 157, 159, 161, 164-167, 183, 218, 225,
 230-231, 233, 235-257, 294, 312-313,
 319
Easy Walk Harness, 253
Eating Grass, 307
Eating Habits, 7, 106
Eating Poop, 224, 286
Egg, 98, 179, 184, 188, 201
Egypt, 6
Elective Surgeries, 8
Electric Clippers, 118, 123, 128, 134
Electrical Cords. *See* Cords, Electrical
Electrocution, 55, 210, 285
Electrolyte, 202
Electronic Collars, 253
Elimination, 140
Elizabethan Collar, 161, 166-167
Emergencies
 Artifical Resuscitation, 8, 207
 Car Accidents, 209
Emmetropic, 234
Emotional Health, 139
Endoscope, 218-219
English Ivy, 55, 215
Enilconazole, 190
Eustachian Tube, 236
Euthanasia, 23, 187
Extrusion, 104
Eye Contact, 250, 261, 274, 286, 292-293,
 313
Eyes, 16, 32-33, 35, 37-38, 41, 46, 48, 57,
 62, 85, 87, 92, 124-125, 133, 139, 142,
 159-160, 166, 172-173, 178, 186, 188,
 197, 211, 215, 218, 225, 230, 234-235,
 237, 250-251, 260, 271, 290, 294, 310-
 312
EZ Groomer, 129

F

Falls, 43
Fat, 96-101, 171, 211, 241
Fear, 35, 41, 43, 76, 80, 82-83, 91, 93, 114,
 132, 159, 168, 203-204, 228, 230, 232,
 246, 249, 267, 276, 279, 283, 293-295,
 314
Fear Period, 41
Feces, 101, 140, 172, 187, 195, 198, 201,
 202, 218, 287, 305
Feeding, 39-40, 97, 102-109, 140, 150,
 184, 206, 302
Feeding Trials, 102
Feline Society, 87
Femoral Head Ostectomy (FHO), 176
Fenris-Wolf, 303
Ferret, 172
Fever, 33, 140, 161, 169, 172, 177-179,
 191, 198, 201, 292
Fighting, 42-43, 81, 148, 150, 242-243
Fights, 155, 223, 233, 242, 250
Filarids, 192
Finicky Eaters, 7, 110-111
Fipronil, 185
First Aid, 207
Fish, 67, 90, 98, 109, 111, 305
Flea Products, 129, 148, 185, 192
Fleas, 32-33, 48, 123, 130, 138, 147-148,
 180, 183-185, 198, 200-201
Fluid Therapy, 178
Fluoride, 135
Follicles, 115, 186
Food Labels, 102
Footpads, 173, 195-196
Foreign Body Obstruction, 217
Fox Terrier, 38, 156
Foxglove, 215
Free Feed, 65
Frontline, 185
Fulvacin, 190
Fungal Infections, 122, 139, 189-190
Fur. *See* Coat
Fur Mats, 117-119, 125-126, 128, 138, 159
Furminator, 129
Fur Problems, 138

G

Games, 239
Garbage, 57, 63, 111, 170, 205, 302, 305,
 313
Garm, The Dog Of Hel, 304

H

I

J

Pit Bull Terrier, 187
Plane Travel, 76
Plants, 52, 55, 58, 214-215, 288-289
Play Bow, 85, 242-243, 314
Playing, 45, 47, 58, 67, 82, 86, 92-93, 105,
    128, 198, 203, 207, 213, 239, 241-243,
    280, 289, 291, 292-293, 314
Pododermatitis, 196
Pointers, 18-19
Points (Color Pattern), 122
Poisoning, 205, 213-215, 218, 307
Pomona, 178
Poodle, 16, 20, 27, 116, 119, 128
Posture, 79, 160, 178, 225, 230, 233
Potassium, 101
Potato, 215
Potty Training, 57, 226, 259
Praise, 89, 136, 163-164, 254-255, 257-
    259, 261, 266-269, 272, 278, 281, 283,
    285-286, 289
Predatory Behavior, 21, 88, 90, 97
Pregnant, 14, 29, 150, 153, 195, 197
Primary Hairs, 115
Proglottids, 198, 200
Program, 185
Protein, 96, 98-100, 104, 109, 113, 193,
    286
Pug, 16, 19, 46, 65, 187m 234, 310
Pupil, 234, 310
Puppy Kindergarten, 62, 248
Puppy Mill, 29
Puppy-Proofing, 7, 52, 58, 205
Purebred, 17-20, 24, 26-27, 31, 60, 69,
    121, 149, 156, 174, 264, 317
Puzzle Toys, 67, 169, 285, 297
Pyriproxifen, 185

Q

Quarantine, 170, 177, 202-204
Quick, Of Claws, 92, 133, 146, 163, 253,
    259, 273

R

Rabbit, 200, 238
Rabies, 68, 145-147, 150, 203-205
Raccoon, 172, 203
Radiologists, 175
Random-Bred, 14, 19-20, 27
Rank, 81-82
Rapid Sleep, 310
Recall, 266

Reclining Restraint, 160
Reconcile (Prozac Or Fluoxitine), 296
Registered Name, 60-61
Regurgitation, 205
Rescue Breathing, 208
Resident Pet, 47, 83
Restraints, 160
Retina, 234-235, 310-311
Retrievers, 19, 156
Revolution, 147, 185
Rewards, 8, 62, 80, 109, 246, 255-256,
    261, 265, 267-271, 273, 276, 286, 295
Ringworm, 32, 48, 189-191
Roaming Behavior, 150-154, 204, 302
Rods, 310
Rolling, 305
Romulus And Remus, 303
Rottweiler, 128, 201, 234
Roundworms, 194, 196-198, 200, 307

S

Sable, 122
Saccule, 236
Saint Bernard, 16, 173, 291
Saliva, 172, 177, 184, 203, 216, 276
Salivary Glands, 203
Salivate, 204-205
Saluki, 16
Sarcoptic Mange, 187
Scent, 40, 59, 79, 114, 130, 224-226, 231,
    234-237, 248, 259-260, 276, 284-285,
    296, 305, 308
Scent Communication, 226
Scent Corrections, 279
Scent Signals, 225
Scenthounds, 19
Schnauzer, 121, 234
Schutzhund, 35
Scissors, 124
Scratching, 125, 139, 167, 188, 301
Scrotum, 153, 154
Scruff, 33, 160
Seizures, 172-173, 211-212, 214-215, 218
Selamectin, 185
Selenium, 101
Semi Moist Foods, 104
Semicircular Canals, 236
Separation Anxiety, 36, 75, 295-296
Set (Greyhound-Like God), 303
Setters, 18-19
Sex, 14, 44, 47, 81, 84, 154
Sexual Maturity, 14, 38, 42, 153
Sexual Status, 114, 260

BIO: Amy Shojai, CABC is an IAABC certified animal behavior consultant and a nationally known authority on pet care. She is the award-winning author of more than two-dozen dog and dog books and thousands of articles and columns.

She is the Puppies Expert at Puppies.About.com, and the behavior expert at Cats.About.com, and writes a weekly newspaper column.

Amy addresses a wide range of fun-to-serious issues in her work, covering training, behavior, health care, and medical topics. She also writes the September Day "Thrillers With Bite" dog viewpoint series featuring a German Shepherd service dog.

Amy is a founder and president emeritus of the Cat Writers Association, Inc., a member of the Dog Writers' Association of America, past president and Honorary Life Member of Oklahoma Writers Federation, Inc., and an active member of International Thriller Writers. She frequently speaks to groups on a variety of pet-related issues, lectures at writing conferences, and regularly appears on national radio and television including Animal Planet DOGS 101.

She and her husband live with Magic the German Shepherd, a seventeen-year-old Siamese "wannabe" Seren, and an adolescent kitten Karma (the dog's best friend). Amy can be reached at her website at www.shojai.com where you can subscribe to her PET PEEVES Newsletter, like her on Facebook.com/amyshojai.cabc, follow on Twitter @amyshojai, and check out her Bling, Bitches & Blood Blog at AmyShojai.com.

Please consider recommending **COMPLETE PUPPY CARE** to your rescue organizations and dog-loving friends. Help other puppy lovers benefit from the information in this book by writing a review, too!

CPSIA information can be obtained
at www.ICGtesting.com
Printed in the USA
LVOW09s0029200417
531397LV00013B/321/P

9 781944 423285